BREAKING APART

BREAKING

APART

_____

A Memoir of Divorce

WENDY SWALLOW

An Imprint of Hyperion
NEW YORK

Library of Congress Cataloging-in-Publication Data

Swallow, Wendy.
 Breaking apart : a memoir of divorce / by Wendy Swallow.—1st ed.
  p. cm.
 ISBN 0-7868-6599-7
 1. Swallow, Wendy, 1954- 2. Divorced women—United States—
Biography. I. Title.

HQ834.S93 2001
 305.48'9653—dc21
  [B]   00-047201

FIRST EDITION

10 9 8 7 6 5 4 3 2 1

For C.E.S

Who read an article and fell in love.

APPRECIATIONS

Many people have helped make this book a reality, and I am deeply grateful to all of them. I would like to thank my friends and colleagues at American University, particularly in the School of Communication, where we struggle all the time to make writing matter. Outside of the university my circle of writing friends were instrumental in helping shape this book: Charlie Shepard, Susan Kellam, Nell Henderson, Liza Tucker, Sandy Eskin, Steve Piacente, and my two amazing sisters, Anne Swallow Gillis and Penny Dwyer, who had some of the best insights of all. I must also thank my patient parents, Chandler and Edith Swallow, and my brother Peter Swallow and his wife, Laura Swallow, for serving as outstanding examples of marital strength and commitment, as well as the rest of my loving family, who have supported me in countless ways. Thanks, also, to my agent Flip Brophy, who took this story to her heart and guided it into the right hands. At Hyperion many people made this book better, but special thanks go to Cassie Mayer, for her helpful support, and to my terrific editor, Leigh Haber, who understood this book deep down and who saved me time and again from my own excess. I must also thank my ex-husband, for his courage and support through this project, and my two wonderful children, the best boys in the whole world. And although she is not here to read it, I would like to thank my cousin Jeannie, who was the first person to see the writer inside me. I miss her still.

But the biggest thanks goes to all those brave and wise people who have shared their divorce stories with me over the years, including the many students I've taught who have grown up through divorce and lived to tell the tale. It may look like my story, but it is theirs as well.

CONTENTS

BREAKING APART

INTRODUCTION

I thought I knew how I felt about my marriage and my divorce until I sat down to write this book. But as I dug down into my memories and the few scraps of journal entries and photos, I discovered I wasn't sure of anything anymore. I hadn't taken notes as my marriage disintegrated, and I couldn't check the tape to see if my quotes were right. Instead of a pile of research, I relied only on what Hemingway said about getting at the truth: "Try to remember what made you feel that way, then write that." Sometimes it seemed like precious little.

I got the contract for this book partly because few writers have been so bold, or so stupid, as to write a divorce memoir before their parents are gone and their children grown. While the recovery literature in nearly every other field is peppered with memoirs—about alcoholism, eating disorders, mental illness—the divorce genre is thin in such work. There are a few memoirs, but not many. I know, because when I was getting divorced I wanted desperately to read a book about what it really felt like. Most of the divorce literature is relentlessly focused on the road map for the journey, the steps it takes to recover from the disruption and trauma of divorce. These are helpful, important books. I relied on them often, but I also wanted to know if others had felt what I was experiencing: the look in the eyes of my friends when I talked about joint custody; the echo of my son's sadness down a telephone line; the loss of a sense of home as I bounced from rental to rental. The longer I wandered through the landscape of divorce, the more it felt as if the conventional wisdom was not only outdated but just plain wrong. Mothers didn't always get their kids; married people seemed to envy me as much as they pitied me; and it certainly wasn't true that my children would be happy if I was happy.

I thought there was a story to be told, a story other divorcing people would want to hear. So I wrote a piece for *Washingtonian* magazine, clearing the idea with my ex-husband first. He said what he always says about my writing: "As long as you tell the truth, it will be okay." I wrote the piece with little angst—with only six thousand words it was difficult to get into too much trouble—and published it to a low rumble of approval. "So balanced," people said, "so refreshing." "A divorce piece that isn't angry or bitter; it's about time." People sent me e-mail, mailed me letters, left me messages. Single fathers called and sent me pictures of themselves with their children, asking for dates. I had struck a chord.

My ex-husband, Ron, thought it was good, but I saw that it also made him sad. Seven years out of our marriage, we were over this stuff, but here I was, dredging it up again. By agreement, we didn't show the article to our children. The boys didn't like it when I "talked about them."

And then a friend suggested I send the piece to her publisher in New York. I thought about that a bit, kicking the article around on my desk for several months, then sent it off one day mostly on a whim. I have nothing to lose, I thought, except a little postage. No one is really going to think this worthy of a book.

Two days later an editor called me. "I'm sitting here in my office crying. We love it. You need to hire an agent."

An agent? Me? A two-bit freelance journalist who teaches so she can pay the rent?

"Yes," she said. "Hire an agent, clear the project with your ex-husband, then call us. We'll be waiting."

Which was how I ended up, several months later, staring at my computer screen, alone at last with my big, sad story. And that was when the real trouble began, because the truth, it turned out, was sly and uncooperative. In writing a magazine piece you can skim over the hard parts. I had dispensed with my marriage in one paragraph so as to get to the good part—the divorce part—quickly and painlessly. But in a book you can't do that. The contract with the reader is different. The story needs to arc from start to finish, it needs to make sense, it needs to reveal the pieces that make up the puzzle, even if those pieces feel like unexploded shells. I sat in my office for months, struggling to make sense of my marriage, my pain, my life. I wrote about the moments that had mattered most, the times when I saw something in a new way. I wrote about the times my children balked; about the turning points, those heart-stopping moments when I looked over the edge and saw nothing but air. Each time I sat down I would try to strip away the outer rinds of the story and get to the core. It felt like searching for pearls in deep water, and there were many mornings I looked at the words on the page and knew I was drowning. The voices of the people I loved buzzed around me in an imagined murmur of disapproval. "Don't tell that. Do you really see me like that? Do you need to say that?" I doubted Ron was right: The truth was not okay; it was downright dangerous.

I knew I was in trouble when I mentioned the project to other people. As both an academic and a journalist, I'm supposed to write for publication, so most people were thrilled to hear about the book. "How wonderful, a contract," they would say, their faces lighting up with approval. "What's it about?"

"My divorce. It's a divorce memoir."

"A what?" they would stammer, and their smiles would fade. "A divorce memoir? Boy, that must be, well, interesting." That was about the nicest thing people could find to say. Then there was always the next question: "What does your ex-husband say? Does he know?"

"Of course he knows," I would answer defensively. "I'm not about to threaten our relationship. I couldn't do this without his okay."

But then I would go home and look at what I had written and wonder if this truth was anything close to what he remembered. I worried about how I characterized our children—what would they think when they read this? By writing about them I felt I was pinning them to the page, half-formed, butterflies caught forever as caterpillars. Would they think this was the only way I saw them? And what about the story itself—would they learn more about their parents' divorce than they needed to know? How do you portray your parents, your siblings, the people you will sit down with at the next Thanksgiving dinner? How do you face your colleagues at the next departmental meeting after they've read about your sex life?

Memoirs are hot in this era of personal revelations, and many are nearly exhibitionist in what they reveal. I cringe before what some call the "showing my privates" genre of television and magazine writing, and I am troubled by what sometimes appears to be the trap of telling the personal story—people who tell their story over and over but don't seem to grow or heal in the process, people whose stories become their personality, their excuse, their destiny. In Greek myths it often takes a hero to rescue people from the endless retelling of their sad story, someone brave and confident who can see past the story to the wider world beyond. I worried that the story would come to define me, become a dangerous, repetitive loop, and that there wouldn't be a hero to pull me out. I doubted I could pull myself out.

At the same time, though, I knew that crafting a story could reknit the shattered soul. When you divorce, you lose so much: your place, your identity, your foundation, and your anchors. Some people experience more fragmentation than others, but all need to find a way to put the pieces back together. It's not just telling the story, but making it make sense that is redemptive. What the hero learns from molding the story is what ultimately heals.

Many of my friends asked if writing this book was cathartic. To be honest, it wasn't, mostly because I had buried my hatchets long ago and by writing this book I found I needed to dig them up and examine them again. But I didn't like having them lying around my house. Sometimes I would sink into a difficult period in my past, trying to find the strings that would unravel the story, and I would feel the old angers stirring. Then I would have to snap back to the present and sit next to Ron at David's Christmas concert and barely be able to stay in my seat. I felt like a spy in the house of forgiveness. Ron and I were past this part, yet here I was, digging around in all those sad memories. It didn't seem honest; it didn't seem fair.

Eventually, the book began to emerge out of the pieces. I cut some parts and found unexpected links between others. There were some things no one needed to know, other bits that didn't fit in the story or didn't seem to matter. I don't believe we need to reveal all to tell a coherent truth. Mostly, I hope this story rings true for Ron and our boys, that it feels like our story. But I also hope they know it isn't the only story, or even the full story. As with any life-altering experience, the story of this divorce will shift and change over time, as we all revisit it again and again. It will never be over.

So where does the story start? With a pair of pictures. A pair of pictures I keep on my desk, like bookends for my life. The first is recent, from just a few months ago. It's a shot I took one afternoon when my two boys and I were at the National Zoo on a warm spring day. It's our favorite place and we are regulars there, but this day I remember as unusually contented. My children have always had a strong affinity for wild animals—there is something about untamed and vulnerable creatures that feels familiar to them—so we wandered about, checking on the otter pups, hoping the wolves would be out, watching the gibbons for a long time as they ricocheted around their enclosure. We ended up playing on a steep hill, running and rolling down it until we were covered with grass. The boys, tired for the moment, climbed inside the letters of a stone ZOO sign and I snapped the picture as they looked out at me. David, twelve, is sitting inside the first O, leaning against the side and smiling gently. Jesse, ten, all sinew and energy, is crouched inside the second O, ready to spring like a leopard and grinning in anticipation.

Happy, relaxed, their lives carried effortlessly on their sturdy shoulders—like anybody's children. But they are not anybody's children, they are mine; and because of choices I made when they were little, they will never really move through life effortlessly. I hold on to this picture as a talisman, as proof that my children can be happy, yet I cannot really be sure. I cannot know how they will think of their childhood when they are grown, whether they will see it as good or safe or happy. Maybe it will be best if I never know.

Because there is the other picture, a more haunting picture. In this photograph it is years earlier, the summer of 1992. David is five and Jesse three, and they are perched on a rock above our favorite New England beach. In the picture, they are aglow with the happiness of another lovely day, this one spent chasing gulls and scooping sand. The late-afternoon light glints off their tousled hair. I've caught them in a game, so they aren't smiling as much as just looking up for a moment, looking up out of the deep heart of a happy childhood.

And I knew, as I clicked the shutter, that they would never look that way again. It is the last record of my children's true selves, the last time they were whole and innocent, because it is the last picture taken before their parents divorced.

1

DIVORCE FANTASY

As a fantasy, divorce has a lot to recommend it. A good divorce fantasy can feel like an open window in a life otherwise shuttered in on itself. It can comfort a heart stinging from marital strife. It can be intensely private and perfectly controlled, unlike reality, which may be spinning apart. A good divorce fantasy can take up a lot of time.

During the twelve years I was married, I spent many hours fantasizing about divorce. At first it was just a whisper of an idea, held guiltily for a moment and then dismissed, but as the years passed it became something of an obsession. Whenever my marriage made me unhappy, which was often, I escaped in my head into the world of divorce.

It was a place where women were free and could choose, where women decided everything from the mood of their day to what to watch on TV or where the family would go on vacation. It was a place where I didn't have to compromise with a difficult spouse. It was a place where I could make my children infinitely happy, a halcyon world of simple pleasures and contented days. I knew it wouldn't be an easy life—money would be tight and I would have to learn how to mow the lawn—but I imagined the inevitable hardships as lessons that would somehow make us all stronger and bind me closer to my two little boys. With middle-class parents who were still alive and willing to help, I didn't have to worry about ending up in a homeless shelter.

This fantasizing was the perfect antidote to a marriage that had become a struggle for power over the smallest of choices. The problem with my life, as I saw it then, was my husband, and I imagined divorce as a process that would remove him but change little else—a sort of neutron bomb that eliminated men but left the rest of the world intact. When my husband went on business trips, I played at being divorced, reveling in the freedom his absence afforded and the peace that would descend on our little world when he was gone. It would be so simple, I thought, so pleasant. There would be less yelling. The boys and I would stay in the house and I would get my parents to help me fix the things my husband never got around to fixing. I would get a nice student to live in the basement apartment and help out with baby-sitting in exchange for a lower rent, so I could get an occasional break from the kids. I could re-arrange furniture to my liking, perhaps get a dog. If the mortgage got too oppressive, I could rent out the attic as well, maybe to another single mother. We could sit to-gether in the kitchen at night, soul sisters chatting about our kids and conspiring about men. Compared to the cold war of my marriage, it sounded pretty wonderful.

Most people, though, will tell you that divorce is a night-mare rather than a fantasy. Many, in fact, will tell you it is *the* American nightmare of the late twentieth century. And in many ways they are right. Divorce is, unarguably, a deeply troubling trend in society, a corrosive and often unpredictable force that erodes families and cripples children. It has become so ubiquitous that it threatens even strong marriages, as if it were something that could be picked up in crowded malls or during the coffee hour at church. Yet despite the wide experience of divorce in our society, most people who've been through it don't talk about it much—outside self-help circles and therapists' offices—because other people don't like to hear about it. They don't like to think about how it happened to their parents or how it changed their friends, and they can't bear the thought of what it would do to their children. It's one of those taboo subjects—like cancer or war—too difficult to explain to those who stayed home, too depressing to ponder for more than a moment.

And so it gets pushed down into the collective subconscious, where it rustles about like a monster under the bed. But like every nightmare, divorce has its fascinations. There is hardly a married person I know who has not confessed to me, in a whispered aside, that they have been tempted by divorce. Just my presence in a room full of married friends is enough to make people uneasy, especially if I appear happy or talk about what I do in my free time when my children are with their father. Marriage is complicated, and sticky with hurt and disappointment. Divorce, from the outside, looks simple, neat. Like suicide for the depressive, divorce is something unhappy spouses dream about with a mixture of fear and longing. Someday the monster will break out, sowing destruction in its wake, but it also will sweep aside all that is old and knotted and unfixable. The monster will bring renewal because there will be nothing left to do but start again and make it better.

For thousands of unhappy people, this has actually worked. Divorce has liberated them, given them a chance for a startling rebirth, a chance to correct debilitating mistakes made early in life and restabilize children shell-shocked from the marriage wars. Divorce can save lives. Divorce can even, iron-ically, save families. Divorce can be an astonishing blessing.

In the last few years of my marriage, that seductive voice intensified and my fantasy began to harden into a plan. I watched with a clinician's interest as my older sister strug-gled out of her marriage and set herself up in a tiny cottage with a breakfast table just big enough for her and her little boy. I spent countless hours reading up on divorce, sitting cross-legged on the floor of the library because I didn't dare take the books home. I talked with friends, talked with my counselor. I plotted and planned.

Through it all, I came to believe that I was prepared, that I knew what divorcing my husband would bring. I knew I would be alone. I knew I would have less money. I knew I would be a single parent, and that divorce would be difficult and painful for my children. I knew that, even-tually, I would have to tell my husband what I was doing.

And that was when it all blew up.

Divorce, like marriage, turned out to be a game with two players. In all those years of silently indulging in my divorce fantasy, it hadn't occurred to me that I needed to consult my husband, that divorce was something we were going to do together. Divorce, as it turned out, was the last act of the marriage, the final dance. And true to form, we had a lot of trouble agreeing on the steps.

When I finally stumbled out the front door of the comfortable brick house that was the only home my children knew, I found myself in a place so removed from my fantasy divorce it left me breathless. Everything I'd anticipated—the money problems, the loneliness, the pres-sures of single-parenting—turned out to be true, but even so I had no real idea what divorce would be like. Over the last seven years I've moved from a secure, two-income life where everything predicted success for my children to a place that is financially vulnerable, with the deck stacked against us. I didn't know what the days would feel like, how many small but significant things I would have to give up to buy my freedom, or how little I would ultimately be able to keep safe. Even my departure, planned for months to cushion the impact on my little boys, tumbled out of my control, knocking down best intentions with every turn.

More than that, though, was that divorce threw me into a remarkable and unexpected emotional landscape, a place outside normal society. It is a shockingly unprotected place, windswept and empty. There is little to lean on for support.

It is the very privacy of marriage—that no one else can really know what is happening inside a marriage—that makes it either a place of freedom or a prison. When a marriage begins to break down, that old privacy becomes part of the cage. When the bonds of marriage are broken—and they are stronger than most imagine, even in the worst marriages—one is utterly alone. There is no longer a shared experience or, more significantly, a shared drama. You find yourself on the stage that has been the final years, still speaking your lines but playing to an empty house. The play is not concluded, or wrapped up. Somebody just shuts off the lights.

So you find yourself in a new place. Either the old house of the marriage, now bigger and emptier, or a new place that looks suspiciously like the places you lived in when you were young and just scraping by. And you begin to wonder if instead of moving forward you are falling back, instead of starting over with a clean slate you are starting over with all the responsibilities of middle life but no way to pay for them. Divorce robs you of much. It takes away your mid-career wealth. It takes away your place in society. It takes away the easy reassurance of two-parent child rearing and all the benefit of the doubt we give to intact families. For many people it even takes away their children.

Yet loss creates space, and emptiness brings possibility. All people who divorce ultimately seek renewal, but it is hard to understand that the transformation will be to something entirely unexpected. What it takes to get out of an unhappy marriage is not what it takes to rebuild a life, and sometimes what it takes feels impossible. The challenge, I've come to discover, is believing anything is possible when it looks like nothing is there.

This story is about a divorce. It's about a descent, an excruciating choice, and a recovery. It's about rebuilding my life so that my children can live within a structure that gives them strength and support and the courage to thrive. But it is also about the dissolution of a marriage, and that is the hardest part. Even today, seven years after Ron and I separated, seven years of working together to find the strands back toward each other so we could trust again, the death of my marriage is still the hardest part. And make no mistake—divorce is a death. It kills the dreams of your youth, those innocent beliefs that your marriage can weather sickness as it can weather health, that life will be kind and fair, that the joys will be shared and the vicissitudes bring you closer. I can't even imagine now what it would be like to live through my middle age still believing those things, still having them be true for me. I know that some marriages manage to hold on to those beliefs even as they are squeezed and burnished by experience, because I can see them burning like gold at the core; and I know I will never have that. I left my innocence behind that still September day when I walked out the door of my house. Left it behind with the wedding presents and the Christmas ornaments and the memories and all the familiar corners of my life.

2

THE WEDDING PICTURE

My youngest son stands in the doorway of my bedroom, a large photo album held out in front of him.

"Mom," he says, a puzzled look on his face. "Who are these people?"

I take the album and open it, and there we are—his parents on their wedding day.

Jesse is ten now, but he was only three when we separated. This album has been buried under a pile of piano music for years and I suspect he has never seen these photos before.

"That's me and Daddy, the day we got married," I say, trying to sound nonchalant, as if this discovery is a small thing. But Jesse isn't fooled.

"No, that can't be you," he says, disbelieving. "You never looked like that." He holds the book open, riveted by a picture of Ron and me kissing exuberantly on the chapel steps. My sister Anne, who read us our vows, stands in the background in her ministerial robes. My other sister, Penny, decked out as the maid of honor, is tripping down the steps. I'm front and center, in my mother's elegant satin wedding dress, the family's heirloom lace veil cascading from my head as I lift my face toward Ron. He's in tails, his arms clasped around my waist. We look deliriously happy.

This picture is beginning to make me nervous, so I reach out to flip to the back of the album, where most of the photos are of family and friends, but Jess stops my hand, won't let me turn the page. "Daddy is skinny! You are so young!" He's mesmerized. "Boy, you really look different." He pages silently through the book, then turns back to the first picture. Finally he looks up at me. "You're happy," he says, his voice cracking. "Did you really kiss?"

I pull him into a hug and he leans against me as he tries to collect himself. This child holds his emotional life deep within, and I know this isn't easy. "Yes, of course we kissed. That's what being married is about." I don't know what else to say.

"When did you stop kissing?" he says. "When you got divorced?"

"No," I say, because I try to be honest with my boys. "We stopped kissing before we got divorced, but I'm not sure when. It's hard to say." We sit together quietly for a few minutes. I remember other last times—the last time my husband and I had sex, the last time we went out together as a married couple, the last time we sat with our boys as a family around the dinner table, but I do not remember the last time we kissed. Probably I don't want to.

Jesse isn't the first person to ask me this kind of question. Nearly everyone who knows me has asked if there was a moment, a single moment, when my marriage died. Our culture views divorce with a mixture of fear and fascination, and people are curious about how it happens, how a couple who starts like Ron and me—radiating happiness on the chapel steps—ends up embittered and angry, squared off in opposite corners and grabbing whatever marital possessions they can get their hands on. This question, "Was there a moment?" doesn't only spring from curiosity—it rings with the hope that if you could identify the critical moment you could go back and fix it. You might be able to shove the fragile vessel that is a marriage back off the sandbar of disappointment and heartache and prevent its foundering.

Perhaps. Perhaps for some marriages there is a moment, a moment when one discovers a spouse is having an affair, or when someone gets angry enough to hit a partner for the first time. I waited for such a defining moment for years. But for many of us who have been through a divorce, this question is a bit like asking if there is a single moment when a cancer starts. One night in the middle of my marriage, in those years when I was unhappy but unable to change it, I heard a line in a play that made me ache with recognition. I don't remember the play but I'll never forget the words: "A drought doesn't begin on a single day." The simple answer is that there wasn't a moment. There wasn't a moment that could be fixed, or that could even be understood apart from the million other moments of my marriage. I don't remember when we stopped kissing, but at some point we did. And from that point on, nothing was ever the same.

My friend Kay is walking with me one morning, talking with me about men, our favorite topic, when all of a sudden she says: "So how bad was it, really?"

"How bad was what?"

"Your marriage. How bad did it really get?"

Ah. Of course. This is related to the "Was there a moment?" question, but it goes deeper, I think. It reveals the dark corner of worry that seems to haunt most of the marriages I know today, partnerships that are fundamentally strong but which are taxed daily by the demands of children and jobs. These friends want to know where their problems lie on the spectrum of marital misery. They want a scale that will tell them what is tolerable and what is not. They want to know what others have endured, whether a husband who never changes a diaper is bad enough to get the boot or if he has to commit greater sins. Is yelling okay? Is an affair an automatic out? And what about illnesses like depression or alcoholism? My friends seem to be looking for reassurance, for a comparison that will put their devils into perspective. They want to know where the threshold is, the pain threshold that absolves them of blame if they need to divorce.

The problem is, I never know quite what to say in answer to this question, because the pain seems so private, now, so far removed from my present life that it is tough to describe or explain. Sometimes my children ask this question, usually in the form of "Why did you leave Daddy?" and I'm left to struggle with an answer. Because there better be a good reason. My children suspect there are skeletons in a closet somewhere; in fact, they want skeletons, otherwise it doesn't make sense. Why else would their loving, rational parents do something this awful if there wasn't a damn good reason? "Daddy and I were not happy together," I say. "You would not have been happy growing up with Daddy and me together in the house." Trust me, I try to tell them with my eyes, because I don't know how else to say it.

When my parents celebrated their fiftieth wedding anniversary last summer, Jesse asked me how long Daddy and I had been married. It was the first time he had thought about longevity and marriage, and I wasn't sure what to tell him. Like many couples of our generation, Ron and I lived together for two years before we married. We lived as a married couple for twelve years, then lived apart for five before the divorce was finalized. That had been two years earlier.

"Daddy and I were together for fourteen years and we've lived apart for seven," I told him.

"So, twenty-one years," he said. "Are you going to have a party?"

Indeed. For him, his parents are still "married" in essential ways. We share custody of our two boys, so we talk often and make all the important decisions about the boys together. When my family gathers for birthdays or holidays, Ron is often invited over for a drink. He and I occasionally sit on his screened porch—once the setting for the most intense arguments of our marriage—and sip wine while we catch up on our news. We appear to be friends, and I tell the boys we are friends. Yet we are friends in limited, carefully scripted ways. Every now and then one of us stumbles and crosses a boundary, and then I'm reminded of all that went before, of all that couldn't be solved. Every now and then one of us commits one of the old crimes, and the other flares in annoyance. If I had to stay inside this circle of tension, I think to myself, the dispute could blaze into something destructive, something hurtful. Instead, I disengage. I say a polite good-bye, kiss the kids, then skip down Ron's front steps and jump in my car, thankful that I have my own bed to sleep in that night.

Being married to Ron didn't turn out to be like the fantasies I had of married life.

When I was in college and beginning to think of myself

as being a marriageable age, I would imagine a life of wedded bliss. I saw myself living in a big old house, ramshackle but comfortable, open to the breeze and the numerous friends and neighbors who would be drawn to my warm hearth. My husband would be the witty, charismatic, college-professor type, someone who could take my breath away with his insights on Tolstoy, then turn around and tie a child's shoe. He would be gentle but strong, the pilot of our life, the one who envisioned things and brought wonders to my doorstep. I would wear soft cotton dresses and my hair in a long braid down my back, dividing my time between baking cobbler and writing something significant—this was the vague part—on an old typewriter set up at the kitchen table. There would be dogs and children underfoot, and a beat-up old Volvo in the drive. There would be lots of books. When someone made a mistake, everyone would laugh gently. No one would ever get angry.

The key to how hopelessly unrealistic this dream was is the idea of wearing my hair in a braid down my back. My hair has always been short, a curly mop barely long enough to tuck behind my ears, and I've never looked good in billowy dresses. As for the rest of it, I got some of the pieces but missed others. My husband turned out to be the witty, college-professor type, and he could take my breath away with his insights not just on Tolstoy but Dostoyevsky, Metternich, and Stalin as well. He had a strong spirit and personality, and he brought many wonders to my feet. He was the pilot of our life, even though I turned out to have a steadier grip on the controls. Eventually there were children and a Volvo, but the dog was out of the question and I could only write behind a closed door. He didn't like cobbler, and when I made mistakes he got mad. When I sat down to write something significant, I struggled with stories about how anger and depression could warp a marriage.

There are many simple ways to explain why my marriage didn't work, and over the years I've probably used all of them. I was too young and he was too old; he was intense and spontaneous, where I was calm and controlled; his family life was so badly managed he left home at sixteen; I came from a family whose wisdom and love extended their influence over me well into my thirties. He was private and solitary, I wanted a life dense with family and friends. He was brilliant, I was not; he was depressed, I was not; he had fought for all the advantages in his life, I had not; I was lucky, he was not.

When we met he was thirty-four, a brooding, bearded intellectual who had just returned from living and teaching in Europe for four years. I was twenty-four, just two years out of college and still trying to figure out who and what I was going to be. Ron seemed infinitely worldly and interesting, the angry young man who was angry for all the right reasons. I was just his type—young, pliable, happy, stable, the perfect young protégée, the attractive student at his knee. We quickly discovered that we shared many interests—literature, politics, drama, and music—and a foundation of common values.

To the outside world, we seemed to fit together like hand and glove, and we did fit together. But over the years I found that some of that fit came from long-simmering conflicts inside us rather than healthy needs. Our problems fit together with the same loud snap as did our dreams and our joys.

The truth was, Ron and I had distinctly different personalities, had grown up in very different family cultures, and had daily needs that were so divergent I still puzzle over why we married at all. Most divorcing people struggle for years to understand why they chose a particular partner for the most central acts of their lives—having children, buying a home, settling in a community, building for retirement. But people marry for deeply complex reasons, reasons that often elude the lost kids we are when we make those decisions. Unraveling those subconscious motives, cracking open those early years, can be tough indeed.

When I look at our wedding pictures now, I peer at that younger self and try to remember what she knew about this man standing next to her. I thought I knew him, and I thought I knew myself. We had lived together for two years, moved twice, been on vacation, visited with family. I knew he was moody, that he sometimes needed to retreat from me into his books or his papers, but it didn't seem to be a significant problem. I knew he was both envious that I had a loving family and resentful of their meddling, that he was much more independent and solitary than I was or ever wanted to be, that he loved me but sometimes struggled to stay close to me. I knew he wrestled with a quick, sometimes bitter, temper. I knew all these things and still I married him. I married him because I was blindly optimistic about my life. I married him because I thought I could handle anything. I married him because the person I didn't know very well was that laughing girl with the curly hair and the vulnerable eyes, the one in her mother's wedding dress.

My marriage was a confusing, unhappy journey, and my divorce a painful struggle to regain the open air. But somehow they were what finally forced me to grow up, the crucial passage that stripped away the trappings of who I imagined I was and forced me to accept who I would always be. I thought I knew myself when I married Ron nineteen years ago, and I thought I knew him, but I had no idea. I was a child when I married, then woke up one day twelve years later, alone in a barren apartment surrounded only by the mover's boxes, and I knew then that I was just beginning to see life as it would be.

3

N A V Y   B R A T

It is a chilly February morning in 1964 and my father is going off to sea. I am ten years old, a tomboy who prefers her sneakers and marbles to dresses and Barbie dolls. On this gray morning my mother has hustled us out of bed in the predawn darkness, bundled us into our jackets, and dragged us down to the beach a few blocks from our house. Now we are standing out along the line of seaweed left at high tide, clutching our stuffed animals and gazing toward the west as my father's navy destroyer steams out around the North Island Naval Air Station in San Diego, out past Point Loma, and off over the horizon. My brother, Pete, two years younger, gets bored and skips rocks. I crouch down to get out of the wind, but still it happens faster than I expect it to. One minute the ship is there, her radar spinning, her pennants whipping in the wind, the next minute she is as small as a toy, and then, suddenly, she is gone. I'll never forget the kick of that instant—the speed with which my beloved daddy disappeared right before my eyes, not to return for nine months. Gone.

.   .   .

It wasn't the first time he had disappeared like that. In one of my earliest memories, I'm four, sitting in the front seat of our station wagon in my yellow rain slicker, Annie next to me, watching the water course down the windshield as we wait for my father to appear at the head of the gangplank of his ship. One sailor after another lopes down the ramp, but Daddy doesn't come. "He's the captain," my mother explains. "He has to make sure everything is right before he leaves the ship. He'll be here soon." At the time we were stationed in Newport, Rhode Island, and my father's ship was on rotation: home for two weeks, then out at sea for the next two, chasing Russian submarines around the North Atlantic. It was there that I first learned the rhythm of military life. Sometimes he was at home, playing the piano at night while Anne and I dropped off to sleep, other times he was so far away, so deeply hidden in the government's vast scheme to thwart the Soviets, that he was beyond even radio contact.

When we moved from the East Coast to California when I was five, we settled in a neighborhood just beyond the high barbed-wire fence of a large navy air base, where the planes took off at the rate of one a minute, screeching over the house and leaving behind clouds of jet-fuel dust. At school we learned to dive under our desks during the air-raid drills, and in the afternoons, horsing around with the neighbor kids, we played a game called London, where we pretended we were caught in the blitz of World War II. Every time a plane approached, we would scream and leap for the bushes, or grab each other's hands and try to make it, against hope, back to the front step before the planes dropped bombs on our yard. My brother developed a spooky imitation of a man being machine-gunned to death, held up against the pull of gravity by a thousand stinging bullets.

By the time I was six, I was dreaming about ships, but not the kind of hero dreams you would expect a child to have. In my dreams ships fell out of the sky, huge, gray warships dropping onto our house and crushing everyone inside. It was the very winter of the cold war and none of us questioned my father's duty to go to sea; we just put our heads down and weathered the loneliness.

At the time I was the second daughter in a family of three kids—my younger sister wasn't born until just before we moved back east several years later—and the five of us were a tight tribe. We were bound together by the vagaries of military life, new schools and playgrounds every few years, different communities, different homes. The one fixed pole was the circle of faces around the table—except that sometimes Dad was there and sometimes he wasn't. In California the rotations lengthened and he was gone for longer periods. The Vietnam War was heating up, and the American presence in the western Pacific was sustained by a steady stream of ships out of San Diego and Pearl Harbor.

Despite his uniform and his commitment to the navy, my father wasn't a stereotypical military man. He was gentle and quiet, a man who spent his leisure time painting watercolors and chasing tumbleweeds with us on the beach. The day before the ship left my father would line us kids up and, in a serious voice, tell us to be good to our mother while he was away. For an officer he wasn't much of a disciplinarian at home, and we were always awkward with a sense of loss that, as children, we couldn't express. Instead, we would break rank and dance around, laughing and saying, "Sure, Dad, we'll be good," while rolling our eyes and trying to make him smile.

I don't think he ever realized that his family closed in like a knot while he was away, and that none of us would have made life any harder for our mother than we already knew it to be. But she was just the kind of wife a navy officer needed: strong and loving but also uncomplaining and no-nonsense, the kind of mom who could get you to quiet down just by raising an eyebrow. She came from a long line of independent women and is still, at seventy-one, one of the most competent people I know, a woman routinely called to lead volunteer causes, who might have been a corporate executive if she had been born in a different era. She ran her house the way my father ran his ship—well-organized, and with as little hysteria as possible. Unlike mothers today, her generation wasn't big on talking about feelings, but she was a master at managing them. She knew we were lonely for Daddy, and to cheer us up she tossed surprises into our everyday lives—pancakes with maple syrup for dinner instead of the usual hamburgers or pork chops, a late-night trip to the park to play hide-and-seek among the palms, special treats in our lunch boxes like marshmallow creme in our peanut butter sandwiches. Sometimes, as we romped in our pajamas before lights-out, she would round us up and say, "Okay, monkeys, you can sleep with me in the big bed tonight," and then there would be an hour or so of giggles and shoving, and only when she threatened to banish us to our dark bedrooms down the hall would we settle down so that we could all get some sleep.

When my father was away, our favorite place was the beach, particularly in the fall and spring when it was empty and my mother could draw large mazes in the sand for us to run through. One day we started building a sand castle, and soon we were building more than a castle—a whole city, like Venice, my mother said. We stayed late into the twilight, working in the wet sand until the tide crept in and filled the canals with water, then slowly flooded the houses of the little town. We felt closer there, on that beach, to my father. From there he seemed to be just in the next room, just beyond that close horizon, instead of several thousand miles away. I have a picture from those years of my mother and me standing on the beach looking out to sea, our legs spread apart, our heads back, me nestled against her like a small replica of her.

In 1965, when I was eleven, our world shifted again, this time more radically. My younger sister, Penny, was born and a month later we moved back east, to Arlington, Virginia, where my father was now stationed at the Pentagon. We settled in a house surrounded by woods, on the edge of a neighborhood with other big families and good schools. This time my father was home for a few years, and we got used to having him around, although we missed California and the sound of the surf out our windows. I remember lying in bed at night, talking quietly with Annie and listening to the wind in the naked winter trees outside our window. We felt as if we had been forced out of paradise. Then, in 1967, my father was given command of a frigate out of Jacksonville, Florida, a ship that would be detailed to the Mediterranean fleet. We went down over spring break to find a place to live, my mother muttering under her breath that uprooting us all again was hardly her idea of a holiday. We stayed for the week in a trailer park surrounded by trees that dripped Spanish moss and snakes. My mother went out one day to visit the local schools, met with a real estate agent, and then got stopped by a cop who bragged about how many black people he had shot in his years on the local force. I don't think my mother had ever encountered anyone like him before. She came in that night and announced that we weren't moving to this backwater—we were going home to Virginia. Dad's ship wasn't going to be in port that much anyway, and his next assignment was likely to be back at the Pentagon. We might as well stay where we were, where the schools were good.

It was the right decision, but it meant nearly three more years with my father away, this time home only for long weekends or his official leaves. We went down to Florida for the summers, but it wasn't like living together. By the time Dad returned for good, Penny was three, I was a moody preteen, Annie was sixteen and sneaking out at night to meet her boyfriend, and Peter was eleven and struggling with learning disabilities that masked his innate intelligence. I remember those years as the dark ones, the years when my mother seemed besieged by my brother's problems, Penny's baby needs, my older sister's rebellion. One day Annie came to sit with me on the piano bench where I was practicing, her face glum after another argument with our mother, and she said simply, "I need a father. I can't wait for Dad to get home." Then she looked at me. "Don't you need one?" I turned away, back to my music. I didn't know what to tell her, because by then I had already figured out that my job was to be the easy child, the one who didn't need anything.

For a long time, through most of those years without my father, I struggled to remember when he was away what he looked like, thinking that if I ever forgot his face he would die out at sea and we would never see him again, not even his dead body. My continuing dreams of ships falling from the sky seemed to confirm these fears, but because I didn't want to worry the others, I kept my anxieties to myself, obsessing over them in the middle of the night. I wonder now if my mother was struggling with similar fears during that time, and, if so, how she managed to keep going day after day. When I found myself, many years later, swallowing back tears and smiling her smile as I tried to manage a husband who was absent in other ways, I thought about those dreams anew. This time it was my family, not my father, I feared was dying.

I know my father better now. He has been there for me as an adult as he could not be when I was young. Together we have dreamt up plots of novels, walked through city streets until even the bars closed, sat for hours on darkened porches, beaches, and docks, not speaking sometimes, just absorbing each other's company. And the week my husband lost his moorings and cried until the doctors gave him tranquilizers, as I sat up late each night sipping bourbon, my father would call to make sure I was okay.

But there is still a child in me who watches the horizon, watches for a ship and a father who will miss my next birthday if he doesn't return soon. I learned how to wait for happiness in those years that he was gone, learned how to push my sadness under the pillow with my pajamas every morning and turn around and face the day. Learned how to play for hours on a chilly winter beach, not thinking about the ship that wasn't there.

And many years later, when I faced the cold reality of divorce and knew it meant my children might lose a parent, I felt the echo of my father's absence. Somehow, despite all my good intentions, I had brought my own children to the same lonely place.

4

M I S S I S S I P P I

I don't know where I picked up the idea that I needed to save someone.

It was in the air when I was growing up, that sense that one's life could be a mission, if one cared enough. I was thirteen the year Martin Luther King Jr. was shot, the year I woke up and saw that the world was not a simple place anymore. The afternoon the news broke, my mother and I were going to pick up my brother from judo class. Mom, late as usual, was racing up the highway. "Oh my God," she breathed, when she heard the report. She slowed down and pulled over, forgetting Pete. "No, oh no, this can't be," she muttered, listening intently, suddenly pale. I was just beginning to tune in to the events swirling about me. It was 1968 and as far as I could tell the world seemed to be coming apart. I knew who King was, but I didn't really understand why my mother was so upset. When the report was over she just sat there, looking as if she'd been hit. "This is going to be bad," she said.

Two nights later my father and I stood on a hill above the Potomac, on the Virginia side, watching the city of Washington burn in the distance. It was March and he must have been home between deployments. The haze from the smoke hung in the air, and Dad was unusually quiet. "Do you think the rioters will come to Arlington?" I asked him, worried by his silence, thinking of rumors I had heard at school. "No," he said, shaking his head. "They are taking it out on themselves, on their own city. Their hope has died. It is very sad."

There is a strange arc across the early years of my life, one that starts in that moment on the hill, leads straight to a small town in Mississippi, and ends, years later, with my marriage to Ron. It's faint, difficult to see in places, but powerful nonetheless. This arc is about giving something back, about using one's life to make others happier. I learned it from my liberal parents, heard about it on the evening news, practiced it in church youth groups. It's a glittery, self-effacing quality, this desire to do good. It plays well with adults, looks good on a college application. It can be worn as a badge, as a shield, as camouflage. There is a lot you could hide behind it—vanity, the need to please, the intense hunger to be a hero of some kind. And for me, all of that got stashed behind it, although I was too young to understand it then. I worked as a lifeguard, volunteered with environmental groups in my neighborhood, taught Sunday school to an unruly bunch of five-year-olds, always searching for someone to save.

Then one day a Peace Corps volunteer came to talk to my high school Spanish class about her experience working with native Indians in Peru, high on the Andean plateau. She had pictures of llamas and babies in colorful blankets. I was mesmerized, by her and by the opportunity of such a thing. By dinnertime, I had a plan. After college, I would join the Peace Corps. I would take my Spanish and my big heart and go to South America.

When I graduated from college four years later, I did

apply to the Peace Corps, by then feeling like an anachronism—now most of my friends were heading off to business school. The sixties were over and at that time—1976—the great waves of social reform that had buffeted my childhood had largely ebbed. Still, the Peace Corps was alive and well, and offered to send me to teach music in Kenya.

"Music?" I said to the recruiter. "Don't you need me for something, well, more critical?"

"Actually, we need people to work here in the United States, in VISTA, the domestic counterpart of the Peace Corps. Everyone wants to go overseas. No one wants to do the hard work here," he told me. "I've got several assignments in the South."

The South. I'd never been to the Old South. Brief visits to Florida, land of palms and tourists, hardly counted. Being from true Yankee stock, I thought of the South as a foreign land, unfamiliar, probably hostile. It was a long way from llamas and native peoples in colorful blankets, but I said yes, then packed up. Just days before I left for my assignment to a small Mississippi town, Jimmy Carter, the governor of Georgia, was elected president. As I flew south I read a cover story in *Time* magazine about the resurgence of the South as an economic and political engine. It was wonderful. I was on the edge of a revolution, part of a renaissance for this poverty-stricken part of America. I was going to make a difference.

Fayette, Mississippi, was made up of just a handful of people living amid tall oaks and pines just across the river from the bayou country of Louisiana. Most of its residents were poor, most were poorly educated. No one, it turned out, had read the *Time* article that had so inspired me. Rebirth? Maybe that was happening in Atlanta, but not here. One look around and it was easy to see that the *Time* reporters had missed a few things.

Fayette was the county seat for the third-poorest county in the United States, a small cluster of decrepit storefronts and a jailhouse at the main intersection, which still had a spot out front where they had lynched people only a few decades earlier. In the park across the street stood a Civil War statue of a Confederate soldier, which the black residents referred to as "the Anonymous Bigot." The population of about two thousand was eccentric, gossipy, and deeply divided along racial lines. The town had a black-owned bank and a white-owned bank, black liquor stores and white liquor stores, black churches and white churches, black schools (the public ones) and white schools (the private ones). And yet it wasn't that simple, either. The local grocery store owner was a white guy from Connecticut who had come south during the civil rights years and married a local black woman with two girls from a previous marriage. I ended up giving them piano lessons, along with the children of several other middle-class black families. There weren't many of those in town, however, because there were few jobs to hold men in the South—many had migrated north to Chicago. Often they had settled up north, some even had second families there, but most still sent money to their Mississippi wives and kids. Still, there wasn't much to go around. Fayette, it turned out, was filled with single mothers on welfare, most of the population so poor that the town qualified for just about every kind of federal assistance available. The mayor, a charismatic man who was the first black mayor elected in a biracial town in Mississippi, said he was looking for someone who could help get federal grant money for social services. He wanted me to write the grant proposals, to crack the federal treasury.

I moved into a house with two local schoolteachers and jumped into my task, running around town compiling data to support our case, planning programs, talking with the single mothers about what kind of services they needed and how they might improve their lives. The work was interesting and straightforward, the needs obvious. Like my mother, I was good at the executive chores—writing the proposals, organizing the programs, and putting together support from local leaders. But when I left the mayor's office in the evening, I found myself fumbling through a social terrain I couldn't understand. The black community was mostly poor, with just a thin veneer of educated middle-class people at the top, people who usually came from other parts of Mississippi or somewhere else in the South, many of them teachers. The white community was something so foreign to my experience I never did understand it. The elderly people had seen my type before—the Yankee college kid, air-dropped in to make a difference. They regarded me mostly as a curiosity, but a few of them felt they needed to make a point. One evening I was eating dinner at the grubby diner in town, talking with Kenn, a bright, politically astute young black man from Jackson who was a close associate of the mayor's and was working with me on the federal grants. An older white man, who I knew owned the white liquor store and gas station, came up and stood beside our table, his face working. I thought he might be drunk. There were lots of drunks in town, white and black, and they occasionally sidled up to me to say things. Usually, though, they were polite and harmless.

"Whore," he finally whispered.

"Excuse me," I said, not sure I had heard him.

"Whores, that's what you-all are, you Yankee girls. That must be why you come here." Then he spit on the floor at my feet.

He stumbled away. I looked at Kenn, and all of a sudden I didn't know who I was. I had never been in a place where my reputation had been so grossly misunderstood, where it had not been defined by my family and my class. For the first time I saw that I had grown up wearing my upbringing, and my education, as a shield against the world. Here, I was stripped of it and made to stand alone before a judgmental crowd. Here, I was just a twenty-two-year-old confused about the world and her place in it. Here, I didn't know nothing. And it was true—I didn't.

"I'm sorry that happened," Kenn said, clearing his throat, his face a mixture of pain and resignation. "There are still lots of cretins left. You just have to ignore them."

Even among the younger people, those of my generation, the social terrain was difficult to traverse, a minefield of racial faux pas, of cultural differences I strained to understand. I was one of a few people in town allowed to walk on both the black and white sides, who had friends in both communities, who was welcome at both churches, but that was because no one expected me to stay for long. People were polite but remote. Eventually I was befriended by a group of aging white musicians and artists, hippies who had retreated to the backwoods of Mississippi to live in ramshackle houses with bad plumbing and low rents. They played music, painted their canvases, worked construction when they needed cash, and drank. Beer and bourbon. For most of the year it was too hot to do much else. I fell in love with one of them, one of the few with a real job. He had been raised as a child in Fayette but had moved to Washington, D.C., during his high school years and gone on to Harvard. He was back in Fayette because his mother still lived there, and was teaching at Alcorn University, a black college. He taught English and had written a novel. He was one of three white professors at the school.

By the time the year was out, I had helped develop and get the financing for a day care center for children and a day care program for senior citizens. The programs brought more than $150,000 of support into the town, but the programs bogged down in petty politics and fights over resources. I was discouraged by these bigger problems, and there was no long-term commitment from the government or the state to pick up the costs after the federal grants ran out. The mayor asked me to renew my VISTA contract for another year, but I felt worn out by the strain of living in such foreign territory and doubted there was much more I could do. My boyfriend had been good and kind to me, but he drank too much, and he gambled, which made me wonder about a life with him. He was saving so he could quit his job and go live in Europe for a few years, writing and teaching for pocket money. He invited me to go with him.

"Does this mean you love me?" I asked him.

He smiled. "I like you a lot," he said. "I think we are good together."

He was right, we were good together, relaxed and easy, but he could not say he loved me and he made me feel rootless, ungrounded. I might have gone with him if he could have said he loved me, but perhaps not. I knew, deep down, I needed to go home and figure out who I was.

So I returned to Washington, jobless and confused about whether I had failed in Mississippi. I worried that I didn't have the guts to continue in social service work and, if I didn't, wondered what the hell I was going to do next. I knew my work in Fayette was largely futile. Unless I was willing to stay and dedicate my life to that community, I was not going to make any lasting change. And I knew I didn't have that kind of courage. I came home after my year was up because I couldn't face the poverty anymore. Mississippi beat me, stripped me of my youthful illusions and left me resentful of the world experience that replaced them.

Race relations are different in the South than in the North, and I also came home more troubled about them than ever, humbled and confused. After working almost entirely with blacks for a year, I now felt like an alien in white society. I tried to fit back into my comfortable, middle-class life in northern Virginia, but in truth I was not the same person. Even a trip to the local supermarket made me nervous—too many luxury items, and all the prosperity that had once seemed completely normal. I hadn't fit in, back in Mississippi—but I didn't fit in at home anymore either.

I got a job at the Peace Corps headquarters in Washington, where there were other returned volunteers trying to make sense of their lives, but none of us had any real idea how to get on with things. I dated a few lawyers, but to me they seemed to be worse than the suburbanites—overly satisfied with their wealth and status and only mildly curious about my experience in Mississippi. "Tell me what it was like working with poor people," they would say, ordering rare scotch and sending it back when it wasn't right. I drank cheap bourbon, the cheaper the better, because it reminded me of humid nights sitting on the sagging front porches of Fayette, and wondered if I would ever feel better. I missed Mississippi yet knew I couldn't bear to go back.

And then Ron walked into my life, and he had the answers.

Sometimes that happens. Sometimes there is someone who, you only understand later, becomes your keystone, who becomes the central, gravitational force that keeps you from spinning apart. Someone who makes sense of your life when you can't.

I met Ron in an acting class. On a whim, I had enrolled in an improvisational workshop at a local theater in Washington the summer of 1978, just six months after I returned from Mississippi. In my day job at Peace Corps headquarters, I did little more than answer phones and compose letters, so I had started writing a play in my spare time. But it wasn't going well. I had little feel for the rhythm of drama, no sense of how to capture events through dialogue. I hoped the workshop would correct that. Most of the other participants, however, including Ron, were there to learn how to act, and they brought a range of abilities to the stage. I didn't notice Ron in the first few days until he stood up one night and started quoting Victor Hugo from memory, filling the black theater space with a tumble of bitter words while contorting his body and transforming himself into a broken old man. When it was over he straightened up, shook himself, and turned back into Ron. I was impressed. Who was this guy? Nobody else in the class came close to having his power and presence. No one else had a mind like his—lightning fast, often showering the group with witticisms, impersonations, bits of poetry and philosophy. But I noticed something else—a tension, a pent-up energy that threatened sometimes to spill out in anger. I have a clear memory of sitting on the other side of the class from him, considering him, wondering if getting to know him would be like playing with fire.

A few days later he came over to where I was sitting on the grass, away from the rest of the crowd, eating a sandwich for my supper before class began. He asked if I wanted coffee. He held up a thermos and two cups and suddenly this impresario looked like he needed a friend. I said,

"Sure," and we started talking about the book I was reading—the letters of Isadora Duncan. Soon we were talking about other books, theater, music, writing, then about his life in Europe, and finally I told him about Mississippi and my disorientation at being back home. We missed the first hour of class, but by then it didn't seem to matter.

Over the next few weeks Ron and I met each night before class to share supper on the lawn outside, talking about our pasts and what we thought of the world. He smoked French cigarettes, stubby Gauloises with smoke thick enough to curl up between us as we huddled over our coffee cups. He had laser-blue eyes and that leading-man look, handsome and athletic. Best of all, he had a puckish humor, and an exotic European intellectualism. He talked about philosophers and history with a passion and understanding I had only glimpsed in college. He was thirty-four, ten years older than me. I was hungry for his insights and felt privileged to hear them—he seemed to disdain most other company. He talked about his childhood on Long Island and about leaving home at the age of sixteen. He told me about his years as a campus activist in the early sixties, about raising money to pay the legal costs of a friend who had gone to jail as a conscientious objector to the war, about the thrill of organizing a political crusade. He told me about his disappointment when the antiwar movement seemed to disintegrate in the early seventies, and how he had retreated to Europe to work on his dissertation and then later to teach. He had lived overseas for much of the decade, and seemed to understand the deep feeling of disaffection I had for the suburban, middle-class life I was expected to live now that I was back in Washington. Although he seemed cultured and worldly wise compared to me, something else came through when he stopped talking, a loneliness and a rootlessness I could understand. He knew what it felt like to have grown beyond everything you had learned before. Then one night he said something that really got to me, because it was about trying to find a way back. We both, it turned out, desperately wanted to find a way home.

"I came back to the States because of baseball," he said. "I want to raise my kids in a place where they play baseball."

I began watching him more closely.

In our acting class he was the star of the troupe, bright, creative, spontaneous, and funny as sin. His characters hummed with expressive power, turning quickly from anger to joy, tenderness to fury. When we sat alone together before class, his feelings flickered between us like quicksilver, and he often watched me to see what effect he was having. I learned early that part of my job was to be the appreciative audience. Sometimes it was hard to tell if what passed between us was theater or life.

But this didn't bother me. Indeed, there was something intoxicating in this, particularly the anger he expressed so freely. Before I went to Mississippi, I had had little experience with angry people. Anger, along with most other unpleasant feelings, was given little room in my mother's house. We had occasional angry moments, but conflict at home was usually resolved through earnest talking. My parents were compassionate people, always willing to listen even when they didn't like what they heard. They were particularly civil with each other, rarely raising their voices, rarely disagreeing openly. On the infrequent occasions they had what my mother called "discussions," they argued fairly, always on rational ground.

Ron didn't come from such an experience. His father had also been in the navy, but only during the war. After that he held a series of jobs, some that closed out from under him, others that left the family strained for money and security. Ron's mother, Evelyn, had grown up as the only daughter of parents who had worked as housekeepers for a Connecticut couple with no children of their own. Lonely and rich, they indulged the girl with violin lessons and garden parties, the spoils of a life that wasn't really hers. Marriage to Ron's father must have been like having a bucket of cold water thrown in her face: tight finances and the five children who soon filled their house on Long Island. Ron was the middle child, the third of three boys spaced just a year apart. She told me once that by the time Ron came along, she was tired of teaching the boys everything. "He learned to swim and ride a bike all by himself, because I was done with that by then," she said. He also learned how to manage his older brother's epileptic seizures, using advice his baseball coach showed him. Ron remembers his mother as depressed and overwhelmed by the family's needs. His father was distant, either working nights and sleeping days, or angry about the chaos in the house. In high school Ron hung out with a gang of juvenile delinquents and worked odd jobs while worrying about his future. He left home one night after a fight with his dad at the dinner table, dropping out of high school and driving all the way to Las Vegas, where his older brother was stationed with the army. He worked his way through high school and college in Las Vegas, then won a fellowship to graduate school in Illinois. By the time his father died of a heart attack in his early sixties, when Ron was in his late twenties, they had been estranged for several years.

I didn't piece this story together until years later. At the ⁓⁓⁓sed that Ron was more independent of family than anyone I'd ever met, and I envied that. He had free rein to express his opinions and passions without concern for whom he might offend. Mostly he used his anger to rail against the injustices of the world. Embittered by the complacency I felt around me in Washington, I was impressed by Ron's honesty and courage. I saw that he was angry but I was too naive to understand what that meant. At the time, I sensed that Ron could be the resonating box for the unresolved feelings I had brought home from Mississippi. My anger was little compared to his, and fit inside his like a nesting doll. Maybe he could hold all this anger for both of us.

I had been doing fairly well in acting class, until one night. There was one thing I couldn't do, and thinking back on it now it seems almost apocryphal because it revealed something I didn't want anyone—especially Ron—to know.

We were practicing stage fighting, and to get the exercise going the leader of the group called each of us individually to the stage, where she insulted us until we started throwing punches—stage punches, of course, and stage insults, but it felt like conflict nonetheless. I sat in the stands watching the others take their turns, including Ron, who threw his entire soul into the fray. Then the teacher called on me. I had a sinking feeling as I stepped into the spotlight and shook my arms and hands, which were unusually tense. She started insulting me, taunting me, trying to get me to hit her. And I did, but instead of using my fists I lashed out with words. I couldn't throw a punch. She shouted, she called me names, she impugned my honor—none of it worked. I couldn't do it. I could think up lots of mean things to say, but I would not fight. Finally she stopped the exercise, shaking with frustration.

"Why can't you do this?" she yelled. "Why are you

afraid to hit me? I've insulted you every way I can think of and nothing works! I've never seen someone who couldn't be goaded into a fight."

I crept back to my seat, deeply humiliated, wanting nothing more than to run and hide. I didn't know why I couldn't hit her, but it felt like something so deeply ingrained it was unmovable. If I could have, I would have. I just couldn't.

That night Ron offered to drive me home. When we got to my apartment, he asked me if I wanted to go out for lunch the following Friday.

Our romance, now that I look back on it, was like everything else in our marriage: intense, deep, serious, and something that had to be done right away if Ron was ready to do it. I was halfheartedly dating an old college friend that summer, and was getting letters from my Mississippi boyfriend. When Ron asked me out, I hesitated at first—I was vaguely troubled by his contradictory nature but attracted to it as well—then agreed. Lunch, after all, was relatively harmless as dates went. We ate at a sidewalk cafe in Georgetown and after a glass of wine Ron told me he was in love with life, with the weather, then he turned toward me and said, "And with you." I smiled. It was flattering to see that he was smitten, and I didn't stop to ask myself whether I liked him back. Neither of us went back to work that afternoon, but walked through the city streets talking and holding hands. We went out both nights that weekend, talking intensely over bistro tables sticky with beer. By Sunday evening I was scribbling in my journal that I had found the man I would marry. Compared to the others, Ron seemed to be offering me something substantial—stability, shelter, strength. The other men I knew were as lost as I was, still trying to figure out who they were. Ron knew exactly who he was. On the strength of his brains and his willpower, he had pulled himself out of the lower-middle-class world of his childhood and re-created himself. He had marched in labor union strikes in Paris, lived for a time with a group of expatriates in Madrid, tossed Italian phrases into the conversation like pepper. Thoughts of the college friend and the English teacher were fading quickly.

Ron also said he was ready for change. He had come back to the States, he said, to make a new life for himself, to bury that old bitterness and start again, fresh. Secretly, I believed his anger would go away if he was happy. It was a powerful challenge, and linked to what I had not achieved in Mississippi. There I had tried to fix a town and failed. But maybe I could save one person, one special person. Maybe I could save Ron.

5

R O N

Ron wasn't the first of his kind to fascinate me. I had been drawn to volatile, creative people all my life, as if seeking my opposite or someone who would help me voice the passions I kept bundled up inside. I had my share of dependable friends, but there was always another group I was secretly in love with, people who were different, even difficult, but talented and exciting; people who seemed to need me to hold still so they could orbit around something solid.

Aside from my own family, one of my closest ties was to my cousin Jean. Of the many siblings and cousins in our large clan, Jean and I had always been a pair. We were the same age and both second daughters. We were talkers and secret keepers, and agreed at an early age that we would grow up to be writers. But beyond that we were as different as the two sides of the moon, and that was where the real bond lay. She was the shadow, with her sadness and strange mix of fear and boldness. She could be angry, rigid, difficult, then just as easily turn playful, funny, and loving. I, on the other hand, was the sunny and easy child, consistent in mood, unflappable. I was the light, but it felt like a tepid beam against her rich tapestry of color and darkness.

She was quite gifted as a writer and early on learned how to watch the adult world for evidence of illness and unhappiness, which she would weave into bizarre stories that seemed far above her ken. I remember once, during a summer visit when we were about eleven, hiding under the bedcovers with flashlights so she could show me a story she had written. It was about German guard dogs ripping the limbs from young girls who spoke out of turn while waiting to be herded through the gates of a Nazi concentration camp. I remember the surreal juxtaposition of the light reflecting off the rose-patterned sheets, the glimpse of pink rug and pink slippers tucked under the edge of her bed, and in her mind the horror of this story. I had no idea how such a story could have come to her. We were not Jewish, after all. But she insisted that the story was the best she had ever written. It was about things she felt every day. She looked at me for confirmation, her dark eyes burning, but I couldn't hold her gaze. It was the first time in our lives I felt her move away from me because I couldn't say I felt those things too.

Over the next fifteen years of our relationship the differences between us collided more and more. She split from her family and worked her way through college, emerging an angry alcoholic and a lesbian. Over the years we kept in touch by phone, sent each other cryptic, overwritten letters, and occasionally visited for intense binges of talking, drinking, and tears. I loved her because she both needed me and challenged me, but there was often a scrim of tension. I felt bullied by her emotionally, and while I was often exhausted by her incessant need for attention, I knew that in some way I was her voice of reason. There was too much between us for either to let go.

It was from Jean that I learned how to love someone like Ron. When I met him I was certain she would love him too, because they shared the same caged intelligence and creative fire. Shortly after we started dating I wrote Jean and invited her to visit. "I've met the man I'm going to marry," I said in the letter, thinking that would get her attention. She had always been protective, even a bit jealous, of my affections, but it was worth a try.

The first time I took Ron home it was a Sunday evening and our neighbors, several families we had been close to for years, were gathering for a potluck supper. The talk was witty, familial, and fast, and Ron dazzled everyone with his comments and charm, or so I thought. But my parents were not people who were easily taken in.

My mother didn't approve of Ron, and my father seemed wary too. They had an instinctive negative reaction to our ten-year age difference and sensed that his family background was considerably more troubled than mine. They knew things they couldn't articulate, and I was impatient when they did articulate them.

"What has he been doing for the last ten years that he is only now getting a permanent job?" my mother fretted. "Are you sure he hasn't been married before? Maybe he has a wife and child somewhere."

I was offended, and let her know it. "He's been getting his Ph.D., and then he taught overseas because he couldn't get a teaching job here," I explained through gritted teeth. It didn't seem fair that they were questioning his integrity. "He's tired of an itinerant life and came back because he wanted to settle down," I added. Ron's history didn't seem odd to me. In truth, it seemed romantically bohemian. He was both the gifted professor and the angry young man, wrapped into a person now seeking the magic elixir of marriage and a home. As for his family's obvious problems, I was too young then to understand the deep troubles that can reverberate for generations down a family tree. I had no idea how intransigent such problems could be, mostly because I had not yet questioned my own family history, or tested the strength of my own inner circle. The family differences didn't seem to matter.

To my parents, who had known each other as children and were from similarly well-educated, stable New England families, there was something distressing about Ron that was less about him than it was his chaotic childhood in a lower-middle-class section of Long Island. Ron's parents had not managed their family well, and my parents knew that an unhappy past could haunt someone, even if that person eventually pulled themselves out of the family quicksand, as Ron had done.

They had similar concerns when my older sister, Anne, got engaged to a man who had grown up and out of a difficult childhood with a weak and dependent mother who jumped from marriage to marriage. He was charming and bright, but there was something troubling about him that they couldn't quite name. On the surface he seemed perfectly acceptable—he and Annie were both training to become ministers and social workers—but he could also be manipulative and domineering. When he and Anne first got engaged my parents sent her to join me for a short vacation. They were hoping I would talk her out of it.

But if I was supposed to get her to rethink her commitment to Jack, I'd missed my cue. Over the long weekend together, we talked more about our work and the challenges of social welfare jobs than her relationship with Jack.

When it came to men, we were both so lost we wouldn't have known what to say to each other even if we had tried. We couldn't see it clearly then, but we were both seeking the same thing: someone strong to help us escape the gravitational pull of our tight family circle, but also someone needy, someone who would be grateful to have married us. My mother—bossy and strong-willed—was hardly the model of feminine goodness that most men preferred. In our childhood home it wasn't father who knew best, it was my mother. She ran the household single-handedly for years, and without complaint or resentment. As if it were her job. She understood things that made most women shake their heads, like plumbing and motors, and she was quick to confront anyone who underestimated her. As children we had cowered in embarrassment when our mother argued with mechanics or hardware clerks, swearing to ourselves we wouldn't be like that when we grew up. She was independent and fearless, a natural beauty who scorned makeup and feminine affectations. In many ways, she was born a generation early. She could have flown fighter jets or run for local office. Most of my friends didn't have mothers like her.

For Annie and me she presented a formidable and contradictory message. We had inherited many of her strengths and talents but were afraid to own those powers. Men didn't like bossiness. It wasn't a model that sold well. I would not understand this until years later, but I believe we sought out men who would not tolerate it as a way of keeping it in check.

But there was another agenda. I can see now that both Annie and I needed someone to rescue. If we weren't going to be the boss in the relationship, then we had to have another source of power. We would be the rocks, the stable and patient ones. Our spouses would provide the entertainment and excitement, and we would be the supportive wives when they crashed and burned. And they would be grateful, even in our debt. They would need us. Perhaps then they wouldn't go off to sea.

At the time, though, neither of us had the self-knowledge to understand what we were doing. We were young and we were hopeful. Maybe, in an odd way, my parents' happy marriage left us naive—naive about trouble, naive about what a bad marriage would look like. We didn't expect it because we didn't know it could happen. I know that runs counter to the accepted wisdom—that it is the children of divorce who are more likely to divorce later in life—yet I think there was something about growing up under the halo of a healthy marriage that left us too innocent and too trusting. We didn't really understand that my parents' marriage worked because it was a marriage of equals. We didn't have any appreciation for how much effort, how much patience and goodwill it took. They made it look easy.

A few months later I stood at Anne's side as she married Jack over my parents' protests. Two years later I also would marry a challenging man. It would then take both of us the next two decades to recover from the unhappy consequences of those decisions.

Within a few weeks of our first date, Ron began talking about moving in together. My parents were alarmed that it was moving so quickly and said so. But I was an independent adult and they couldn't stop me, so they didn't try. In some fundamental way, I had already made a deep and abiding commitment to Ron. Before I really took the time to question what I was doing, I leapt and didn't look back. I broke the lease on my efficiency apartment and Ron found a small town house with a garden and room for a study, in a neighborhood of other young professionals. I grew hopeful; maybe this was a place where we could start to build something permanent. We both had stable, interesting government jobs. I was now working as a special assistant to the national director of VISTA, and Ron was a policy analyst on urban transit for the Transportation

Department. We planted a yellow rosebush in the backyard, bought a hibachi, and sipped wine in the evening as we waited for steaks to cook. It felt grounded, like a home. This was how life started, this was where it would all begin.

Now that we were under one roof, however, the relationship began knotting up in surprising ways. After the first few honeymoon months, Ron grew increasingly moody and sometimes seemed irritated to have me around. I found he was easily offended, either by some common annoyance or, more and more, by things I said or did. If I commented on something, I was usually wrong. If I reached out and touched him when he wasn't expecting it, he would pull back as if scorched. He seemed to need me to be quiet for long stretches so he could concentrate on his reading or the work he carried home from the office. He loved me best when I was sitting at my desk working on my hopeless play, when I looked like I was getting closer to living up to my potential. These problems puzzled me at first, then I realized that they hurt as well. But I decided to be patient. We were both adapting, I told myself. He had never lived with another adult, not in the way we were living together—sharing the hamper, the lease, our future. I didn't appreciate how telling that should have been.

I was Ron's opposite, and we were both attracted and repelled by what the other offered. I think now that he was deeply ambivalent about marriage, and yet wanted the things that came to people through marriage—a house, children, a circle of loving family. He believed his years living in Europe had left him behind, that he needed to settle soon or he would miss out on the American dream. I wonder now if he questioned even in those early days whether he had the stamina for the daily intimacy of marriage, the hard work of compromising on everything from cooking methods to sex. He admitted, years after we split up, that he didn't really like having another adult in the house, that I had been an annoyance. To this day he has a hermitlike quality, an ambivalence about the joys and frustrations of connections, and I understand it better. As a young woman, however, I didn't know what to think. I was still struggling to separate from my family and find a career, confused about what my adult life would look like. I had risked my parents' displeasure by moving in with Ron and now I didn't know how to retreat or even how to name what was wrong between us.

I didn't share these thoughts with anyone at the time, least of all my cousin Jean, because she was often harshly judgmental about men. Then one day she exploded into our fragile world, curious to meet Ron and ready to dislike him. She came dressed in leather motorcycle gear and carrying several bottles of scotch, straight from a job working in a chemical factory in Connecticut. It was shortly before she stopped drinking, and it was the angriest I ever saw her. She ranted about the chemical industry but flaunted her newly minted blue-collar status. She and Ron drank, talked, and soon were arguing, about labor practices, politics—and what I should be writing. I didn't dare leap in, and no one asked my opinion. I just sat back, my stomach churning when the words got ugly. Cleaning up the kitchen later, Jean told me Ron was full of shit and trying to control me. That night in bed Ron told me he thought Jean was full of shit and trying to control me. I went and sat on the floor in the bathroom and cried. On some level, I knew they were both right, yet I loved them. They were the hot stars in my sky, the people who set the darkness ablaze. I was troubled that they didn't like each other, but in an odd way it made sense. Part of the bargain with both Ron and Jean was that I reflected back what was good and helped them forget what was bad about themselves. Yet here they were, holding up the mirror for each other and demanding I acknowledge what I saw. What I saw in both of them was so mixed, so promising but so difficult, so contradictory a portrait. How could I tell them what I loved in them when I didn't understand it myself? All I could think was that I would lose them both. I washed my face and crawled back into bed with Ron, feeling disloyal to Jeannie, whom I could hear moving about downstairs. I had never before chosen a man if she disapproved. The next morning we could barely meet each other's gaze. I hugged her good-bye anyway, and watched her screech away in a cloud of exhaust.

I don't think they ever saw each other again. Less than two years later, when we married, Jeannie moved west to California the weekend of my wedding. She was the only important person in my life who wasn't there.

By the end of our first year together, my relationship with Ron had taken to dipping and shuddering like the roller coaster it was, an apt metaphor because it whipped from highs to lows and because I had so little control over it. After a year in the town house with the rosebush, Ron got impatient with the suburbs and we moved downtown, to a small one-bedroom apartment near the National Zoo. We were surrounded again by young professionals, but this felt less like the start of family life. He began staying after work at a bar near Dupont Circle, his secret place, he said. I wasn't to know where it was, mostly, I think, because he didn't want to have to share it with me. He needed space, he said. He didn't drink much at the bar and usually came home for supper, but his need for secrets troubled me.

I had always kept a journal, but during that period I began to write more often, trying to sort out what I was doing that was driving him away. Looking back at my journal entries from our first years together is painful, because they track the early stages of a relationship that should not have continued. I struggled for balance and, in an odd way, learned to cling to Ron to keep from sinking under the problems that rose all around us. He seemed to love and hate the world at the same time, and all that was in it, and I soon began filling my journal with similar messages, often separated by only a day or two. They read now like letters from someone drowning. "I love him so much," I would scribble in the dark after he went to sleep, writing only by what little light came from the window so as not to disturb him. Then a fight the next day, usually over something I had done, and I would pen harsher words. "Why is he so hateful toward me? It makes me hate him back." This, just a year into our relationship. It chills me, even now, to think of those nights hunched over my journal, trying to make sense of something that couldn't be solved.

And yet, it wasn't all bad. It never is; and therein lies the snare. When he was happy and worry-free, Ron could be like a mad elf let loose in a garden of earthly delights. He could spin yarns or lectures or hilarious free-wheeling flights of fancy from the thinnest material, and always for my entertainment. He would regale me with stories, or interesting things only he seemed to know, or challenge me to think about conventional wisdom in new, often heady ways. He could be generous and kind; he could be deeply understanding and supportive.

Although my parents had their doubts about us, they gradually grew to know him, his good and his bad, and understand better why I loved him. My younger sister, Penny, who was eleven when I first brought Ron home, remembers him as a comet streaking across her world—

charming, fascinating, artistic, bohemian. There were wonderful times together, sailing on the Chesapeake, holidays in the big house in McLean, cross-county skiing whenever there was enough snow to cover the grass. We were the happy family Ron had always wanted, and he moved into their hearts the way he had moved into mine, pushing aside the doubts as he barreled through the front door, grocery bags in hand, shouting to the assembly that he was planning to roast a duck. Drinks at six, cassoulet at seven. Everybody, hold on to your hats.

But sometimes it was too much, for Ron, for all of us. Sometimes the wine and the intimacy would sour late at night and Ron would argue with my mother or get angry with me—for little things, for big things, for still being so tied to that familiar circle. One night, at a birthday dinner for me, Ron took on both my mother and my older sister in an argument over the politics of the Soviet Union. He used his knowledge like a prizefighter, hammering his way through their more pedestrian views, and in the process exposing a curious contempt for their intelligence and character as he pursued the truth. It was not how we treated each other in my family. By then I had escaped to the other room, aching with tension just hearing the voices rise.

The truth was that Ron treated me the way he treated the rest of the world: hot toward it one day, cold the next. Because I had grown up in a stable emotional environment, I had little understanding of Ron's changeling nature. Sometimes the tension would rise to new highs and we would fight, usually starting with some infraction on my part. Most of the times our fights ended with both of us sullen, beaten down, but occasionally we ended up in an exhausted clearing of understanding, where we could both see the problems and find sympathy for each other. We would agree that I was young and immature, and that he needed more freedom. We would agree that I was too dependent on my family and too sensitive, and that he was unfair and sometimes cruel. He would feel sorry and I would forgive him. He would soften his criticisms and I would accept them. Sometimes in that hard-won space I would ask the impossible question: If we had so many problems, why did we stay together? And he always said one thing: "Because I love you." It was so simple. I thought it was enough.

After a year in the apartment, my government job changed and I grew bored. I knew I couldn't stay at a government desk much longer, and Ron pushed me to apply to graduate schools in journalism in and around Washington, to do something constructive with my instinct to write. I had thought of getting a master's of fine arts in creative writing, but Ron scoffed at such a plan as a waste of time and money. "If you were any good," he said, "you would just write and get published. You wouldn't need to go to graduate school for that." So journalism it was. I picked several schools and applied, praying that one would see fit to accept me even though I had little journalism experience.

Waiting to hear if a future would come through for me, however, made for a difficult time. I was unhappy at work, unhappy at home, and I began to wake up at night, afraid to disturb Ron but unable to go back to sleep because of the worries running through my head. I tried, briefly, to get some counseling through my limited health insurance, but was told I only needed to exercise more to cure the insomnia.

"I don't see anything really wrong in your life," the young counselor told me. "The only thing I don't understand is why you are so nervous."

I looked down at my hands, twisting in my lap. I desperately wanted the counselor to say I was okay and at the same time see how much pain I was living with. "Oh," I said, suddenly fearful he would think I was nuts. "You're right. I'm fine." And I made my hands go limp. There was nothing here I couldn't handle. Get a little exercise, go to graduate school, make something more of myself so Ron could be proud.

A few weeks later I was accepted into the graduate program at American University, just a mile from our apartment and my first choice of schools. Ron made a picnic of chicken and champagne, and as we celebrated under the spires of the National Cathedral we found ourselves talking about marriage. I looked at him and the jagged fragments of my life started to come together. "Are you asking me to marry you?" I said. There wasn't a ring and he wasn't on his knees. "I guess," he said. "Yes. Do you want to?" So I said yes. Yes, because my life was beginning and to say no might stop it cold. Yes, because I was ready to wear my mother's wedding gown, ready to end the debate in my head, ready to commit to something. I believed our problems were linked to the ambivalence we both felt but couldn't admit. I said yes because I was blindly optimistic despite the early warnings, because I still believed I was lucky. It might take hard work, but I was smart and unafraid. Hearth, home, marriage, children—that I could do. I was sure of it.

Our wedding was a big, relaxed, confused party, the house filled with cousins and old friends, my sister Anne officiating, Ron's mother playing her violin, and everyone sweating too much in the August heat. With the closure our engagement brought, Ron had seemed happier, more stable. The summer spent in preparation for the wedding was a busy, contented time for all of us, and my parents had mainly come to accept Ron, even with their reservations. I felt as if something necessary was unfolding, my destiny, my fate—almost as if I didn't really have control over it. So I didn't question it or try to stop it. One of our neighbors said that after the traditional kiss I literally jumped off the altar steps, the happiest bride she had ever seen.

6

___

BREAKDOWN

It didn't work. Marrying, despite our seriousness about the bond we had formed, failed to solve anything, never worked the magic we expected. We continued to operate as single people on a hundred levels. We didn't take a honeymoon because Ron started an intensive acting class right after the wedding. I was free until graduate school started the following month, so I went traveling in New England with a German friend and her boyfriend who had come over for the wedding. We went to visit my aging grandmother and she, knowing I had been married just a week earlier, assumed the German boyfriend was Ron. When she caught him and my friend smooching in the kitchen after dinner, she nearly fainted. When I explained that Ron was at home, she gave me a searching look. "But aren't you married now?" she asked. "Yes," I replied, not sure that fact was getting through to her. "Well," she said, "you should be with him, not traveling with friends." What had felt modern and open suddenly felt dangerously stupid, and I fretted over what that said about our relationship.

I thought being married would resolve my remaining ambivalence about Ron, but instead our distrust of each other produced a new series of walls. Instead of merging our identities, financially and officially, we kept our separate bank accounts, separate cars, separate names. Escape hatches, I called them at the time. We even divvied up the costs of the mortgage and groceries, like roommates.

Along with the financial escape routes, we also maintained our emotional distance. I still did many things with my family—leaving Ron at home if he didn't want to go sailing or to my parents' for dinner—and that riled him. He often said that I never really left my family, and that was true. I have my reasons, I would think to myself as he muttered about my immaturity and lack of independence. The truth was, I felt safer at my parents' and freer to be myself. I could talk openly with them without fear of criticism or rebuke. I needed someone who loved me unconditionally and I wasn't getting that from Ron.

While I retreated to my old family circle, he pulled back into the solitary life of the books and hobbies that had sheltered him from loneliness in the past. Not surprisingly, when we were together our intimacy was often jerky with hurt and misunderstood intentions. He was often frustrated by what he considered my weakness, my inability to stand up to demands from my bosses or my mother, and perhaps even from him. On top of that, he often seemed embarrassed by my more limited understanding of the intellectual pursuits that were so central to his identity, and he would berate me for knowing little about philosophy or politics, often calling me stupid or naive. At other times he seemed desperately grateful to have married someone who could weather his varying moods, and would come to me like a supplicant, begging forgiveness for being angry or hard. I was, undeniably, weak and immature at that time, and not nearly as well educated as my Ph.D. husband, but I was also just twenty-six, only beginning my career as a journalist and unsure of myself. Now that I know what people know at thirty-six—and how immature twenty-six-year-olds sometimes sound—I marvel that we lasted as long as we did.

Ironically, as my self-esteem withered at home, it began to build in my professional life. I did well in graduate school and then went to work for an upstart community newspaper in northern Virginia. My editor was a former *Washington Post* reporter, and he found in me the ambitious young cub reporter he needed to make a mark with his fledgling newspaper. Fueled by the praise I earned from him, I stayed late at county board meetings or spent hours at the office laying out pages and writing articles. Ron, on the other hand, was taking more acting classes and getting cast in local productions. He loved the exposure and experience, but it meant long evenings of rehearsals and weekends spent in production. We weren't together as much as newlyweds should have been.

Even when I was home I found myself avoiding Ron, going to bed early or working late at my desk on busyness I would pull up out of the stack of unfinished short stories on my bookshelf. It was in that first year of my marriage that I learned to live with the painful contradiction that would ultimately prove so exhausting: I acted and made decisions on the basis of an abiding commitment to Ron, and yet I questioned the relationship relentlessly in the privacy of my own head. I flirted with the idea of divorce even then, an unhealthy preoccupation that built gradually over the years. I could not leave Ron in little ways—demand better treatment, challenge him when he bullied me—so I left in big ways, even if only in my imagination.

But this hidden life, so separate and dishonest, troubled me. My journal grew dense with self-incrimination, sadness, and a creeping depression.

Then one cold February night early in our marriage, Ron woke me at about two in the morning and said he needed to tell me something important. He had me come sit in the wing chair in the living room, opposite where he had been hunched for hours on the sofa, unable to sleep. I sat down obediently, rubbing my eyes, a vague sense of dread creeping up through my body.

"I can't do this," he said without preamble.

"What do you mean? What can't you do?" I had no idea what he was talking about.

"All this," he said, waving his hands about the apartment. "I can't do this married thing."

I looked at him there, across from me. His eyes burned beneath their thick brows, his jaw was clamped tight with tension and determination. He stared back at me.

We had been married only two years, and often talked of our dreams of children and a house. I had my own internal doubts about our marriage, but it hadn't occurred to me that he also dreamed of getting out. Now he was saying that children and I would enslave him, and he couldn't do it. I was struck by his choice of words, and looked around the comfortable apartment wondering what part of our life together felt like slavery. He said something about how he didn't want to give in to sentimentality, that such a life would compromise him. Sentimentality seemed to be what it was all about, all this loving and marrying and dreaming of family. It didn't seem to be about me as much as the idea that a conventional married life was just too narrow, too claustrophobic. He presented his case, seemed to be saying clearly that the marriage was over, and then sat back to see what I would say.

I couldn't think of anything to say. It didn't seem to be open to debate. Instead, I cried, with Ron watching me from the other side of the room, apparently unmoved. For the first time it occurred to me that divorce would be an enormous, astounding failure, a very public humiliation. How could I get divorced when so many people had sent me out into married life with so much goodwill? Now that the possibility of divorce hung between us, I had no idea how I was going to get through it. After a while I ran out of tears and stumbled back to bed. In the morning I got up early while Ron slept like someone dead, made some notes in my journal, and headed out for work. I suddenly felt resolved. It wasn't going to be easy, but I was getting divorced, that was all there was to it. As the day went on, I made more notes and began planning what I needed to do. Hire a lawyer, pack my things, tell my parents. It was over. I felt an odd combination of sadness and efficiency.

But when I got home that evening, Ron was clattering around in the kitchen, making me dinner. He seemed happier, even lighthearted. I was stunned. "I thought we were getting divorced, right?" I asked, baffled.

"What do you mean?" he said, genuinely surprised.

"Last night—didn't you tell me you couldn't do this, this whole 'married thing,' as you put it?"

He was puzzled. "Last night I was depressed, and I just needed to tell you that. But it doesn't mean we're getting divorced. Why would you think that?" Why indeed.

Later he tried to explain that I shouldn't listen to him in the middle of the night, when his demons got the better of him. He said he needed to be free to tell me the darkest things, but that they didn't necessarily mean anything. He had a difficult time being married, but that didn't mean he wanted to get divorced or didn't love me.

We stayed married for almost ten more years, got a cat, bought a house, buried the first cat, got more cats, had a baby, remodeled the house, had another baby. But I never forgot the night he said he couldn't "do this married thing." When he began to struggle with real depression, when he seemed overwhelmed with responsibilities during the years when the kids were young, when he railed against life, I never forgot that there was a part of him that didn't want to be married. And I kept my list of notes on getting divorced. Just in case.

On the surface Ron and I pushed ahead with our life, looking for a house to buy in Washington and talking about the children we both hungered to have. But these large decisions, however happy they seemed in the dreaming, became minefields of tension in the doing. If we saw a house we liked, Ron would fret that someone else would buy it before we could sign a contract, and he would not allow me to talk about it with anyone else, even people who were not looking for houses. We were not poor, by any means, but neither were we rich, and driving through Washington's neighborhoods often made Ron sad, depressed that we couldn't afford the lovely old Victorian houses that seemed to represent happiness and success. At the time I couldn't understand why Ron chose to be sad. His life, after all, was sunny and promising by most standards. I didn't see then that mood, for him, was rarely a choice. I didn't understand the sense of claustrophobia he felt around me at times, or the deep restlessness that powered his endless searching—for the right house, a better job, a different life. His anger, I know now, sprang mostly from fears he barely contained—fear of failing, fear of falling back into the lower-middle-class life his parents had lived, fear of losing the connections he needed, fear of connections because they left him vulnerable to loss. In his lucid moments he would admit that he was difficult to live with. The central joke of our relationship was a line he repeated often, usually after some flare-up or fight: "The only thing worse than living with me is being me." It was so true it made me cry. No matter how unhappy I was, I knew it was worse for him.

Perhaps Ron would have done better with someone stronger, someone with better emotional boundaries who would have stopped him from saying too many damaging things, someone who would have refused to listen. My mother, who occasionally witnessed Ron berating me for some failing, often asked why I let him treat me that way. At the time I was bewildered by that question, unable to imagine how to make him stop, but in retrospect I think it was a fair request. I was probably a stronger person than I dared to be, and I contributed to the dynamic of the marriage by abdicating my power to build something better. I was trapped by my own cowardice, and on some level I knew it. I began to have unusual dreams, sometimes violent, always emotionally intense, dreams of people coming into our house and killing Ron while I hid under a stairwell, dreams of being responsible for horrible accidents that happened to people Ron liked, dreams of losing babies. The most common dream, however, was one I came to think of as my disability dream. In this dream I was slowly going blind, or sometimes losing the use of my legs or arms. That was bad enough, but most troubling was that no one would believe me. Everyone, including Ron and my family, kept telling me to quit complaining and get on with things. No one could see me stumbling, or acknowledge that I was sick, no matter what I said. And I would feel this panic rising because I couldn't see or move and no one would listen.

These dreams, I think, marked the start of an ugly internal process that I could not consciously acknowledge.

My untenable marriage split my personality wide open, creating a rift between the side of me that refused to fail, that thought I could solve the problems if we worked hard enough, and the other side, that of the young woman who knew the marriage was eroding her self-esteem, who knew she had to get out before her self-worth melted away.

As I lay in bed dreaming my tangled dreams, Ron took to sitting up late at night more and more often, troubled by things he couldn't articulate. My watchful mother, ever concerned, took me to lunch one day and asked how things were going for us. I admitted things weren't great, but didn't want to give her too many particulars. I remember feeling suddenly ashamed that our problems were so transparent and made a silent pledge to hold my cards closer in the future. I tried defending Ron. Yes, he was sometimes harsh, but he always regretted it later, always apologized, seemed haunted by things I didn't always understand. But she was on a mission and insisted I listen. To be blunt, she said, she thought Ron needed psychological help. At the time she was serving as chairman of the board of a local mental health clinic, and was learning more about the tide of depression rising in middle America. She passed me the name of a psychiatric nurse who was willing to talk with me. "Call her, sweetie," my mother said. "You might be able to get him some help." And then she said something I never forgot: "You can forgive him a thousand times and then one day you'll wake up and all your love will be gone, all used up. You don't want that to happen."

I took the card home and, after several weeks of nervous ambivalence, called the nurse. I felt like a traitor, as if I was breaking a code Ron and I had silently agreed to uphold. I described Ron's behavior and she said he might be fighting some serious depression, might in fact be bipolar, or manic depressive, and that he probably needed to see a psychiatrist. I instinctively feared Ron would scoff at such an idea, and questioned whether he was that ill. From what I knew of manic depression, it was the kind of mental illness that sent people to loony bins—people who couldn't tie their shoes or do their jobs or see the world clearly anymore. But I agreed to call the doctor she recommended because there was something in what she said that rang true. It turned out the doctor's office, by a stroke of luck, was in the building directly across the street from our apartment.

Awkwardly, because I felt guilty calling the doctor without Ron's knowledge, I dialed the psychiatrist. I explained my concerns, some of Ron's behavior, and then asked him if I could set up an appointment for Ron. "Well," he said carefully, in that patient way shrinks have, "he will need to call me. I can't see him unless he wants to work with me. Have him call me to set up an appointment."

I said I would, but I already knew I wouldn't have the courage to tell Ron about the doctor. This was an obvious invasion of his privacy, and by initiating such a thing I was launching a covert attack against him. I kept the doctor's phone number in a secret drawer in my desk, but I didn't tell Ron about the conversation. I didn't want him to know I was beginning to question his sanity.

I first learned about nervous breakdowns from my cousin Jean. We were visiting her family when they still lived in Massachusetts, so I must have been about nine. Jeannie and I were out in their driveway making lazy circles on our roller skates when Jean, ever interested in the adults around her, pointed to a woman across the street who was helping a toddler ride a tricycle. The woman, she said, had had something called a "nervous breakdown" that winter. I had no idea what a nervous breakdown was, so Jeannie described it in full. "Screaming, crying—she even tried to jump off the roof. Mom said she heard voices telling her to jump, but there was no one there."

"Did she jump?"

"No. She chickened out."

I watched the woman as she pushed her little boy up and down the sidewalk. She seemed calm and patient, her hair tied neatly behind her head. She didn't look like the maniac Jean described. "Well, she was," Jeannie insisted. "Her hair was out to here. You should have seen her."

I began to wonder about nervous breakdowns and imagined that women I knew—my mother's friends, my friends' mothers—might be leading double lives, calm and patient around the dinner table but crazy and self-destructive in the deep of night. My mother was nothing like that, of course, which may explain my fascination. It is odd to think that I learned much about how to be a single mother from watching my mother manage our military life—the moving, the packing, the effort to build friendships in each new setting because she needed both the support and the comfort of the neighbors around her. I know she had low moments, but she rarely indulged in unhappiness and never seemed the least bit in danger of cracking. She kept herself busy with her children and her volunteer work, knew how to relax at the end of the day, and seemed thankful for the life she had found. Nervous breakdowns, I somehow deduced, were for women who had more time and fewer people counting on them. They were for women who could afford them. As a literature major in college, I specialized in reading the works of women notorious for their emotional disorders, from Sylvia Plath to Virginia Wolfe to Zelda Fitzgerald. Depression seemed to be a woman's disorder.

But I still knew little about depression. I thought of it

as having two essential forms: the everyday blues we all occasionally struggle with, the sadnesses and disappointments of life, and then the real thing, serious mental illness, the door through to the other side that transformed people into angels or madmen.

When mild depression hit me, as it did during that period after Mississippi and during the early years of my marriage, it took the form of a low-grade numbness rather than an exhilarating craziness. It didn't make me exciting; it made me dull. It didn't make me write better; it made me seize up before the blank page. It was more like a nagging headache—blunting my enjoyment of life but hardly disabling me. In the summer of 1983 I could feel the pain building for both Ron and me. He had been diagnosed with an ulcer and was beginning to worry about the heart disease that had killed his father at an early age. I began to suspect we were heading toward some kind of catastrophe. I didn't know what, but I could feel it coming, as if our shaky marriage would be blown apart by either a natural disaster or some calamity of our own making.

In my journal scribblings I noted Ron's deepening depression and wondered what would happen to us if he had a collapse of some sort. For several weeks in early August he became desperate to keep me home, angry if I went out with friends or even to work, although when I was there he didn't pay much attention to me.

Then one night I came home after a tense day at the paper to find Ron sobbing on the sofa. He was laid out, as if sick, and crying steadily. There was a glass of wine in his hand but he didn't seem to be drinking it.

"I don't know what's wrong with me," he gulped. "I can't stop."

I took the wine away and knelt down next to him. I thought perhaps he had had terrible news.

"Ron, has someone been hurt?" I could barely utter the words. "Has someone died?"

He cried harder but shook his head. "No, it's nothing like that," he choked out. "It's me. It started at work and I had to shut the door to my office because I couldn't stop."

He didn't stop all evening, and he couldn't tell me much about what was bothering him. He finally fell asleep on the sofa without any dinner. The next morning the crying started again and I urged him to stay home, but he insisted on getting dressed for work, although he needed my help in doing it. "I have to go. If I don't, I'll die," he told me. I didn't argue. I tied his shoes for him and then helped him get a cab. He didn't want to cry on the subway.

That evening he was home, crying, when I got back from work, so I went to my desk and got the name and phone number of the psychiatrist I had spoken to a few months earlier. I had no idea what Ron would say. Normally I would have been afraid he would be mad at me for talking with a psychiatrist about him, but he was so broken up he didn't seem capable of anger.

I gave him the name, explained briefly who the doctor was, and said I was going out to the corner store for milk. I was only gone a few minutes, but when I came back Ron was on the phone with the psychiatrist, agreeing to see him the next morning.

When he hung up he was white.

"He asked me if I was suicidal," Ron said.

I put down the groceries. "Are you?" I remember feeling like a clinician, detached from the answer.

"I don't think so, but I said I wasn't sure. He said you should call him if you think I'm in danger."

"Give me the number, then," I said. "I don't want to have to go looking for it at a bad moment." Ron handed it over like an obedient child. Something had already shifted between us, although it would be months before I would recognize this.

Ron cried off and on for nearly a week, going into his office each day but hiding there behind his closed door. Each morning I would help him into his shirt and tie his shoes, and each evening I would get him to eat a little bit and then help him into bed early. After he was asleep I would pour myself a stiff bourbon and wait for my father to call. As soon as my parents knew Ron was having a breakdown, my father took to calling every night to find out how I was doing. He had battled a brief but intense depression years earlier when he'd faced some difficult career choices, and his sympathy for Ron ran deep. I didn't know what to tell him, it was all still so new, but the nightly phone call felt like a lifeline.

Ron saw the psychiatrist each day, and by the end of the week was beginning to pull himself together.

As breakdowns go, Ron's was minor. One of my editors quizzed me about it when I tried to explain why I had been late for work several days running.

"Did he hallucinate? Hear voices? Try to cut himself?"

"No," I replied. "He cried. All week."

"Oh, that's nothing," she said with disdain. "Breakdowns are only really serious when they hallucinate."

We left for a vacation in New England the next week, and by then Ron had mostly recovered—thanks to the psychiatrist and some medication he had prescribed—but now I was beginning to fray. We traveled around our favorite haunts, staying in old country inns and going to summer-stock theater at night, and the minute the houselights went down I would start to cry. And now it was me who couldn't stop crying.

7

CONTAINMENT

SPECIALIST

It would be several years before I would fully understand my response to Ron's breakdown, and even what it was about me that made that response feel so natural. In unraveling it later, I saw there were lessons I had learned as a child that worked in subtle ways to encourage me to stay and fight his illness. In my mother's world, having the gumption to stay with something and work out a solution was a central value, and Anne and I have often wondered how our lives might have been different if we hadn't stayed so long in our first marriages, struggling to correct unfixable problems.

But it wasn't just that. There was something else about me in particular, a deep capacity to cope with untenable conditions, that I learned as a child. There were things in my past I didn't want to face, that took me decades to acknowledge and understand, but which I now see shaped the way I managed my marriage. It's a small part of a larger picture, not a dominant force, but significant, essential.

It's a cool November evening in 1967, just a few days before Thanksgiving, and I'm in the backseat of the family station wagon, still smiling from an afternoon spent playing with my best friend, Nancy. Peter's beside me, pestering me as usual, but it doesn't matter. I'm happy and contented, my world feels perfect. I'm in the sixth grade, eleven years old, starting to get small buds on my chest. Nancy and I spent the afternoon making cliff dwellings out of her bookshelves for a collection of tiny stuffed mice, which seems almost childish for a sixth-grader, now that I think back. I am clearly at that in-between age—sometimes old enough to talk with the grown-ups at the dinner table, and ready for my first bra, but also young enough to play with dolls. It's a vulnerable age.

What I remember next is that we pull up in front of the house, all lit up with the glow of people at home and getting dinner on the table, and my mother says to us: "Go inside and say hello to Cousin Cliff."

And my heart sinks.

I had forgotten he was coming. I had forgotten that it was almost Thanksgiving. I panic slightly.

"Is he staying in my room?" I say, trying to keep my voice from squeaking.

"Of course, honey. That's really the only good place for him," Mom says, getting out of the car and holding my door open for me. "Come on, sweetie. He'll be happy to see you." She doesn't have any idea.

We go in and there he is, my cousin Clifford, heavy, sweating, breathing hard. He wraps me in a bear hug that squeezes my breasts tight against his chest, making the little buds hurt. He smells of sweat and bad breath and English Leather aftershave. After a moment he lets me go. I keep my head turned away so he won't kiss me. The hug is bad enough. I manage a few polite questions: "How are you? How was your flight?"

Cliff is a distant cousin, someone left behind by a family that disintegrated several generations back. He's slow, possibly slightly retarded. No one is sure. He holds down a modest job, lives on his own, but only marginally. He is difficult to have around, dependent, and whiny. His life is empty of friends and everyone in the extended family feels sorry for him. My mother and my aunts pass around the responsibility to include him, invite him to visit. The family long ago gave up trying to find out why he was slow, seems to accept him as one accepts a disability. He's a problem, but one they manage.

To a child, though, Cliff is an enigma—an adult but someone treated like a young child, treated even like a bad child—someone unruly and unpredictable. Someone you have to watch.

After a few pleasantries, I escape the scene in the living room and go down the hall to Annie's room. She looks up from her desk. "Hi," she says, eyeing me closely. "Are you okay?"

"I forgot he was coming," I say nervously. "We've got to go down to my room."

"I know. Mom brought most of your stuff up, but I'll go down with you."

Peter and I have rooms in the basement, next to the recreation room and the laundry, and when Cliff visits he gets to sleep in my bed. I move upstairs to Annie's room for the week, sleeping in the double bed with her and worrying about what Cliff is doing down below.

Annie and I slip downstairs, away from the hubbub of dinner, and into my room. He's only been here a few hours but it already smells of him. I grab a suitcase from my closet and pull open the dresser drawers. I scoop up all my underwear, all my shirts, all my pants and dump them in the suitcase. I don't need nearly half this clothing for the time he'll be here, but I don't want to leave it down here.

The year before, he left twenty-dollar bills wrapped inside my underpants and a *Hustler* magazine slipped inside one of my shirts. I figure it will be harder for him to hide things if the drawers are empty.

Here's the irony of this: Cliff loves me, adores me. I've been his favorite, ever since I was little. He steals my school papers out of the trash can next to my desk and takes them home to his apartment. I suspect that he also steals my underwear, although I'm still young and not yet possessive about clothes, so I'm not sure. When he gets the chance, he hugs me, often surreptitiously sneaking in a bump to my breasts, a hand that gets loose and slides across my bottom. Sometimes, if he catches me alone in a room, he says things that shouldn't be said to a twelve-year-old girl. He can't help it, he says. He loves me. Don't tell your mother, he says.

So I don't. But Annie knows and Annie protects me. He doesn't visit often, but when he does, usually for a holiday like Thanksgiving or Easter—she goes on patrol, making sure I'm never left by myself, sitting with me in the living room while I practice the piano in the afternoon. She helps me go through my drawers after he leaves, helps me figure out how to throw away the girlie magazines. The year he leaves the money, Annie says we should keep it, but I tear the bills into tiny pieces and we flush them down the toilet. I cannot bear to look at them.

This strange dance goes on for years. Family holidays get divided into the happy ones—when he isn't there—and the others, when he is and I retreat into my shell. I don't talk as much, don't laugh as much, because if I forget and act like myself I find him gazing at me from across the room, loving me. I can't stand it, that glint he gets in his eyes when he looks at me, so I contain myself, muffle my bubbliness. Attention can be a dangerous thing.

So here is how I handle this: I learn to manage it. Over the years I learn how to pull away, how to squirm just enough, but without being obvious about it, so that he can't quite reach what he wants. I learn to feint to the left, then slip away at the last minute so someone else gets stuck sitting next to him at Christmas dinner. I learn how to whisper back at him when he comes up beside me, mean things I would never say to anyone else, things that make him go away. I learn to contain the problem, and it is contained. It never gets any worse. He never does anything beyond blundering into the bathroom when I'm bathing or going through my underwear drawer or grabbing for my breasts momentarily in the front hall.

Annie is tall and blond and beautiful, and yet it doesn't happen to her. I'm not a beauty, yet there seems to be something about me, something I cannot control, that attracts men, both good and bad. Maybe it is friendliness or openness. Maybe it's a passive, vulnerable quality, like a house with the front door standing open. As I've grown older I've learned how to mask it. Men don't bother me in airports anymore, as happened when I was a young reporter and traveling for the newspaper. Maybe it's because I'm older, but I've learned how to shut myself down, how to tamp down my personality. I rarely go out in public without that protective wall around me.

As a young teenager, I think it doesn't happen to Annie because she has a steady boyfriend, a gentle young man who spends a lot of time in our house and is often there when Cliff visits. I begin to think of a boyfriend as protective, someone who can shield you from other men. So I grow up hoping to find a strong man who will protect me. The day I tell Ron about Cliff he says that if Cliff ever tries anything with me again, he'll deck him. I say no, no. He doesn't do it anymore, now that I'm grown up. But secretly, I'm relieved. Now I'm safe.

8

M O M M Y   L I O N

When we got back from the vacation we took after Ron's breakdown, I was depressed and worried about everything—Ron, myself, our partnership, our fragile future. The disaster I had anticipated had happened but it hadn't cleared the air or released the tension. It had only revealed what I hadn't been able to see before: that Ron had a real illness, that his changeling nature was perhaps more permanent, more serious than I had suspected. Instead of the strong, supportive man I thought I married, I now found myself bound to someone with a depressive illness. It raised all sorts of questions—about having children and buying a house—but there were few easy answers. Because if it was an illness, I was trapped. I had pledged to stay with him in sickness as in health. I just never thought sickness would look like this.

Ron's breakdown, minor though it was, turned out to be a watershed event in our marriage. It upset the power balance, reordered the relationship, brought us closer yet also drove a wedge of worry between us. It left us hoping things would get better, a deep-seated hope that became the center of gravity for our relationship. If he could get better, then I wanted to stay in the marriage. And I wasn't the kind of person to leave before we tried.

So we tried. Ron saw various doctors and was diagnosed with anxiety and a chronic, low-grade depression that could be expected to flare up at times, perhaps on a seasonal basis. February and August had always been difficult months for him, so this made sense. It was nothing psychotic, they said, nothing particularly life-threatening. They prescribed an antidepressant and talked with Ron about his past.

At the same time Ron's psychiatrist suggested I start counseling, because the partners of people like Ron—he said—often suffered from their own depression. The idea of turning the spotlight on me was disconcerting—I was the strong one, after all, the one who didn't lie sobbing on the sofa—but I was also relieved. I needed someone to help me sort out what was happening.

I started seeing a gifted psychologist that fall, and we began to unravel the strands of experience and family history that left me passive in the face of a strong, volatile spouse. My psychologist, Ursula, asked me point-blank why I was so afraid of confrontation with Ron, my mother, or, for that matter, anybody in authority. She suggested that Ron's bark was worse than his bite, that I should challenge him more and push harder for what I wanted in the marriage. I found it maddening when people suggested I shouldn't let Ron treat me like a child, because I couldn't think how I was supposed to stop him, but her question instead was "Why do you stay?" I hoped therapy would confirm my sense of victimization, and instead it forced me to confront my own role in polarizing our relationship. She helped me acknowledge the vanity that fed my need to be the good partner in every pair, that enabled me to hog the moral high ground. She suggested early in our sessions that my unhappiness was my own responsibility, even if I couldn't control or anticipate Ron's moods. I was astounded by that thought, by the idea that the trap had a way out if I would only look for it. For the first time I started thinking about what I could do to make my life better rather than obsessing about the things I couldn't change—Ron's outlook, Ron's moods, Ron's happiness.

My parents, sensing these challenges, took me aside one afternoon and asked me to consider putting off the idea of kids until, until—no one really wanted to say until what. My father was hopeful that therapy and antidepressants would stabilize Ron, but he knew it might take several years to work. My mother was perhaps more cautious. "Wait and see how he does," she said. "Bright people often benefit the most from counseling, and he is certainly bright. But don't jump into anything right now."

I promised, relieved, deep down, to have an excuse to delay, but I was also disappointed. I was already nearing thirty, and Ron and I had been married for three years, three difficult years. He was still loving, but still just as often critical and bitter about my inadequacies. I couldn't understand how someone who claimed to love me so much could only love me conditionally. As if to balance myself emotionally, I longed for children, could feel the rising hunger to have someone in my life who loved me no matter what. I watched kids in the grocery store, talked with friends who were having babies. There always seemed to be a cocoon wrapped around these families, a cocoon of preoccupation with the dailiness of it all—reading stories at night, rocking the child through the last bottle. This cocoon seemed warm and cozy and protective, and I wanted to live inside such a place, wanted those little arms around my neck, needing me, distracting me. But I knew my parents were right, so

I packed those dreams away. I didn't tell Ron about the promise. I wasn't telling Ron much of what was in my head or my heart.

By then I had outgrown my job with the small community newspaper and was freelancing as a stringer for the *Washington Post*, covering a farming region northwest of the city that was being carved up by big developers. The experience was good but the pay was lousy, and I didn't get benefits. I couldn't afford to continue stringing for long, but the thought of job-hunting with my battered ego and nagging depression was more than I could bear. Day after day I sat at my borrowed desk in a far corner of the *Post* newsroom, talking with sources and filing my stories, hoping for a lead to something better. Then one day the editors of the financial desk called me over. They said they wanted to hire me to cover local growth and development, a beat that was just taking off in the early eighties. "You're nobody," said *Post* executive editor Ben Bradlee when he interviewed me. "But you know what you're doing and the editors want you." It seemed too good to be true, but it was, and the day I typed my first *Post* byline I felt my depression lift. I wasn't stupid, as Ron sometimes said, or untalented. If the editors at the paper thought I was capable, then maybe I was.

Now that we had two decent incomes, Ron began pushing to buy a house. It wasn't as big a commitment as having children, but because our down payment was mostly mine—money I had inherited from my grandfather and that had grown in the stock market—it felt like a test of faith. If I was going to stand by him, he seemed to be saying, then I would willingly put my money on the table.

I knew my parents found the idea of a serious financial commitment nearly as troubling as having children, but when I talked with Ursula about it I saw that I couldn't live my marriage with one foot out the door. Besides, I believed in the power of psychotherapy. I believed our hopes would be fulfilled, that Ron would get better now that he had been diagnosed and was getting help. There was every reason to think change—the cure that would make him a happy person—was right around the corner. Maybe a house and kids could help that along.

Ron and I searched in the neighborhoods we liked and soon found a brick colonial within our price range that was airy and light. It had a small nursery upstairs, space for a study in the attic, and a rental apartment in the basement that would bring in extra income. We closed on the ides of March, and that night, after eating a supper of Greek takeout on the floorboards of the bare living room, we opened the windows to the spring air and danced gleefully together in the dark of the empty house. Ron, who had been anxious about the closing and the financial plunge, was as high as a kite now that it was over. So I was happy too. As with our wedding, I let events carry me along, reluctant to question the tumble of activity or consider if this was what I really wanted. Making Ron happy was my job, and through me he could get the house and the children he had always wanted. Despite my work with Ursula, I wasn't ready yet to wonder what it was costing me to make Ron happy. I still believed my happiness would piggyback on his.

But there was, once again, a dark side. Although the closing went smoothly, moving triggered all of Ron's fears and anxieties. He was tense, and we were both tired from a week of packing and cleaning. My brother, Peter, offered to help us move, and on a rainy Sunday we wrestled everything into a moving van and then wrestled it out again and up the steps of the new house. It was an exhausting day, and at some point that afternoon things broke down and suddenly Ron was raging at me, yelling about something now long forgotten. All I remember is that Peter suddenly stepped in between us and faced him down. Later, Peter told me he did it because he thought Ron was going to hit me. "I hate him when he treats you like that," Peter said, shaking his head.

"But he wouldn't hit me," I remember saying, oddly defensive and at the same time humiliated that Peter had witnessed such a scene. I trusted that Ron would never raise a hand to me, but I also knew he had little idea how scary he was when angry, his face contorted in contempt or rage, his body shaking. Like so much about my marriage—about my life—I reacted to Ron's outbursts with opposite feelings, and I could hold them in my heart at the same time. I was both afraid and unafraid of him. I knew his limits but I questioned his control.

The next day I stayed home from work, sick and overwhelmed. I remember lying on the mattress which had been tossed flat on the floor because we hadn't had time yet to put the bed together. I looked out at the sun shining down on this pretty neighborhood, the trees just beginning to leaf, the daffodils golden in the neighbor's yard, and I felt hopelessly trapped.

Houses can long for children. It's not just the adults who live there, but the houses themselves that can ache for the hubbub of kids. Houses without them are too big, too empty. Especially unhappy houses.

We waited several years before we started trying to have kids, as I had promised my parents, but it was not an easy time. We each worked on our own therapy, heads down in our individual stories, not sharing much of what we uncovered. We were also consumed by our jobs. Ron rose steadily in the policy office of the Federal Transit Administration, writing papers and directing research, while I scrambled to meet the demands of my editors at the *Washington Post*. My work at the newspaper was intense, dominated by the tyranny of deadlines and the complexity of financial reporting. I covered both the boom and the bust of the real estate explosion of the eighties, criss-crossing the Washington region chasing vanishing farms, mortgage scams, environmental hazards, and failed savings and loans. It was often exhausting work, and the newsroom was a competitive pressure cooker, but the *Washington Post* gave me something I hadn't had before—success and the deep self-respect that came from overcoming my fears. Writer's block, shyness, self-doubt—all evaporated in the hot glare of the work. Never again would I doubt my abilities, even when Ron questioned them, as he still did.

On the surface Ron and I were like nearly every other professional couple we knew: We had friends over for dinner, went to the theater, met at a sidewalk cafe in Dupont Circle each Friday night for dinner and a movie. But the perennial friction of our relationship was wearing us down and we were growing apart. Old hurts often sat stubbornly between us, and I worried often about how best to manage Ron rather than just enjoying him. If I had something depressing or bad to tell him—a friend ill with cancer, a summons from the IRS—I would spend hours strategizing about how and when to do it. I worried over what he ate and drank, whether he took his pills, whether he exercised. Ursula suggested it would be hard to be Ron's psychiatric nurse and his wife at the same time, but I couldn't stop. I'm not sure that by then I knew any other way to live.

.　.　.

One of the mysteries of divorce is why so many couples fail to face their problems until after they have kids, after they make that commitment that binds them together forever. It is one of the ironies of bad marriages that many of them barrel along with all the activities that signal good marriages. Couples on the verge of divorce do things that look crazy from the outside: They sign a contract to build an addition to the house, move to another state, or even get pregnant with a third child. Yet there is a subtle logic to such plans, a logic many divorcing people recognize. In truth, it is hard to stop a life while one considers divorce. Most people who divorce start the process in secret, holding a silent debate with themselves that may last for years. All the while, life crashes forward. Decisions have to be made, children grow up, houses slowly but inexorably fall apart. Life is a dance, and it all goes whirling on, even as we consider stepping away. Because the minute you stop dancing, the partnership breaks. We know that, and so we keep our feet moving.

Sometimes friends ask why I had children when I was so unhappy in my marriage, and the question makes me squirm. Probably I shouldn't have, if you listen to the sociologists, because kids of divorce are vulnerable to everything bad—drugs, low achievement, poor self-esteem, suicide. You name it, they tend to suffer from it more than their peers whose parents have intact marriages. The conventional wisdom is that people in bad marriages have kids hoping they will provide the missing glue, keep the marriage from spinning apart. When I hear this I think, How stupid, how selfish, and that is true, it is stupid and it is selfish. People in bad marriages are notoriously self-focused, often obsessed with their problems and oblivious to the rubble they leave in their wake. But maybe it is less conscious than that. Most people don't bail out of unhappy marriages until they have tried everything, or nearly everything, and unfortunately that includes children. Maybe I pushed on into parenthood because kids were the one true test. Everything else I could escape or recover from, even financial ruin. But not kids. I knew that was a lifelong commitment. With kids, I wouldn't have permission to divorce Ron. I could quell the debate in my head once and for all. Selfish, yes, if it is selfish to try and save one's marriage.

Maybe the motive was deeper than that. Perhaps the very act of creating progeny—raising children to fill a life and fulfill the tug of biology—was more important to me than whether my marriage survived or collapsed. I could feel the years slipping away. If I didn't have children with Ron, I might not have them at all. I had had some problems with my cervix and my gynecologist suggested I go ahead and have kids if I was planning on them, "in case we have to take all the equipment out later," he said. I began to panic. Ron was my chance. I was now past thirty, needed to get on with it, especially if I wanted more than one child. Besides, it is much easier to have children than to get divorced, especially if one is on the fence. I knew kids would bring joy and happiness to my entire family, including Ron. If I got divorced instead, everyone would be miserable and it would be my fault. I didn't think this out consciously—few of us do—but these hidden motives proved powerful enough to stifle my doubts. We threw my diaphragm away and began charting my periods. Within a few months I was pregnant.

When I called my sister Annie to tell her, she sounded unusually subdued. She congratulated me, trying to muster her usual enthusiasm, but then suddenly started to cry.

"What is it?" I asked, startled. She had had a baby the

year before, Adam, the first grandchild, a golden boy with huge brown trusting eyes. Maybe something was wrong with Adam. "Is it, is it . . ." I didn't want to put my fear into words—it was too awful.

"Oh, Wen, I think my marriage is coming apart," she said, gulping air, trying to control her sobbing. "Jack told me today that he's in love with someone else. But he says it's just an affair of the heart. They haven't slept together." She stopped to collect herself. "He told me this like he was some kind of fucking hero, being in love with her but not acting on it."

My heart froze. Annie and I had suspected something like this. When I had gone to visit her in California shortly after Adam's birth, we had stumbled across Jack one day having lunch at a shopping mall with this woman, and then seen him driving with her in the next town two days later. Another time Annie had pictures developed and there, among the baby shots and photos of friends, was a picture of Jack and the woman, whom Annie recognized as a family friend, holding hands surreptitiously under cover of a picnic table while in the background Annie pulled hamburgers off the grill. Whoever took the picture probably had no idea what they were capturing.

"What are you going to do?" I had no idea how I would handle something like this.

"I'm pissed but I'm trying to be open-minded," she said. "He said he would stop seeing her." We were both silent for a minute. "I don't know what I think," she finally said. "All I can think of is Adam."

Despite the warning signs in the news from my sister, being pregnant made me happy in a way that I had not felt for years, a deep-down, for-always kind of happiness. A happiness that couldn't be touched by the daily tension of living with Ron. Not surprisingly, I threw myself into the pregnancy with the same perfectionist gusto I brought to my work. I made a chart of foods to be consumed for maximum nutritional benefit and hung it on the fridge. I started special stretching exercises and interrogated experienced moms for the inside dope. I was going to do this right. Maybe I wasn't the greatest wife, but I was going to be a phenomenal mother.

And then I started to bleed. I bled for a week, brown spots appearing on my underwear but drying up quickly. My doctor told me not to worry and to try and rest more. I was under deadline for several stories and felt torn. On the one hand I was unwilling to give them up, but then again I was angry that the paper was pushing me so hard. Then one morning I woke up and I was bleeding seriously, big clumps of bright-red knotted stuff. I called my doctor and he said I might be miscarrying. I called Ron at work and he met me at the doctor's office. The technician turned on the sonogram machine and rubbed the cold probe across my belly, but nothing showed up on the screen. After ten minutes the doctor cleared his throat and said, "There's no baby here. I don't think the fetus ever really developed." He sent me home, saying I would probably bleed heavily all night. "If it gets bad, call us."

I cried quietly during the drive home, with Ron watching me from the driver's side. It was one of the ironies of our relationship that Ron was often at his best when I was at my worst, or during one of those crises that makes all the bullshit fall away. He put me to bed and brought the television into the room, propping me up and feeding me Advil to quell the cramps. He brought me soup and cookies, tried to cheer me up with jokes. I finally told him to go away and fell asleep early, but I woke up in pitch-blackness several hours later, my body trembling with cramps and cold. I was bleeding at a prodigious rate, soaking through pads and underwear in minutes. Ron called the doctor, who told us to meet him at the emergency room.

With Ron at the wheel, we sped across town, careening through lights and around corners, and I gripped the door handle in an attempt to breathe away the pain. Ron prattled nonstop about whatever goofy nonsense he could dream up, trying to get me to laugh. As we waited for our doctor in the emergency room, he began mimicking people we knew, pulling medical devices out of drawers for props and prancing around until I was laughing so hard I was afraid I would pee in my pants. The doctor was surprised to find us in hysterics, but he just shook his head and gave me a shot to stop the hemorrhaging. They checked me in and did a D and C later in the morning. Ron, now wistful and melancholic, picked me up that afternoon and took me home. I was still woozy from the anesthesia and lack of sleep, but he insisted we go out for supper that night. He had made reservations at my favorite restaurant, for dinner and a comedy show. I remember sitting in the restaurant, my stomach still too upset to allow me to eat much, considering this husband who seemed desperate to pull me through this disappointment. He was wonderful, he was intense, he was pushing me. I needed to crawl in a cave and grieve.

Our miscarriage was a bitter disappointment. Perhaps I should have taken it as a second chance to reconsider, but instead the miscarriage hooked me into a fierce determination to have a child. It wasn't easy for us to get pregnant again afterward, and I began to wonder if I was ever going to be able to have the happy family life I longed for. Sometimes I felt cursed, successful at work but fated to be unhappy at home. When Annie and Adam came to visit, I played with the baby and cooed at him while Anne huddled with my parents in the other room, talking out the problems in her marriage. It was hard for me to hear all that, since it raised so many questions about my own life, so I would piggyback Adam around the yard and wish he were mine.

Finally, after struggling for months with basal thermometers and ovulation charts, I got pregnant again. At first I didn't quite believe it was true, until we had a sonogram and could see David in there kicking and rolling about, his little spinal column strong and supple, his fists flailing. Even when he was born, nearly nine pounds and as healthy as a colt, I held back a bit, worried that somehow this miracle might be snatched away as well. I didn't feel safe enough to be happy.

But on my last morning in the hospital I woke up early and carried David over to the window to watch the dawn. I began telling him about other dawns we would see together, about the one over the lake at the family cabin on Cape Cod, the one from the deck of his grandparents' sailboat, the one from inside our house in Washington. He gazed up at me with his round, dark-lashed eyes, and I began to believe he was really mine. He was here to stay, and he needed me. I would take him home and raise him in that cocoon of love and care I yearned to create. I would be his protector, the mommy lion. I would make our family work.

And for a while, it did work. I scaled back to part-time editing at the *Post*, working three days a week. The days I worked, I spent the mornings with David and I edited into the evening and helped put the paper to bed while Ron gave David his supper, then put him to bed. I often came home at eleven to find Ron asleep on the sofa with the baby on his chest, the two of them snoring away. Ron adored the baby and wanted another.

Meanwhile, in California, Anne's marriage had finally collapsed and she was moving to a small cottage in a nearby town. She wanted custody of Adam, now three, but her ex-husband demanded having Adam half the time. On the phone Annie sounded beaten down, resigned. My parents thought she was crazy to agree to joint custody, but Anne would explain that she couldn't deny Adam's dad unless she was willing to fight for full custody, and to win she would have to prove he was an abusive father, which he wasn't. Her hands were tied.

A few weeks later my family convened for a reunion at a conference center in California near where Anne lived, nearly sixty of us together for the first time. It was an intense weekend, and Ron seemed overwhelmed by the crowd, uncomfortable and remote. He would take David for walks on the beach and avoid the group activities. Anne, humiliated to be the first in the extended family to divorce, wandered through the group like a ghost, unusually thin and tense. Adam threw a temper tantrum the afternoon he had to go to his dad's, kicking his trucks around the parking lot as his parents tried to get him into the car, too angry to look at each other and too saddened to know what to do for Adam. I stood aside and watched, and an odd feeling came over me. Yes, it was awful. Yes, my heart ached for Adam and what that small child faced, but mostly I watched Annie and I was jealous. Her difficult husband was driving away in his car, while mine was sitting next to me at dinner, angry that he had to vacation with my family, irritated when I spoke to others, morose and unfriendly. I went with Annie to see her new little house, and my envy deepened. It was a doll's house, just big enough for her and Adam, a small table in the kitchen and windows all around. Sunny, clean, private. She had set up her easel in the dining room space and was painting again. When Adam was away at his dad's, Anne would walk down to the beach at night and watch the sunset. I couldn't believe how jealous I was.

The day the reunion ended Ron, David, and I headed north through San Francisco and up the winding coastal road. I had made reservations at a small motel months earlier, but at that time we had no idea how isolated it was or how slow the trip would be, and by mid-afternoon it was clear we wouldn't get to the motel until very late. With the sunset the fog rolled in, and soon Ron was clutching the steering wheel, desperately afraid he would miss a turn in the road and send us over the cliff. I peered at the map in the fading light, trying to find a road inland, while David fretted in his car seat. Soon, Ron and I were fighting, a long, tearing fight no doubt powered by the tense reunion as well as my jealousy over Anne's divorce. Ron was anxious about the drive and angry about the planning I had done for the trip; I was defensive and resented his barbs. I was stupid, he said, should have gotten help with the itinerary, should be mature enough to not need to vacation with my family, should have foreseen these problems. I parried, saying he should have helped me with the planning, should have said something if he didn't want to go to the reunion, should be able to open up more instead of always retreating from people. It went on and on, Ron's contempt for me, and my resentment of him, ballooning until it filled the little car.

David went silent in the backseat, his eyes wide with worry. Finally we stopped yelling and I stared out at the fog as Ron kept the car tight against the side of the cliff and cursed when he couldn't see the road. In Annie's life I had seen the other side, and suddenly it didn't look so awful, especially when I looked at the bitterness in my own marriage. Eventually we found a gas station and a place for dinner, but later, by the time we finally got to the motel, a plan was beginning to form in my head. Ron felt better, and invited me to come sit in the hot tub with him after we got David into his crib, but I was so angry I just climbed into bed by myself. One of the missteps in our relationship was that Ron, hot-tempered but loving, often bounced back quickly from his angry outbursts, truly sorry for the things he had said and seeking forgiveness. Sometimes it seemed that his emotions created a firestorm in his head, and when it cleared he was surprised to see the rubble around him. For me, though, recovery was slower, and I was seldom in the mood to forgive as soon as the incident passed. Instead, I would retreat, put up walls, and refuse to let him in. The hardest thing for me was to open my heart and be vulnerable again, and I didn't push myself often enough to be courageous and just do it. It was easier, and safer, just to shut down.

At the end of the week, despite several nice days hiking in the redwoods and driving through vineyards, I was still bitterly hurt over the things Ron had said during the fight. We stayed the last night in San Francisco with an old high school friend of mine, and as we sipped wine in a fancy restaurant that evening, I took a moment alone with Jamie to tell him I needed to get divorced. He looked at me, aghast. "But what about David! You just had a baby! You can't do that!" Later that night, after Ron fell asleep, Jamie and I sat in his kitchen and he talked me in off the ledge. "Don't do it," he said. "Ron has his moments, but he loves you and it isn't all that bad." I nodded. People were often telling me it wasn't that bad, but these were people who didn't live inside my marriage. It made me feel so alone, so isolated. Yet I also understood what Jamie was saying, and when I looked at David's trusting face, I knew I couldn't leave Ron. I couldn't do that to my precious boy.

We went home, and within a few weeks Ron began talking about having another child sooner rather than later. In truth, I thought it was crazy, too much for us to manage—but I gave in, more out of weariness than anything else. I did want another child, I told myself. This time it took only a few days, and suddenly there I was, pregnant with Jesse. The kids were going to be just nineteen months apart. Ron was thrilled. When I told my sister Annie, she just said, "Oh, Wen!" She didn't need to say much more.

9

S T E A L T H   W I F E

The week before Jesse was born Ron announced he was going off his medication. I looked at him, astonished. The pills—a muscle relaxant and a mild antidepressant—helped him sleep, brightened his mood, and provided a stabilizing force when the going got rough. He had been taking them for five years, since his breakdown. They hadn't worked miracles, but they had obviously helped. I didn't want to imagine what would happen to Ron without them.

"But Ron, having another child is going to be a lot of work, and we aren't going to get any sleep for weeks, and . . ." My voice trailed off.

He glared at me: "I don't want to live my whole life on medication," he said bitterly. "My doctor and I have discussed it, and we agreed that this was a good time. I'm much better now. We'll have the kids and things are going well at work. I need to try this."

I went into Jesse's delivery sick with the flu and worried about David, who was barely old enough to string words together and had little idea what was coming. I knew having two children close together would seriously strain any family, and we had little resilience. That fall I had questioned every mother I spied who had kids who seemed close in age, asking for tips and advice. "It's hell for the first year," they all said, rolling their eyes at the memory. "But then it gets better." I wasn't reassured. I wasn't sure how I would take care of everyone. Part of the box I built for myself in my marriage was a conviction that I was the hub of the family, and that without my ever-present attention and effort things would quickly spin out of control. I was also worried that I couldn't love two children, that I would have to "divorce" David to make room in my heart for another baby. David was so young and dependent, it seemed unnatural to break with him to care for another.

But when I saw Jess, with his coppery blond curls and intense gaze, my fears evaporated—at least my fears about the boys. It took thirteen hours to push him out, and by then I was hoarse and exhausted, but there he was, calm and self-possessed in his papoose of baby blankets, looking about the delivery room. He was a wonderful little bundle, and I knew the minute I held him that I would have no trouble loving two. Ron was overjoyed and sprinted around the neighborhood that evening telling everyone we knew that we'd had another boy.

Managing two, however, turned out to be harder than I'd imagined. The first few months were exhausting, as the other mothers had predicted. Juggling a nursing infant and a demanding toddler took a presence of mind and soul I hadn't anticipated. I had arranged a three-month maternity leave from the newspaper, but after four weeks of a nonstop stream of nursing, baby food, and diapers, I called my editor and begged him to let me come back early. I was only half-joking.

But when the haze of exhaustion lifted, I began to see how wonderful it was to have two. Jesse was different from his brother, more tuned in to the world from the very start, eager to move and easily frustrated when life got boring. David, too young to care that he had been displaced, found the baby endlessly fascinating. He watched me, then dragged his big white bear through the house imitating me with Jesse—feeding the bear in the high chair, giving it bottles, strapping it into the stroller, and wheeling it around the living room. Jess, wiry and determined, learned to cling to me like a little monkey while I went about the work of the household. Now I had two faces that lit up when I came into a room, two sweet cubs to snuggle with. They went a long way toward filling the empty places in my soul.

Both Ron and I found in the boys the love we had lost in our marriage, and for a while it revived the household. Ron bonded with the boys profoundly from the very beginning, buying them baseball gloves that he put in their cribs like stuffed animals, and dancing them around the living room at night when they fussed. In his dark moments he worried about them, checking the house for hazards, installing gates and fences, berating me when he didn't think I was being careful enough. Perhaps he felt the joy they brought was too ephemeral, too fragile, as if life might snatch this gift away just as quickly as it had plunked it in our laps.

Ironically, the happiness of the kids threw the pain of my marriage into high relief, and I began to wonder what I was settling for in my life. The stronger I became, the more Ron and I struggled, and we struggled over everything, from how to manage the children to whether he should take his pills to the meaning of life. We took to caring for the boys as a tag team, each of us handling one boy then trading him off: David for a walk with Daddy while Jess gets a bath; then the handoff and David goes in for a bath with Mom while Jesse gets a twilight walk with Dad. Night after night we split them up, unknowingly practicing our single-parenting skills.

As our problems escalated, I began to question the bedrock assumptions of my marriage. Would therapy really make Ron better? Would love and patience win out in the end? Was this relationship a good place to raise my children?

But now when I thought about divorce the equation was different, because the boys had changed everything. Before we had them my life was simple—complicated on the surface but fundamentally simple—because it was all about Ron and me. Then, in less than two years, there were two small dependents, and my life exploded with ramifications on a thousand new levels. It was no longer about me, or even Ron. Now our problems needed to be solved for a tight web of people, and the old solutions—stay and be miserable, confront the issues head-on, or screw up my courage and leave—took on ominous overtones.

So I found myself imagining, instead, that Ron might die.

Not that I wished him ill; I just couldn't think of any other way to end the story.

I was astonished to find myself thinking this way, but the odds were in my favor. Ron was nearly fifty, had a family history of heart disease, had struggled with high cholesterol and smoking. He also fit the description of those people doctors said had "angry" hearts, people with type A personalities at risk for heart attacks because their hostility and anxiety triggered adrenaline burns that wore out their systems. Sometimes, when he was late coming home from work, I wondered if the worst had happened, both dread and hope flickering through my veins.

One evening when he didn't show up on time, I sat imagining a medical team leaning over Ron collapsed on a subway platform somewhere. Then I suddenly looked around my snug house, knee-deep in building blocks and toy trucks, and felt a chill run through me. What was happening here? What kind of monster was I becoming? Someone who wished the father of my children would die? This was me? My mother's warning about running out of forgiveness rumbled through my echoing heart. I felt like that now, empty of love, empty of feeling, empty of forgiveness. Ron had said once that he married me for my big heart, and even that rankled now, because I knew it meant he married me because I would forgive him again and again. I sat in front of the Disney videos with my small children and wept because I didn't live in a world where people were always good and kind. I knew it was silly but I also knew it was tragic, and I knew it couldn't go on.

My sister Annie, newly in love with a wonderful guy and beginning to appreciate the opportunities divorce could bring, came east for a visit. She seemed shocked by how she found us. Ron and I, overwhelmed by the work of the boys and too many nights with little sleep, scrapped with each other over everything, from who would grocery-shop to when Jesse should nap. One morning, after Ron had blown up at me and then stomped out of the house, Anne turned and asked how much longer I was going to live like this. The boys gamboled at our feet, Jesse just barely crawling, David bouncing around on his little toddler legs. I was surprised by how quickly I cut to the chase: "I can't get divorced now, Annie," I said, shaking my head. "They are too little. I can't handle them alone. I have to wait a few years."

But it wasn't just that the boys were too young. I was paralyzed by the insanity of my position. Here I was, with two small children, fantasizing about divorcing their father. I had known stupid people in my life, had always felt sorry for stupid people, but I had never felt like one—until now. What had I been thinking? How could I have gotten here? And then, just below this layer of humiliation, were the real fears, the fear of what divorce would do to the children, the fear that I couldn't make it on my own, even the fear that separating would destroy Ron, that he couldn't live without my help. Because, when I really thought about it, I didn't want to destroy Ron. I didn't want him to die.

All my life I had thought about love as a box, safe but confining. As a young woman I sought out relationships with men because I felt I needed protection, needed someone who could help me negotiate the challenges of life— argue with auto mechanics, drive in bad traffic, protect me from other men. I hated doing these things myself, and didn't feel safe alone in the world. So I had boyfriends— one after the other. Some nice, some domineering, all protective. The box worked.

By the time I married Ron, however, the fantasy of escaping from this box had become an old habit. It was how I coped with living in a relationship that was both protective and confining. If this gets too claustrophobic, I would tell myself, I can always leave. It was how I managed that inner voice that began to ask uncomfortable questions about the box—why I needed it, whether I saw how it was warping my life. That voice was a real problem, disruptive and depressing. So I would tell it to relax, that I was there by choice. But inevitably, I began to daydream about what life looked like outside the box.

With Jesse's birth Ron bought a video camera, and he often set it up in a corner of the room to capture the activity of the household. The boys still love to watch these videos of themselves crawling and careening around the house, but I find them depressing reminders of how stressful our life had become. There I am, in nearly each one, sullen, angry. I sit hunched on the sofa, nursing Jess while David falls and hits his head on the coffee table. Or there I am, leaning over the tub, trying to soap one while the other teeters unsteadily to his feet. My voice is tense, and I'm often asking Ron to put down the camera and help. We were not a happy family, and it's all there—in the background, but present to anyone who wanted to see.

I had stopped seeing my therapist before David was born, but I knew the old issues still festered inside me, so I started reading self-help books, looking for clues about myself, trying to find the key to my unhappiness and what I could do about it. Within months I stumbled onto several books about co-dependency, and was riveted by the description of classic enablers, people who compulsively run around fixing the problems and cleaning up the messes left by alcoholics or drug-addicts, smoothing over relations with family and friends. They sit virtuously at home, hoping the other will change, waiting for them to come home and ask for forgiveness. They are the morally superior, smug and blaming, usually consumed with the other's problems, rarely looking to themselves as a part of the problem.

When I looked at my own behavior, I was astounded to

see that that was me. I spent most of my waking hours thinking about Ron and his problems, focused almost entirely on him. I tiptoed around, trying to manage Ron's emotional state with an array of bewildering behaviors. I spoke to my mother only from work, because I didn't want Ron to know how much I still depended on her. I flip-flopped between commiserating with others who found him difficult, to defending his behavior and honor. I alternately heckled him to do more for the boys, or held them close to me in an effort to shield them from him. It was exhausting me, driving Ron nuts, and leaving a residue of resentment between us. I needed to let go.

My counselor, Ursula, had tried to get me to take responsibility for my own happiness and not worry so much about Ron's, but I had resisted, in part because I suspected that pursuing my own happiness could be a highly revolutionary act. It could, possibly, upset everything. But now I saw that I had to find a way out, and focusing on myself seemed to be a key.

Which is how I started thinking of myself as a stealth wife. I began working on a simple agenda in secret: I would try to be happier. I didn't know where it would lead me, or what would come of it, but I hoped that if I was happier, the children would be as well.

While Ron didn't drink, I began to suspect I could learn something from Al-Anon, the support program for spouses of alcoholics, and started looking for a group to attend. I didn't tell Ron. There are many Al-Anon groups in the Washington area, but by instinct I sought out a group just for women and found one that met in a church in the suburbs, far outside the professional circle I moved in through my job as a reporter. In the cold, linoleum-floored basement of the church, graying women with coffee cups gathered on metal chairs and told stories that sounded hauntingly familiar. They spoke of the silent pain, the broken promises to re-form, the loss of family and friends because of the bad behavior of spouses. Most striking, many spoke of their hope that their spouse would die. There were worse things too—beatings, theft, bankruptcy, suicide. Some just sat and listened, their pain either too big or too depressing to share. In that circle of strangers, none of them women I would have chosen as friends, I found a subtle but resilient kind of strength, and began to learn the lessons of Al-Anon. There were many things that helped, but the most important was that I began to disengage from what I had seen as the business of managing Ron and began to view myself as a separate, autonomous adult—an adult with choices, with courage, with resources. Al-Anon helped me find hope again because it brought me back to myself and gave me permission to let go of Ron.

I gradually noticed that, compared with many of the women in the circle, I was much better off. Ron wasn't nearly as bad as he could have been, wasn't nearly as bad as many of these spouses. He didn't drink; he didn't gamble or use drugs. He held down his job and was financially responsible. He adored his children and was a good daddy, it was just me he couldn't seem to live with. Most of the women in Al-Anon didn't have husbands with that kind of record.

I also had my work, and I could see now that it was a valuable asset. Although I was growing bored with the stress and pace of daily reporting, my job provided both economic stability and a base of support. Even with its problems, the newspaper was a place where intelligent, successful people valued my contributions. My work, in many ways, saved me. Without the strength I gained in that world, I would never have mustered the courage it took to divorce.

I also had a strong circle of friends and family nearby

that I could rely on. My parents had retired to a town on Maryland's eastern shore, but that was only two hours away, and my sister Penny lived in Washington with her wonderful husband. I had my support group of Quaker women, with whom I had supper on a regular basis, and many other understanding women in my life. And so I began to think that maybe I could let go of my unhappy marriage. In my frenzy to manage everyone I had underestimated Ron, and myself. Maybe it would be okay.

A few months after I returned to my part-time job at the paper, my editors began asking when I planned to come back to work full-time. "You've had your fun," the business-desk editor told me. "Now you need to get off the mommy track and tackle something more challenging." They dangled plums before me, possibly a job covering national banking, but to me their offers looked like prison terms. Jesse was just six months old, David had just turned two. The thought of going back to work full-time gave me the willies, because I knew I couldn't manage the boys and the pressure of a national reporting job. Besides, now that the boys were getting a little older, I loved having the time with them at home in the mornings, and free days when we could picnic on a blanket in the backyard, visit with neighbors, explore different playgrounds. I hadn't had children to turn around and pass them off to a baby-sitter for sixty hours a week.

Then one day I got a call from one of my old mentors at American University. They had a teaching job in the journalism department and wondered if I was interested. I had taught several courses there as an adjunct before I had the boys, and had daydreamed about full-time teaching but had never thought a job would open up at a school anywhere nearby. Now, here was a job in my old department, at a good university, right in my backyard. I still wasn't thrilled about working full-time so soon after Jesse's birth, but I knew it was a rare opportunity. I interviewed with the dean and guest-lectured in a class on investigative reporting, and before I knew it, was offered the job. I was the first woman hired in their print journalism department, and a good bit younger than most of my colleagues. The newspaper gave me a two-year leave so I could make sure I really wanted to teach. In those two years I would have to earn the right to a tenure-track job at the university, so it was hardly going to be less pressured. But it felt right—the hours would be better for the boys and it wouldn't be the same level of stress. Besides, teaching was so much fun it didn't feel like work. I packed up my notebooks and files and said good-bye to the paper. Now all I needed was good child care.

As with all of my job advancements, Ron both celebrated my successes and chafed at my good fortune. In his work he struggled with the inflexibility inherent in bureaucratic government jobs, and envied the ease with which I moved about. He didn't feel he could risk exploring other opportunities, and in fact felt shut out of the teaching jobs he had always wanted. It rankled that his wife, with just a master's degree and ten years' reporting experience, could land a teaching position with a respectable university, although we both knew how much harder it was in his field of political science. He told me I better watch how I talked—that my grammar could well prove an embarrassment. I just shook my head and went about preparing for classes.

To solve our child care problem, we hired a young French girl as an au pair for the year, and prepared the attic as a room for her to live in. Marion turned out to be a godsend for the children, capable and loving, but having another adult in the house proved awkward for everybody. It was obvious to her that there were serious problems between Ron and me, as much as we tried to hide them. She was sweet and efficient with the children but cool with us, and one could hardly blame her. I worried all year about exposing her to our conflicts, so we kept it mostly tamped down, arguing only when she and the boys were away. But we weren't fooling anyone. Tension lingered in the corners like a poisonous gas and I knew instinctively that we couldn't host an au pair for another year. Our marriage was breaking down, and we needed our privacy.

My first year at the university was a delight but, like the birth of the children had, threw the unhappiness of my marriage into high relief. I hadn't been able to imagine single-parenting as a newspaper reporter—too many demands, too little time at home—but I could imagine handling it if I was teaching. I began to imagine it more.

And then, one day, something happened that finally tipped the balance. It was a small thing, in retrospect, but proved to be one of those moments that suddenly allowed me to see beyond the common terrain of everyday life, to glimpse my future.

It happened the day our French au pair left to return home. Despite everyone's best intentions, it had been a difficult year and had only grown more so as her time with us waned. As she packed, I suddenly felt giddy with a dangerous kind of freedom, as if I could now get on with the serious business of fighting with Ron whenever I needed to. Now the gloves could come off.

Instead of going to the airport with the rest of us, Ron spent the day in bed, sick perhaps, but probably also depressed. August is one of his bad months. The boys and I waved Marion off at Washington National Airport, then came home and spent the heat of the day inside, playing quietly downstairs while Daddy slept in the darkened bedroom upstairs. David had just turned three and Jesse was only eighteen months old. They were sturdy little bundles of boyness, unaware and happy, busy with their toddler lives. Both Ron and I were utterly in love with them.

When the afternoon heat wore off and the evening descended, I took the boys for a walk to the playground. It was a beautiful twilight, the air soft and still, the last brightness lingering in the sky for a long time. We played in the park until nearly nine o'clock, past bedtimes, in a world that was, for the moment, protected from the pain that sat stubbornly in my home. As I pushed the swing and helped build sand castles, it dawned on me that I was afraid to go back. I was suddenly so acutely aware of it I could taste the fear and reluctance. I didn't want to face Ron and the darkened house, didn't know what kind of mood he would be in, didn't know how quickly the gloves might come off—or even who would take them off first. I had been afraid of Ron before—his disapproval, his anger, his fear—but now I was afraid of myself, afraid of what I might do. I saw that something inevitable might be just about to begin.

But the boys needed baths, and they were tired. I had to go. As we packed up to leave, however, David pointed to the sky. There, swirling in arcs above us, were suddenly thousands of bats. They were streaming out of a tall chimney across the park, curling up into the dusky sky in a mesmerizing spiral, some diving back down only to emerge again. It was beautiful and wild, and we watched until it was too dark to see. Finally, I plunked them in the stroller and turned home. It seemed silly, now, to be out so late, but the dance of the bats made the evening special, gave us something to share with Ron, a reason for our tardiness. Now that it was dark outside, I could imagine the house alight, maybe even welcoming. Maybe he would be happy to see us.

But when we walked through the door, Ron was beside himself. How could I keep the boys out so late? he asked, barely containing his anger. Why hadn't I woken him for dinner, why hadn't I told him where we were? In my mind the lovely, lazy evening in the park began to fade to black, overshadowed, like so many other things in my life had been. So I squared my shoulders, lifted my chin, and told him about the bats. They had been amazing, I said, he should have seen it, the boys had loved it. David chimed in, "Oh Daddy, there were so many bats!"

Ron just looked at me. "Do you know how dangerous bats are?"

"Oh, Ron. Not these bats. They weren't coming near us."

"They are often rabid, especially if they are doing something unusual like that."

I thought of the swirling cloud, delirious in its action, the bats swooping all around the playground. "I don't think they were rabid," I said, lowering my gaze.

But in Ron's eyes there was no defending my action. It had been foolhardy, risky, dangerous to stay and watch the bats. Ron went back into the bedroom shaking his head and I put the boys to bed quickly, hugging each hard and breathing in the last faint smell of the park from their sandy hair. Then I went downstairs, poured a finger of brandy into a Mickey Mouse cup, and sat in the darkened living room.

Fear was a powerful thing. Fear could make people do and say cruel things, desperate things. Ron's life seemed rimmed with fears, bigger fears than the usual everyday anxieties, and they made him see demons that were not there. Everything good in his life—the boys, his job, the house, our financial stability—all seemed fragile and vulnerable to sudden loss if he didn't stay vigilant. And the vigilance was exhausting.

What I saw that night, for the first time, was that the fear was rising in the house like floodwater, and that if I didn't do something, we would all drown. I had no idea where to start, and I couldn't even think of David and Jesse asleep upstairs in their beds. Still, I knew for the first time that I had to move, had to consider all the options. Something ephemeral but precious was dying inside me, and I wasn't willing to give it up. It had something to do with seeing the beauty in a cloud of bats, something I wanted my children to have, something I knew I couldn't live without. It was about providing that cocoon of love and care I had wanted to weave around my children. For reasons complicated by time and hurt, I saw now that I couldn't do that with Ron. We were too different, too angry, too weary of each other. I went upstairs and crept into bed beside him. How many more nights would I lie there, aching with unhappiness, afraid to move for fear of waking him and his ire? How many more nights would I lie in the dark hoping he would die? Suddenly, I couldn't live that life anymore. I made a quiet pledge that I would get up the next morning and start a new life. I had no idea what it would look like, or even how I would do it, but it would be different. I slid my wedding ring from my left hand to my right, whispering, "Tomorrow it starts—I promise." I didn't want to be the kind of woman who hoped people would die.

10

HOLES IN THE HEART

I went back to the library, but now I had graduated from the self-help shelf and took out books on divorce, on children of divorce, on custody and single-parenting. I pored over the advice, the studies and research, trying to find a way through what seemed to be a minefield. Perhaps, I secretly hoped, perhaps there was a way to do this without destroying my children.

Back at home, I began gambling. I had always played a game of solitaire each night, cross-legged on the bathroom rug while the kids bathed, but now it became a high-stakes bet. If I beat the house, I told myself, I could leave my marriage. If I lost, I had to stay. I kept a tally in my head over the weeks and nursed it each day like a sore tooth.

But no matter how the game came out, when I looked at the boys, rosy and slick with soap, my heart would stop. Every book, every study I read, showed that kids of divorce do worse in all venues of life. They do worse in school, have more behavior problems, more drug abuse, more delinquency. Below that, the studies hint, they are angrier, sadder, more likely to be depressed or unable to have satisfying relationships as adults. One night as I waited in the supermarket checkout line, I skimmed an article on grown children of divorce. "You live the rest of your life with a hole in your heart," said one man. I put the magazine back on the rack and looked at the two little faces gazing up at me from the shopping cart. I can't do it, I thought to myself. I don't want my children to have holes in their hearts. Not holes carved by my own hand.

But there are other studies, not nearly as well-reported, that show children of divorce may do better than kids in miserable marriages. I met a man, a neighbor, who had ended an unhappy marriage and remarried into relative bliss. He had joint custody of a daughter by his first wife, and twins with his second. Their house sat sideways to ours, and during those years when our children were young and getting up early, I would watch him and his second wife in their bright kitchen, kissing occasionally and sneaking intimate moments while the twins sat munching their cereal. I was astounded by him, by the idea that one could pursue happiness as one could pursue success. It seemed unthinkable, until I began to think of it. Then I couldn't stop.

Because that's what it came down to: a tug-of-war between my happiness and the children's. And what kind of mother would put herself first?

All the while my marriage withered. Ron and I barely spoke to each other about anything other than the boys, and every attempt to spend time together—dinner out or a walk in the park—turned us into nervous clock-watchers, both of us anxious to return to the house and the distraction of the kids. I could feel myself sinking, my love of life seeping away into the quicksand that was my world. The sense of power I'd gained at Al-Anon meetings, once so sustaining, now evaporated as soon as I stepped into the house. Unable to move forward, unable to move back, I felt utterly trapped. Life took on a flatness, everything seemed to take enormous effort—just doing a load of laundry sometimes felt like an insurmountable task. Even worse, I could feel my emotions shutting down. For the boys, each day was a bright tapestry of events—a walk in the alley, a new toy, ice cream bars for dessert—but I could no longer mirror their joy back to them. I knew this was depression, and I knew I had to do something, yet I couldn't bear the thought of what moving forward with my life would mean for them. Sometimes I tried to think of the boys as grown and talking with me as equals, and I would imagine asking them what I should do. Sometimes they said go and sometimes they said stay.

There are those who believe it is simple selfishness that leads people to divorce. For those of us who have lived it, it's hard to see why anyone would rip out their veins for some immature or narcissistic desire to get what they want, because that is what it feels like. What I desperately wanted, more than anything, was for Ron and me to be able to live together as loving people, without bickering or yelling, without the residue of acrimony that clung to everything we said to each other. I spent years trying to make that happen, and only slowly, and with great sadness, put it aside. Now what I wanted was to raise my children in a home where I could set a tone of love and consideration, where people said kind things to each other, where the dinner table was a place of calm and comfort. Where I could be happier, and thereby give them a better chance at their own happiness.

I went back to my therapist for a few short sessions, seeking guidance. She didn't seem surprised to find me considering divorce, and suggested that I was at risk for real depression if I stayed where I was much longer. I tried to talk out the options, but none of them was easy. I pressed her for help, for advice. "Tell me what to do," I begged. But she refused. Instead she said, "Either way you go, you'll never know what you saved your children from. You have to accept that—that you'll never know." I left haunted by that thought, the idea that no matter which decision I made, I would never know if I had been right.

The night my older sister married, she raised her glass and said to my parents, "Thank you for giving me the gift of having parents who loved each other." It had been the most precious thing we had as children, and now I was unable to give that to my boys. They were beginning to notice that Daddy and Mommy were seldom relaxed or cheerful around each other. David, in particular, older and more sensitive, was growing into a worried child, watchful of his parents, quick to try and fix problems. I ached to see him try out, in his little-boy way, the same co-dependent behaviors that had so marked my life—brokering compromises, putting aside his own desires if it would buy peace.

I could see that this shadow life we were living wasn't healthy, but from the outside we still looked like an intact family, and it was hard to give that up. If I left Ron, I wouldn't even be able to give my children the appearance of a normal childhood. That may not seem valuable until you take it away and watch your kids struggle with their oddness, the way in which they don't match the stereotype of the happy American family. And that stereotype is everywhere—in advertisements, at school, at church, in the bleachers at the baseball game. They feel their difference every day. Instinctively, I knew this. I knew leaving Ron would throw all of us, no matter how well we handled it, into the great mass of those "others," people whose lives were sorry things, people who could not manage things, people who had been broken by their mistakes. People on the outside.

But the radical act of trying to fix my life was taking on a direction all its own. Over those months that I struggled with this excruciating choice, I was really beginning to prepare, starting the process of adjusting. I didn't know it then, but I was already on my way out.

Imagining my divorce—which now took up most of my private time—was beginning to feel so real that there were few people I dared share it with. In particular, I purposefully shielded my parents and my younger sister, who lived nearby and saw Ron often. I didn't want them to give up on him before I did, and I knew it would be hard for them to behave normally around him if they knew what I was planning.

My parents, as well, were struggling with their own sense of failure. Two of their four children had married difficult spouses—charming but erratic and, often, angry people. My parents had been concerned about both marriages but felt powerless to rescue us, I think, and confused about whether to even try. Marital unhappiness among one's children must be one of the deep griefs of later life, and there is an entire generation of grandparents who have stood by, helpless, watching the damage and destruction of divorce after divorce. My parents had been deeply disturbed by Anne's divorce, by how little control she seemed to have in making decisions for Adam or managing her life. Joint custody had anchored her to California, where her ex-husband worked. It meant years of difficult decisions over every aspect of Adam's life—schooling, sports, moves, vacations. They hadn't seen many divorces up close, and had never seen one like this. It was painfully difficult for them to understand, although they tried and adapted as well as possible. So there I was, two years after Anne's divorce, on the verge of leaving Ron. One divorce in a family is a sad event, but two strikes a blow to its very foundation. Two makes a pattern, and this kind of pattern leaves parents befuddled and siblings unnerved. If divorce can sweep through a family like that, perhaps they have some fatal flaw. I could tell Annie what I was thinking, because she understood, but telling anyone else in that inner circle felt like throwing grenades.

In the years following Ron's breakdown, I had reconnected with my cousin Jean, and she now provided the sounding board I often needed. She had stopped drinking and had finally begun to pull her life together, publishing her first book, and then her first novel, writing and finding stability in the gay community in San Francisco. As my life had filled with its own darkness, Jean's had brightened and flowered in surprising ways, bringing us closer again. We were older now, more patient with each other, more loving, more understanding. But because she disliked Ron, she hadn't visited me. I hadn't seen her more than a few times, all of them in California, and she had never met my boys.

Then one day she called from a hotel in Washington and said she was doing a reading that evening at one of the universities. Would I come to see her? She sounded subdued, so soft-voiced I barely knew it was Jean. She seemed surprised when I said yes.

I took the subway over after work and met her in the lobby of a small auditorium. She was dressed in gentle grays and blues, a necklace at her throat and an elegant earring in one ear. She seemed smaller and more relaxed than I'd ever seen her, but her intensity was still there, burning like a velvety flame in her eyes. With a start I realized she looked happy, something I hadn't seen in her since those long-lost days playing on the beaches of Rhode Island. She hugged me, and the familiar tingle of ownership passed between us. She was reading selections from her book on alcohol recovery in the lesbian community, she said, and she would meet me again afterward. I went into the auditorium and sat down. Not surprisingly, it looked like I was the only heterosexual woman in the room.

After a brief introduction, Jean came out and sat on a tall stool in the middle of the empty stage. She read haunting passages about pain and the healing properties of water. The stories seemed more tortured than she did, as if her troubles had been exorcised from her life and transferred to the tense, aching language of the book. It felt like something out of a magic act, and I wondered how she had done it. After the reading she told the audience it was a very important night for her because for the first time a member of her family was there to hear her. She asked me to stand, and as I looked around at the smiling, clapping women, I felt my heart contract. Why shouldn't I be there? Why was this so unusual, so meaningful to these women? And then, with a sudden blush of shame, why hadn't I been there before? Jean and I were over thirty years old, and this was the first time I had stood with her in support. I had hardly earned the applause of Jean's audience, and I burned with a new understanding: My marriage to Ron had pulled me away from many people I loved in subtle but critical ways. I was beginning to miss people, miss the freedom to love those who mattered to me.

After the reading I went back with her to her hotel room and, over a dinner we ordered from room service, told her that I hated my life; that every day seemed gray with worry despite my wonderful boys and my wonderful job; that I scared myself by wishing Ron would die; that I couldn't bear the growing conviction that divorce was the only alternative. Because I couldn't do that, couldn't do that to the boys.

"Really?" Jean said, leaning back against the pillows of the bed, sipping from a can of club soda. "Do you think you are saving them from something by staying married?"

"Yes," I said, "I do. People who have grown up in divorce speak of it as having a hole in their heart. For the rest of their lives they live with a hole in their hearts."

"Where did you hear that?" she asked.

"I read it, in an article. But it's real—that same feeling shows up in all the studies of kids of divorce."

"And it probably shows up in all the studies of people with every other kind of problem," Jeannie said. "Listen, Wen, lots of people have holes in their hearts and they live full and happy lives. I have holes in my heart. Even you, for Christ's sake. You've got a huge hole in your heart, and every day you still get up and hope that life will be better."

I looked at her, that intense gaze burning into me.

"You should think of what you are not getting," she said.

"Think of love, think of being treasured by someone, feeling respected, having a home that feels like a haven," she said. "Don't you want those for yourself? Not just for the boys, but for yourself?"

This line of questioning felt like being strip-searched, like an invasion into things I had kept secret for years. It had been so long that I had wanted these things for myself, I hardly dared imagine them, hardly dared bring them back into the light. Because if I did, they would take over. They were too powerful.

11

UNTANGLING

Before I got divorced I had never really failed at anything in my life. I hadn't gotten everything I wanted, but I had succeeded at everything I had worked at. Divorce is not only a failure, it's a very public failure. It is perhaps the most public passage Americans make that isn't accompanied by a rite or a celebration. People divorce, someone moves out, and the neighbors skulk by the house for months not knowing what to say.

It was tough for me—the quintessential good girl, the earnest employee, the helper child—to imagine life outside conventional society. Because I could see that divorce would throw me out, mark me as a rebel—possibly even crazy—but certainly as stupid, or selfish. Still Jeannie's words echoed through my heart. I began to imagine divorce as not just a place where I could live peacefully by myself, but as a place where I could perhaps find new love, find someone who would cherish me, who would think I was wonderful rather than an embarrassment, who could support me, whom I could support.

.   .   .

With my heart in full revolt, we left for our usual family vacation on Cape Cod. Ron and I only seemed to connect at the moments we passed the boys off to one another, or when we disagreed about where to have supper or what else to do. The first night at the cabin Ron got angry about a belated Father's Day present the boys and I had given him, and dinner was tense and sullen. It was like the fight in the car in California, one that left me resentful for days. At night I dreamt fear-ridden dreams, dreams of being pursued, of descending to basements filled with lurking threats, dreams of fog and blindness. In the mornings I walked those familiar beaches and played with the boys in the salt marshes, and I could feel the memories of happier times flicker around me: my mother helping me search the shore for a perfect, round stone; my dad telling stories of ghost ships and abandoned lighthouses as we shivered around a campfire. How far away that kind of life seemed now, how little of that I had been able to give to my children. Ron and I could barely speak to each other, and no one was telling the boys stories. People say marriages break up, but mine finally broke down. The machine, fragile and badly balanced from the beginning, gradually collapsed from the weight of the hurt and sorrow it was carrying. I sat on my beach towel, watching the boys digging in the sand, and the conviction that it was over suddenly began to fill my chest. I'll never forget that moment. I don't know if it was a moment of strength or a moment of weakness, but I finally saw that my marriage was over. The next time I brought them to the Cape, I swore to myself, it would be a happy vacation, even if it was just me and the boys. It was over. I blinked, and the world looked different. The quality of the light changed in an instant. It was over and, somehow, I could do this. I resolved to call a lawyer the minute we got back to Washington. The rest of the week

I slept on the sofa of the cabin, not explaining myself to Ron or anyone else. It didn't seem necessary. In a few days we packed up and drove the ten hours home in stony silence.

But back in Washington the old paralysis set in. I couldn't sleep that first night back, I was so terrified of calling a lawyer, which I had pledged to myself to do the next morning after Ron left for work. The niggling fears began to whisper in my head. What if I couldn't afford it? What if just the first phone call cost a hundred dollars? What if the lawyer, who had been recommended by a friend, turned out to be a jerk? What if I couldn't control what he did or said? What if Ron found out?

The next morning I circled around the phone for over an hour, then finally called my sister Annie instead. I needed a guide, someone who could hold up a lantern, someone who knew their way around this cavern I was entering.

"Annie, I need to leave Ron. I've decided. It's time." Then my voice cracked and I started to cry. "But I'm too scared."

"Oh, sweetie," she said. When Anne's marriage had broken up several years earlier, I had stood next to her through some of the worst moments—discovering Jack's affair, helping her set up her new home, buying her a book on how to fall out of love with someone and making her practice the exercises in the back. It had been excruciating to watch, and now I was asking her to do that for me. She let me cry for a bit, then said, "What do you need me to do?"

"Make me do it," I choked.

"What do you mean?"

"Make me. I need to call a lawyer, and I can't, and I need to sit Ron down and tell him, and I can't."

"Okay," she said. "Start with Ron. How about tonight?"

"Oh, God."

"Tonight. Call me before you talk with him, and then call me later. You must call me later or I'll worry."

"Okay," I said, my mouth suddenly as dry as dust. "Okay."

That night I rented *Pinocchio* for the boys and settled them in front of the TV. Then I called Annie, shaking all over. "I'm going to do it now."

"Okay, sweetie. I'm sending you love and strength. Call me when it's over."

Ron was out on the porch, reading. I went out and closed the door behind me.

"We need to talk." He put his book down and nodded, as if he had been expecting it. "I can't, I can't go on like this," I stumbled. "I think we need to split up."

He looked at me with such deep seriousness I couldn't tell what he was thinking. I had begged him several months earlier to go with me for marital counseling, but he had said at the time that he feared counseling would lead inevitably to splitting up. Now, though, he seemed to sense my desperation. "Okay," he said. "Let's talk this out."

Over the next hour, I told Ron in unvarnished terms what was in my head and heart. I told him I felt like an intruder in my own house, that I was so clearly irritating to him that I was walking on eggshells, fearful all the time that I would trigger his anger. He admitted I often bothered him—by the way I talked, by my continued allegiance to my family, by choices I made for the kids, by what he saw as certain lapses of good judgment. Instead of defending myself, as I had in the past, I simply responded that my problems didn't justify the level of anger and distrust in our marriage and that I wanted the boys to grow up with something different. We didn't talk about the lost intimacy between us, the lack of love in the house, but it was there, the monster crouched between us. The shadows of the boys hovered about us as well.

"I have the number of a divorce lawyer," I said. "I'm going to call him in the morning."

Ron flinched. "Please don't do that," he said. "I realize you're serious. I'm ready to go to marriage counseling if you want."

Counseling. A few months earlier I would have welcomed that, but now I could feel my momentum begin to drain from me. Counseling would throw me back into the marriage, back into the cycle of promises and effort, back into the marriage bed. I didn't know if I could do it.

"We owe it to the boys, even if not to each other," Ron said.

"Let me think about it," I said.

I went back inside and found the boys huddled together on the sofa. They looked unbearably worried, still locked in on the movie. "Scary," said Jesse, pointing to the TV. By now Jiminy Cricket was singing and Pinocchio was a real boy, the frightening parts over. Scary, he insisted. It was as if they had picked up the first tremors of the earthquake that would destroy their world, like frightened animals sensing the ground move under their feet. I flicked the TV off, gathered them in a big hug, and then led them upstairs. It took a while to get them into bed.

Finally I called Annie. "I did it, but I didn't get anywhere," I said. "Now Ron wants to do counseling," I said.

"That's good," Anne said. "Isn't it?" I was crying again.

"I don't know," I gulped. "I feel like I failed. I don't think counseling will really help. Does this mean I can't ever get divorced?"

"No," she said. "You can still get divorced if you need to. But this won't hurt, even if you do end up having to leave. This is good, this is forward motion. It's okay."

Ron moved into the attic that night, in deference to the seriousness of my feelings. I got into our big bed, which felt wider and private now that it was mine alone, and tried to calm my shaking body. I couldn't imagine how I was going to do it.

Anne was right, counseling did help, although it didn't bring us to the place we expected. We found a stern, no-nonsense psychiatrist with a wealth of experience counseling troubled couples, and he quickly forced us to own up to our problems and disappointments. Each Wednesday Ron and I would drive together to his office, hardly knowing what to say to each other, then sit in the deep sofas and be surprised by what the other would reveal. The process was like peeling off skin without benefit of anesthesia, but gradually our problems began to surface. Some of it, many of the big things, seemed intractable. We were just too different, our needs and expectations too divergent. We had worn each other out. In the spirit of improvement, however, he encouraged us to do more things together, just the two of us.

By now we were barely comfortable just sitting in the car together, but one evening in April, when the cherry blossoms were at their peak, I talked Ron into a twilight walk around the tidal basin after our counseling session. The cherry blossoms, so beautiful yet so fragile and brief, held a special place in my heart. Every year we were in Washington, my family would make a pilgrimage to see the trees, walking clear around the tidal basin and often sharing a picnic under the flowers. As an adult I had continued the tradition, but usually with friends or by myself. Ron and I had never walked among them together. Now,

I needed to see if we could do this small thing. Ron protested at first, saying we should get back to the baby-sitter and the boys, but he finally agreed. It was a lovely night but the traffic was fierce, the wait for a parking space long. When we got out, Ron walked sullenly a few steps ahead of me, always just out of reach, bothered by something in the counseling session and frustrated that I had insisted on this rite. I was hurt that he couldn't enjoy the walk, but I looked at the trees and the happy crowd and told myself that the first try would be the hardest. Finally, we got in the car and went home.

But there another disaster awaited us: The sitter had locked herself out of the house with the boys and had called a locksmith to get in when we didn't show up right after our session. The locksmith was expensive, and the door had been damaged. Ron was furious with the sitter, but he soon turned his frustration on me. It was all my fault—the door, the counseling, the walk around the damn cherry trees. I listened to him rage at me and felt myself move away, off to a distant spot. I didn't need to be here anymore. I didn't have to hear this. I could choose whether I stayed. It was several hours before things settled down enough to go to bed, but before I did, I took off my wedding ring and put it in the bottom of my jewelry box. I couldn't do it anymore. My mother had been right—the forgiveness had run out. Everything had run out—my patience, my love, my hope. I cried myself to sleep, but somehow I felt better. I knew that the end could start now.

I woke up the next morning and got out the list of things I would need to do to get divorced, the one I had written so early in my marriage: talk to a lawyer, divide up the books, pack my things, tell my parents. Rip up my life— nothing to it.

I was so frightened of going public with my divorce that it took me months to build up the courage to tell my parents. I couldn't say why—I knew they would be understanding and supportive—but whenever I imagined it, a feeling of shame rose in the back of my throat.

Now, though, I needed them. I didn't dare tell Ron it was really over unless I had them there as a backup, in case I needed to move in with them for a few days or take the kids to them in an emergency. What kind of emergency it might be I didn't have any idea, I just felt I needed them on alert. At home, life continued on its jerky course: Ron and I attending the counseling sessions but sharing less and less, the children nervous with the obvious tension between us. Anne was planning a visit east, and my mother and my younger sister and I were to meet her for a weekend in the resort town of Cape May, New Jersey. We had never been away together, just the four of us Swallow girls, and were excited at the prospect. We imagined the weekend spent walking the beach, climbing the lighthouse, sharing tea in quaint little shops, but now I had other plans. I called Annie one evening a few weeks before the trip and told her I had decided to go ahead with the divorce and that I planned to tell Mom the weekend we would be in Cape May. "I need you there," I told her. "I can't tell her by myself."

I could hear Anne sigh all the way from California, but all she said was, "Okay, sweetie. Just warn me a few minutes before you do. At least give me a moment to brace myself."

So a few weeks later, as we sat sharing a bottle of wine in our room at the inn in Cape May, I gave Anne a small signal, took a deep breath, and blurted it out. "Mom, Pen, I have something really important to tell you." They looked up, surprised, unexpecting. I felt as if I was lighting a fuse, starting something that would someday explode. I knew I was changing everything, but I pushed ahead. "I need to divorce Ron," I said simply. "It's over. I can't do it anymore." Then I looked at Annie and burst into tears. She wrapped her arms around me and held me until I could speak again. I could barely look at my mother, I felt so overwhelmed by guilt. I had failed at the most important job of my life, the job she had schooled me for, the sacred task of wife and mother. I was supposed to be the support, the keeper of the hearth. Now I was taking a jackhammer to it, cracking it open so I could escape. I hadn't been able to hold it together through thick and thin, through sickness and health. I was giving up.

My mother sat quietly for a moment, then said the one thing I needed to hear. "I understand," she said, leaning forward to squeeze my hand. "I understand why you married Ron and I understand why you need to leave him."

Later that evening, after the tears and questions and talk, we sat around a table in a restaurant and my mother said: "I can't believe how strong you girls are. I don't know where you get it." Indeed. We just looked at each other and smiled.

Now that I had told my family, the process had to move forward. It wasn't fair for everyone to know more than Ron. When I got back to Washington, I screwed up my courage and called the lawyer. I had gotten his name from an old friend of my parents, who assured me he was competent and understanding, but it hardly helped. Spending money for legal advice meant this was really happening; it was like pushing the start button on some big, unwieldy machine, a machine that could easily lurch out of control.

The man seemed harmless on the phone, however, so a few days later I went in for an interview, shaky and girlish in my uneasiness. He was older, mild-mannered, and slightly bumbling, and—as it turned out—more intent on reassuring me than dispensing the best legal advice. I explained the situation, then said I planned on being the custodial parent and staying in the house, but that I would happily give Ron generous visitation rights. He just nodded, as if that was how all divorces happened. He didn't point out that, as I later learned, custody or visitation wasn't mine to "give" to the boys' father, that Ron had the same rights to custody that I had. Instead he told me what I could expect in terms of child support as the custodial parent, went over some basic finances, and then said I didn't need to worry, the boys and I were going to be just fine. "Children are happy if their mommy is happy," he said, patting my hand. "Do you have a boyfriend?"

"No," I said, flushing with the implications of the question.

"Well, go out and find yourself a date. An attractive young woman like you could do with some fun."

I left in a daze. Dates? Fun? That was the farthest thing from my mind. And I didn't feel young and attractive, I felt fat and middle-aged, though I was only thirty-seven. His urging left an unpleasant taste on my tongue, but the rest of the conversation had been reassuring. It didn't seem as if there would be problems with the custody issue, and the child support numbers were better than I had expected. Maybe I could actually do this without going into the poorhouse.

There was only one thing left to do: tell Ron and the kids. The years of fantasizing, of reading about divorce and weighing the costs, the years of looking at my children and worrying about their future, those countless hours had all led, somehow, to this place, this perch at the edge of the cliff. It was now.

I decided to tell Ron at our next marital counseling session. I was afraid to be alone with him when I did it.

I went home and packed up my most precious possessions, the silver and the ceramic teapot my grandmother had given me and several other breakables, then took them over to my best friend's place. I didn't want them in the house if Ron got angry and suddenly started throwing things. Sandy had listened for years as I had spun my daily troubles into stories, and she understood instinctively why I needed to leave the box in her care, but she seemed worried about me.

"You seem a bit agitated," Sandy said, eyeing me closely as we stashed the box in her basement. "Are you sure you're okay?"

"Well, I'm just nervous. I don't know what Ron will do," I said, pacing around. I could barely stand still.

"Look," she said softly. "I think this will be hard and I think it will be upsetting, but I don't think anything bad is going to happen."

I went home and looked around, trying to talk my panic down to a low hum. Was there anything else I really needed to protect? I packed a small bag, like the one I had taken to the hospital when I gave birth to my children, and stuffed it in the front-hall closet, in case I needed to get out in the middle of the night. I looked around the house, suddenly worried about weapons. No guns, thank God, but there were some nice kitchen knives. I took them downstairs and hid them behind a stack of paint cans in Ron's shop. There were some lethal-looking tools around, but my reason got the better of me. I probably didn't need to hide those. All was ready. I went back upstairs and made dinner for the boys, my hands shaking.

We drove down to our counseling session together that evening just as usual, but we both knew the process was unraveling. The last several sessions had been rocky, angry, accusatory. We sat down and within a few minutes I said I had reached a decision. I looked at Ron. "I can't do it anymore. I've talked to a lawyer. We have to get divorced."

Ron sat in the corner of his sofa and said nothing.

The counselor looked at me, unfazed. He asked us both to talk a bit about how that made us feel, but we could barely sit in the room together. Ron seemed beyond words. We finished early, and I don't even remember if we drove home together. I don't see how we could have.

When I got home I busied myself putting the children to bed, then went downstairs to talk with Ron, braced for the anger and the shouting, the next round in the battle. But he wasn't there. He had gone next door to talk with some trusted neighbors. I sat in the living room looking out the window at the familiar street and our yard, thinking about this home and the painful years we had lived here together. It was over, finally over. After a while the husband of the couple Ron was visiting called me. "We can't believe this, Wendy," he said. "Please think about what you are doing." I knew this man and I liked him, but his words made my hackles rise. As if I could do this without having thought it through, without years of agonized indecision, without trying to parse every outcome, every eventuality. Think about it, he suggested. "No," I remember saying. "I've thought about it plenty." I must have sounded like a coldhearted bitch, but I was offended by his request, by the implication that this was some sort of impulsive act. "It's over," was all I had left to say.

That night I slept on the floor in the kids' bedroom. It was the only part of the house that still felt like home.

12

CUSTODY

"Custody" is one of the most loaded words in the English language. No matter how you dice it—single, joint, sequential—it means somebody gets the goods and the other loses. Custody reduces children to chattel, makes them an asset to be divided, along with the pensions and the furniture. Just the word "custody" puts the concept of parenting in an unnatural box, a box with too many walls, too many closed doors. Custody means that bonds get broken. Custody means that someone who used to have unlimited access to their children suddenly gets to parent only according to a schedule set by a judge in a cold courtroom. Custody means you may not be there the night teddy gets left on the subway, or the day your child breaks his arm, or in those countless moments when your children need the reassuring touch of your hand or your gaze.

I read news stories of people torn apart by custody battles—the Pennsylvania man who shot his beloved son and then himself after a court ruled that the child would bear his mother's last name—and something deep inside me understood how that could happen. Custody issues are usually the most difficult and painful parts of a divorce, the place where a parent's worst fears come to life and stalk the playground. Even now, when I talk with other parents who have lost time with their kids because of divorce, I am stunned by the lasting depth of the pain. Even divorced parents who have good relationships with their grown children cry in restaurants when I talk with them about the impossibility of custody choices, about the days and months they lost.

It seems naive now, but when I envisioned my divorce I never considered that I would lose significant time with my children. Maybe it was because I was good at mothering—even Ron said I was the best in the world. Maybe it was because I was the one who had memorized Dr. Spock, who always kept a few animal crackers up her sleeve. Maybe it was because I was the one who took time off from work when they were born, who nursed them in the middle of the night, who had done the lion's share of the child care. Maybe it was because they had been so young, just barely babies, when I started thinking about divorce.

But by the time we split up, they were getting older. David turned five that summer, graduating from his cozy preschool and headed for kindergarten in the fall. He already was mostly himself—gentle and stouthearted, a sensitive boy clearly troubled by his parents' problems, a worrier and a helper. He had always been a chatterer, nimble with words and able to articulate sophisticated thoughts, but that summer he seemed unnaturally quiet. He probably understood more than we knew.

Jesse, just three, was more of a mystery, still locked up in his toddler world. He had been slower to talk and still had trouble negotiating longer sentences. He spoke to us through his body, spinning, fighting, tensing, or dancing according to the spirit of the moment. Emotions—love, fear, anger, joy—were shared through the vocabulary of touch and action. He lurched through life, struggling to control his impulses and still needing lots of reassurance from the adults around him. It was difficult to know what he understood of our problems. He seemed oblivious yet agitated, sensing trouble but unable to tell what quarter it was coming from.

Together, they were like a pair of polar bear cubs, rowdy and curious, hard to contain in a stroller or a shopping cart. Perhaps that's why I never thought Ron would fight for a significant share of their time. I was arrogant about my ability to handle them, how to manage a trip to the zoo, how to pack for day care in the morning, how to anticipate their varied and changing needs. Ron didn't have tricks up his sleeve. But custody, as I was quickly to learn, wasn't about who knew tricks. It wasn't even about who was going to care for the kids when they were little—it was about who was going to be their parent for life.

After the night I told him the marriage was over, Ron made himself scarce, taking off without comment to meet friends or drive around and think. Despite the year of counseling, my actions took him by surprise, left him reeling and off balance. There is always one partner who is better prepared, and it gives him or her a subtle advantage. I felt it now, for the first time, that because it was my divorce, I was in the driver's seat, and it gave me a satisfying rush of power, the first I'd felt in a long time. At moments I felt almost giddy with power, with the strength of my resolve. I had faced the toughest of the demons and emerged unscathed. I felt now that I could do this, that after the hard parts of telling my family and Ron, that now I could get on with the parts I was ready for. While Ron spun aimlessly about the neighborhood, I sat at home with the boys and began to dream more boldly about my new life. Maybe I would put shelves in David's closet, as I had planned to for years. Maybe I would paint the bathroom. Hope began to sprout in a thousand spots, poking up into the scarred landscape of my life. Maybe I would grow my hair, learn to lift weights. I felt like a separate person again, independent. The abyss in my personality, the deep hole that had opened up over the years I'd struggled with my marriage, had suddenly closed. People asked me later if I ever regretted my decision, ever considered going back to Ron, and all I can say is that I knew instantly that I'd done the right thing. I woke up the day after that terrible night and my soul was healed. Even through all the difficult moments that followed, I never once looked back.

Despite my resolve, the divorce wasn't really moving forward. Ron and I were now caught in a no-man's-land that many couples stumble into, the demilitarized zone between the tension of the breakup and the disruption of someone moving out. It feels like living in a vacuum, as if all emotion gets sucked immediately into some higher atmosphere. I found it difficult to breathe, awkward to be in the house with the shadow of my husband lurking about. I didn't want to eat with him, do his laundry, or stumble into him as I stepped out of the shower. That old, familiar intimacy felt like a minefield, and I watched myself set new boundaries every day: Don't see me like this, don't hear what I say, don't watch me with the boys. I know he found it difficult too, but it was almost as if he needed a break between bouts. I gave it a few days, then sat and wrote out a long letter detailing how I thought we should proceed. In it I listed my "nonnegotiables": that we should share legal custody but that I would retain physical custody, at least through the school week. He could have generous visitation, weekend time, and perhaps one night a week. I would remain in the house, for the benefit of the children. Perhaps he could get an apartment somewhere nearby. I left the letter on the kitchen table.

He took the letter but didn't respond. Instead, he came back from driving around one evening and said he had decided he needed to take a vacation somewhere so that he could think this all out. The next day he announced that he was going to take a week in the Virgin Islands, at a campground where we had gone together the winter I was pregnant with David. It made me sad to think of him there, in a spot where we'd been happy, but then he said something that sent ice through my veins. He wanted to take David with him.

There was nothing I could say, because Ron had every right to take David along, yet the morning my five-year-old boy left with his dad, looking lost and worried as he walked to the car in his oversize T-shirt, I almost couldn't stop myself from running after him. He had never been that far away from me before, and I wondered if Ron would be able to keep him from feeling sad or lonely, particularly if he was suffering from the same thing. We hadn't said anything to the kids yet about the divorce, but I could feel that David sensed something had changed. He seemed subdued, more worried than usual, confused and unhappy. Now his dad was taking him away, over the ocean, to a place where I could not reach him. I fought down a fear that Ron might not return. "That's stupid," I said to myself; but not because I trusted Ron wouldn't steal him. I was stupid because I knew Ron would never leave Jesse behind. I stood on the front steps and waved them off, crying now that David couldn't see me anymore. It was the first time I felt a gap open between myself and my children.

There are so many assumptions we make—when we love, when we marry, when we have children. From the moment my boys first appeared as ghostly shadows on the sonogram screen, I assumed that they would be with me until they went to college. Maybe a week or two of summer camp, an occasional visit to the grandparents, but mostly they would be underfoot and under my wing every day for eighteen years. I always assumed that if they did drugs I would see it in their eyes, because they would be in my kitchen cruising for snacks. If they fell in with a bad crowd, I would know because I would be chaperoning the high school dance. Society also assumes these things about mothers, and reinforces it at every turn. Mothers are encouraged to bond in big ways, from the first fumbling attempt to nurse a newborn to lunchtime visits at the day care center to serving as "room mother" to a bunch of grade-school children.

Mothers, as well, are expected to retain custody of children, despite the fact that custody law in most jurisdictions is now considered "gender neutral." What that means is that mothers have no more right to children than fathers and sometimes lose custody for such sins as earning less income or working outside the home.

I never suspected Ron would want or seek custody, and no one around me did either. My lawyer's exact words were: "Don't worry, he won't fight you. Why should he, when he has you to do all that work?"

· · ·

Ron and David returned from the Virgin Islands a week later browned and bonded, David seeming impossibly grown up as he described swimming with sea turtles and chasing crabs through the underbrush. That evening, though, as I tucked him back in his own bed upstairs, he looked unusually sad. "Did you get homesick while you were away?" I asked, trying to find the source of his unhappiness.

"Yes," he said. "I missed you." Then, in a tiny voice I could barely hear, he said. "Daddy yelled at me at the airport. He yelled a lot on the trip."

My smile faded. "Tell me what happened, honey."

"I dropped my Legos box and he yelled at me."

"Where did you drop it? Were you in a hurry?"

He nodded. "I dropped it as we were getting on the plane. The plane was going to leave without us."

I could see it now, Ron yelling at him, panicking slightly as the jet engines roared overhead and they scrambled to collect the pieces. It made me ache for my little boy, the idea that I hadn't been there to shield him or reassure him. I smoothed his blond hair back from his forehead. I felt infinitely sad, and my sense of power was ebbing away. How was I going to prevent this, how was I going to keep these moments from happening if I wasn't there to pick up the pieces and shield these boys from Ron's outbursts?

"Daddy loves you so much," I said. "Even if sometimes he loses his temper." It was the only thing I could think of to say.

A few days later I returned from work one afternoon in a hurry to change clothes; I was meeting my friend Sandy to see a play downtown. But Ron was there and said he had something important to tell me. I stood by the kitchen table, unsuspecting. He looked slightly agitated, his hands shaking. "What is it?"

"Sit down. This is going to take a minute."

I sat, but on the edge of my chair. "What?"

"I've been thinking about what you put in your letter and I think you should know that I want joint custody of the boys," he said. He stopped to take a breath, then looked at me with a flash of anger. "I don't want to 'visit' with my kids," he said, spitting the word across the table at me. "I want to be their dad. I want them half the time."

I sat uncomprehending for several minutes. "What do you mean?"

"I mean, I think we should each get them half the time—a week at a time, maybe, or two weeks."

I heard these words but they didn't seem to make sense, seemed jumbled in my brain. Joint physical custody? Half the time? I thought of Jesse living away from me for a week and suddenly felt as if he was being torn right out of my arms. I began to hyperventilate.

"You cannot take Jesse away from me," I said, gasping for breath. "He is too young." Maybe David could survive a week of vacation away from me, even a week of school, but not my baby, not my sweet toddler. I suddenly jumped up and left the room because I couldn't bear to look at Ron or be near him. I couldn't bear to look at the man who would take away my children.

Joint custody. I stumbled down the steps to the subway to meet Sandy, unable to see for the tears in my eyes. No, no, no. The minute she picked me up, Sandy knew something was terribly wrong. We sat in a restaurant down near the Washington waterfront and I cried openly over my carrot soup.

She patted my hand across the table. "Come on, you can call your lawyer in the morning. Just because Ron wants this doesn't mean you have to accept it if it's not good for the boys. You don't know what will happen."

"But what if I do have to accept this?" I said, my eyes filling up again. "What if this is my future, living without my kids?"

Sandy had three children of her own, including a two-year-old boy. We met when David and her daughter Becca were just a few weeks old, and being mothers together had formed the bedrock of our relationship. Without needing to say it, she understood who I was as a mom, what those boys meant to me. "Don't panic yet," she just said, in her measured voice. "That's not going to help anything. Besides, maybe you and Ron can work something out." But despite her comforting presence, I sat through the play shell-shocked. To this day I have no idea what we saw that night.

That moment, however, helped me see something I had been blind to before and that would be central to helping me visualize the future. I saw, in that stripped-away second, what Ron was facing: the untenable loss of his children. One of the worst aspects of divorce is how blind we become to the other's reality. It is very difficult to break the bonds of marriage, even unhappy marriages, and I think some of the vehemence divorcing people feel toward their former partners is subconsciously revved up to help the self make that break, help it distance itself from the other. It may help us get out, but it also hobbles our understanding. Until that moment at the kitchen table, I had never considered how Ron would feel about living in a place that was not home to his children, what it would feel like for him to wake in the morning and not have those warm little bodies clambering over him in bed, to lose the blessing of daily chores done for those you love. I would not want to live without them, and Ron—it turned out—felt the same way.

There was another echo, faint, but palpable. I had spent too many days as a child thinking about my absent father, worrying that I would forget what he looked like. When I suddenly saw that same gap opening between my boys and their dad, my heart contracted. It was too familiar not to get my attention. I was still too scared to acknowledge the shift, but deep inside me something had started to change.

To help him stake his claim for the kids, Ron hired a bull-dog of a lawyer, a man who decided I must be a bitch from hell if I couldn't acknowledge Ron's rights as a father. Ron also enlisted the aid of our neighbors, including the man who had remarried and had twins, because he had joint custody of his teenage daughter from his first marriage. Dick came over one night and we argued in the dark of the screened porch over whether Ron had the patience and emotional stability to parent. Dick finally said, "Wendy, none of us is a perfect dad. We all yell sometimes, we all want to spank them when they are naughty. Does that mean we shouldn't be in their lives?"

Ron went over to the University of Maryland library and photocopied every study he could find on custody issues. "Here," he said one evening, tossing them on the table. "Read these. Maybe this will help."

While I was being assailed by Ron and his lieutenants on one side, my family and women friends were lining up on the other, arguing against the idea of my "giving" Ron joint custody. My parents had been appalled to see joint custody forced on my older sister, Anne, in her settlement with her husband several years earlier. The thought that I would also lose control over my children was almost more than they could bear.

Many of my women friends, as well, saw Ron's play for joint custody as pure manipulation, the first move in a campaign that would strip me of everything—the house, the kids, my money. It took my breath away, how quickly he became the devil in their eyes. Several people suggested he wanted joint custody only because then he wouldn't have to pay nearly as much in child support. One friend took me aside and said, "Divorce impoverishes women. You must stand up to him or you will end up poor, and it starts with the children. If you get the kids, then you get the house and the child support you will need."

But when I looked at my life, it wasn't that simple. As Ron and I struggled to find a solution, we were hearing more and more stories of custody fights run amok, and they were chilling. One neighbor counseled me not to fight, saying a battle would leave us both poor and bitter. She had fought for custody of her two children and the result was that she and her husband spent $90,000 in legal fees and ended up with a compromise close to what he had originally offered. "We had to sell the house to pay the lawyers and now we can't speak to each other," she said. "That's what I got from the fight."

Another couple we knew had already escalated their custody battle to full-scale war, with numbing accusations flying from both sides. I saw their children at school and on the playground, and the boys seemed cowed and nervous all the time. If one of the parents had the right to be at a baseball game, the other had to leave, even if it was in a public park. I would watch those little boys shrink in shame as their parents argued on the sidelines, and I knew I couldn't do that to David and Jesse.

I was surprised by how many assumptions friends and acquaintances made about my life and the choices before me, often offering empathetic bits of advice about things they had never experienced themselves. Everyone, for instance, assumed I should get the house, and if Ron forced me out he would go down as a pig and a bully. But I was beginning to wonder if I wanted the house. It was old, rundown, and maintenance heavy. It was bigger than I needed, and the mortgage was more than I could swing, even with full child support.

I also had to admit that Ron, despite his lapses of temper, was a pretty good father. Since the day David was born, he had changed diapers, crawled around on the floor with them, read them stories every night. My neighbor was right—Ron wasn't perfect, but then few parents were. I read through the studies on custody and the results were mixed. Several studies suggested that children whose fathers became "visiting" parents experienced that as a significant loss, like a difficult death that left unfinished business. Denied a daily paternal presence, the kids often fantasized about their dads, investing them with unrealistic hopes that crashed later when the children grew to adolescence and discovered that their fathers were human after all. The one consistent finding among the reports was that kids did better—no matter what the custody arrangement—when their parents stopped fighting. That made sense but it seemed hopelessly idealistic. How, in God's name, were we supposed to stop fighting when we disagreed on so many critical issues?

Ron put a deposit on a garden apartment about a twenty-minute drive from the house, out in Maryland. At first I was encouraged, but as the weeks passed it was clear Ron was thinking twice about moving out. His lawyer, as I later learned, warned him against leaving the family home voluntarily because it would weaken his claim to the children if we went to court over custody.

As June bled into July, I began to get nervous. I had pushed forward in the spring because I wanted to get the separation over and settled during the summer, before David started kindergarten in the fall. I was starting my third year of teaching at American University, and the demands of gearing up for the fall semester would soon be bearing down on me. I was unhappy with the idea of joint custody but had agreed to the concept if Ron would allow the boys to spend the lion's share of the school week with me. I was still deeply concerned about too much disruption in their lives, their need for routine and a grounded space. But Ron argued that such an arrangement pushed him back into weekend status. "I want to help with homework and pack their lunches," he said one night as we argued in hushed tones after the boys had gone to bed. "I don't want to be there for just the fun stuff."

I'm not sure now why I couldn't acknowledge the virtue in what he was saying. Perhaps it was because he wasn't as patient with them, because he didn't baby them as much as I did. I was afraid lunches would get forgotten, or backpacks left behind. That the boys would get yelled at, that Ron would be too overwhelmed with the work of laundry, cooking, shopping, and everything else to do it well. A trip to the grocery with the two of them left me needing a drink and a nap—I couldn't imagine him handling the stress of single-parenting.

To break the stalemate, we agreed to talk with a mediator, nonbinding, just to see if we could reach a settlement. I don't remember now how we found her, but the minute I met her she struck me as cold and unsympathetic. I had carefully worked out a monthly schedule for the boys that I submitted as a compromise. It gave Ron some weekday time but kept me in the driver's seat, with about two thirds of the boys' waking hours. She picked it up and treated it as my opening bargaining position rather than as a compromise. Ron, whose doctorate had been in labor politics, understood the basics of negotiating and started with his original position, that he should have equal time. By the time the session was over, the mediator had created a schedule that I knew instinctively would horrify a child psychiatrist: The boys were to shift households several times a week in a complex, monthly pattern. I felt as if I was the only one thinking about how this schedule would actually feel to the children—the disruption, the lack of routine. I looked at it and said no, there was no way I would agree to that kind of insanity. Although Ron had most of what he wanted with this agreement, he too saw that it was crazy and didn't fight me. We left her office sullen and exhausted. We took our proposals back to our own corners, hardened now in our positions, frozen in opposition.

13

BREAKING POINT

The euphoria I had felt at the beginning of the summer was gone now, pushed out by the growing fear that I had started something that was quickly moving out of my control. I felt like Pandora must have felt in that moment after she opened the box—quailing before the rush of evils that swirled about her head. This divorce was spinning away from me. It was no longer something I was doing and pushing. Now, the divorce was both of ours.

And the reality was beginning to look like nothing I had anticipated. I wasn't sleeping well and began to have problems with my stomach and a sinus infection I couldn't shake. Eczema broke out along my fingertips, leaving behind little calluses that deadened feeling. Finally, almost unable to eat, I went to see my doctor and he told me I probably had an ulcer and needed to think hard about managing my stress. I told him I was in the middle of a divorce, and he nodded knowingly. "It's difficult, but you have to get through it better." Then he wrote out a prescription for something like Valium. "Here," he said. "Take this to help you sleep, and take one in the morning if you know it's going to be a particularly difficult day. This is just to get you through this. We'll talk again before I renew the prescription." I drove home carefully, aware of how distracted I was these days, how often I caught myself about to drive through red lights or change lanes without checking first. It is well known in insurance circles that people going through a divorce are at high risk for traffic accidents, particularly during the six months just before and after a split. I could see how easily that happened. It astounds me, even now, that neither of us cracked up the car that summer.

And then, before I knew it, July was gone. It was clear that Ron wasn't going to move, though he didn't say anything. I was beginning to panic. Was I going to get hung up here, mid-divorce? Living forever in this no-man's-land? Unable to move forward, unable to take it back? I talked with my lawyer again, and he recommended I get an apartment and move out. I told him we were fighting over custody, but he didn't seem concerned by that. He never warned me that moving would weaken my position, or that I could end up without any child support or the children. The session with my doctor convinced me I had to move forward, so I plunged ahead and rented an apartment in a building not far from our house, small but adequate, with an indoor pool in the basement. I figured it would give us something to do on winter evenings, as the apartment barely had enough room to roughhouse. My lawyer cautioned me to take only the things I needed to serve the boys' needs—to leave behind all the wedding presents, the furniture that was jointly owned. Many of the things we had were gifts or hand-me-downs from my parents, so it was possible to furnish a small apartment with what belonged to me. I hired a mover for the piano, then rented a small truck for the Saturday of Labor Day weekend. Labor Day, the weekend before David started kindergarten. I had spent the entire summer trying to reach some resolution well before that day, and now it looked like his first day in Mommy's new home was going to be his first day of kindergarten. I could just hear David, later in life, telling his therapist: "My parents split up the day I started kindergarten. I came home from my new school to find my mother had moved out." I think of divorce now as something akin to a bad traffic accident. Somebody starts out just trying to move to another lane and, before you know it, everything flies out of control and all sorts of innocents get hurt. That was the first of the painful lessons I was to learn—that divorce was something I couldn't control and that it would do damage I could never have anticipated. That no matter how many books I had read, how much legal advice I got, or even how many times I held my tongue, this divorce was getting messy.

I packed as little as possible, but everyone in the house knew something was up. I told Ron that I was going to move out over the weekend, and was going to take the kids' beds and dressers. And them. I said I planned to keep them for the week and that he could have them Friday night, for the weekend. He didn't respond, just looked at the floor. I told him I hoped there wouldn't be a scene at the day care center that evening.

Classes were starting at the university that week, so I was at school when I got the call from my lawyer. "Your husband is going to court later this afternoon to try and get an injunction to keep you from removing the kids from the family home," he said breathlessly, sounding a bit stunned.

"What? A WHAT?"

"An injunction. It would mean that you couldn't take the

kids to your new apartment." His voice cracked. Clearly, he was surprised. Up until this moment this man had only been optimistic. He had never cautioned me about things that could go wrong, or things to protect ourselves from. "I had no idea he was this serious about the kids," he said.

I had to sit down. The air was literally knocked from my body by the shock that a court, a judge, might step between me and my children. This only happened to criminals, to abusers, to evil people. My children adored me, needed me. How could this be happening?

"What do we do?" I croaked. "I'm supposed to teach a class in a few minutes, but I can cancel it." From my office I could see the students filing into the classroom. All the blood had drained from my body. I could not do this, I could not teach right now. It was all I could do to keep from dissolving into hysterical tears.

"Go teach your class and call me when you're done," he said. "I'll try to arrange a meeting with them for later this afternoon. Maybe if we can come up with an agreement, we can prevent them from going to court."

I sat at my desk for a moment trying to calm myself. This was the first class of the semester, these students had never met me before. I couldn't go in there and cry. So I stopped thinking about the boys and Ron and the divorce. I picked up my books and went into that class and, some-how, taught for two hours. It was only after it was over that I got into my car, sped out of the campus parking garage, and headed north up the Potomac River along the parkway. I finally stopped when I was crying and breathing so hard I couldn't drive.

We met that afternoon in a barren conference room at the offices of Ron's lawyer. Even today, when I drive by that building, I get the shivers. If there was a nadir, a single point that proved to be the very bottom of my divorce, it was that meeting in that ugly room. When we walked in, I was startled to see that Ron and his lawyer were visibly angry, hostile and combative in a zealous sort of way. I realized, suddenly, that they considered themselves the good guys in this argument. My lawyer, surprised by these developments and embarrassed to be caught off guard, seemed beaten down from the beginning, timid and conciliatory. I couldn't understand what we had to be conciliatory about. I was the mother, after all, and a good one at that. It all felt off balance, as if I had stumbled into the wrong dimension.

Ron opened the meeting by saying he refused to give up the kids: He wanted them with him half the time and he was going to stay in the house permanently. He proposed we each keep the kids a week at a time, switching them over on Sunday evenings. He would give me a modest amount of child support, what the law required, but only a small fraction of what I would have been entitled to as a custodial parent. The Volvo, which was safer than our old Honda, would get traded back and forth with the kids. Ron didn't want them traveling in any other car.

I sat at the table and tried to fight my panic so I could understand what was happening, but it was almost impossible. The thought of being away from the children for seven days was almost too excruciating to contemplate and I fumbled about, not knowing how to proceed. My lawyer said nothing, just slumped in his chair with a sigh.

"I can't, I can't be away from the boys for a week," I finally stammered. "Could we look at the plan I showed you at the mediator's? It gives you—"

But before I could finish, Ron's lawyer leapt to his feet. "That's unacceptable," he shouted, towering over me.

"Completely unacceptable. Ron will only agree to a fifty-fifty time split of joint custody or we might as well stop this and go over to the courthouse." I looked at my lawyer. He just shrugged and said nothing.

"But these boys are only five and three years old," I said, my panic rising again. "They are too young to be away from their mother for a week—"

But the minute I used the word "mother," Ron's lawyer began to sputter. "There is nothing that makes you a better parent just because you are their mother," he spit out, poking at the air in front of my face. "You think you have the right to decide who gets custody, but you don't. Ron is only asking for what is rightfully his—half the kids' time. Any judge would agree with him."

Was that true? I looked over at my lawyer again, who remained slumped in his chair, apparently defeated and outmaneuvered. I looked at Ron, who sat, grim-faced but determined, across the table from me. He wasn't enjoying this but he had hired this man and was letting him work. Suddenly, I saw what was happening. I was being bullied into accepting joint custody, and I didn't have a bully in my corner to protect me. I was so shocked, so saddened by what I knew in my heart would be a wrenching change for the boys, but there was no one there to help me defend that. The room began to spin and I realized I was going to either faint or cry, so I stood up and said I needed to speak to my lawyer alone. We went out into the hall, to give me a chance to pull myself together and consider my alternatives.

"We don't want them to go for an injunction," he said, talking sideways, to the wall.

"Why not?" I asked. "Could we lose?"

"We just don't. We don't want to get into that." He didn't seem to want to answer my question, and it occurred to me that maybe he didn't want to take on a custody fight himself, wasn't the kind of lawyer who took such cases. Instead, he proposed a compromise. "Why don't you agree to joint custody for a three-month trial," he said. "Just a trial period."

"But doesn't that put Ron in a stronger position if we end up fighting for full custody?" I asked, my voice rising.

He waved his hands at me as if I needed to calm down. "Now you're getting all upset. Don't worry about that. He wants to be the hero right now. He'll get tired once he realizes how much work it is. In a few months' time he'll be begging you to take the kids back."

I looked at Ron through the glass conference room wall, cold and focused in his determination, and I knew that was bullshit. Ron was on a crusade. Ron was trying to hold on to the one thing that kept him connected to this earth, his little boys. Ron felt long and deep and hard, and this wasn't about a few months as the local good-guy dad. My lawyer didn't have a clue about what was motivating him, but I did. I knew he wasn't going to give up.

But in that bleak moment in that awful place, where we stood awkwardly in the reception room and there was nowhere to retreat, there didn't seem to be other options. I wasn't a lawyer, and I couldn't imagine what the options might be. I had never felt so alone in my life.

I went back in, numb, angry.

"Okay, I'll agree to a trial of joint custody, three months, and then we see how the boys are doing." I squared my shoulders. "But we have to make some accommodation in the schedule so the boys can see the other parent for an evening mid-week—my kids can't go for seven days without seeing their mommy. That is just impossible."

Ron's lawyer opened his mouth to protest, but I glared at him and Ron jumped in.

"That's fine, that's great." He seemed on the verge of tears. "I know they need you."

We decided the boys would spend a week at a time with each parent, but go to spend the night with the other parent on Wednesdays. My lawyer seemed visibly relieved to have an agreement. With my heart dead inside me, I signed a letter detailing the arrangements, then walked out without shaking anyone's hand. I couldn't even look at Ron's lawyer.

Three days later several friends helped me load my things into the rental truck and then cart them into the apartment a few blocks away, where they quickly filled the small rooms. Ron had taken the boys away for the weekend so they wouldn't have to watch their mom dismantling their life. We had agreed I would get the kids first, so I took their beds and dressers, half their toys, and a pile of stuffed animals. I took an old single bed from the attic for myself, and my desk and dresser. Sandy lent me a stack of plates and cups. I left behind the stereo, the television, the computer, the camcorder. I left most of the antiques, not because I didn't have a claim to them, but because they wouldn't fit in my new space. I left behind stacks of books, wedding gifts, Christmas ornaments, boxes of photos, and everything in the basement and garage. It was surprising to me how little, in fact, I really needed. Because the boys were starting school the next day, I came back to sleep in the house the final night, helping Ron make them sleeping pallets in their room out of the camping mattresses. "We're getting you new beds this week," Ron said, his voice strained with the effort to make it feel normal. They didn't respond—too young, too confused, too innocent to suspect dirty play.

The next morning I dropped Jess at day care, thankful that he was in a familiar spot, then took David into kindergarten and met his teacher, slipping her a note about what was happening at home. Then I went back and retrieved a few last things from the house. That evening, I picked the kids up at Ron's and drove them to my apartment for the night. I remember thinking of them as tiny hostages, hostages to their parents' failures, hostages to their parents' inability to work together in a better way. I don't remember much else about that day except that I explained what was happening as we sat in the car outside the apartment building. Ron and I had vowed to tell them together, but when the moment came we were so hardened to each other we didn't even try. They sat in the back, two confused little birds, blinking at me in the dark as I tried to explain why they were going to live with Mommy in a new place, and then go back to live with Daddy for a while.

When I said that Mommy and Daddy didn't love each other anymore, David started to cry. I quickly tried to reassure him that we would always love them, that divorce didn't change how parents felt about their kids, but he didn't seem mollified. He asked a few questions about where his toys would be and if he could see his friends again, and then he wondered where he would eat dinner each night. Jesse said nothing until the very end, then he pulled his thumb out of his mouth and said, "What's divorce?"

14

THE TELEPHONE

Jesse is on the phone with me, but he is only breathing.

"Honey, are you there?"

Breathing.

"What did you do in day care today?"

Breathing.

"Mommy loves you, sweetie. You are my best bear."

Breathing again, but more labored. He starts to cry.

"Mommy," he says between sobs. "Mommy."

"What, sweetie? Tell me. Talk to Mommy, Jesse." Maybe if he'll talk he'll stop crying.

"Ahh, uh, uh . . ." He doesn't know what to say, but he doesn't want the connection to stop.

If I were in the room with him now I know exactly what he would do. He would melt forward into my arms, put his thumb in his mouth, and reach around to curl my hair with his free hand. But I'm not in the room with him, and every bone in my body aches to grab the car keys and go to him. This telephone connection, this thin reed of sound and line, is all the access I'm allowed right now, and it is painfully inadequate. He can't talk, but I whisper to him a bit longer, the silly stuff that three-year-olds love. He cries, but somehow he seems better. After a while he stops crying and says good-bye and gives the phone to his father.

"Is he okay," I ask.

"Yeah, he's fine. Well, he's sad, but he was fine until you called."

Jesse and I do not have a good telephone relationship. He doesn't know how to talk on the phone, and I cannot get what I need to know across a phone line. I need to know if he had a good day at day care, but I can only find that out if I can see him, touch him, hug him. If he is agitated or squirms away when I reach for him, that tells me one thing. If his hair is sweaty, if there is ketchup on his shirt, if his pants are torn or his hands blue with paint, those tell me other things. These are not things his father will necessarily tell me, or even notice, and yet they are the clues that help me build in my child's mind the belief that Mommy knows. Mommy knows there is a playground bully, and the torn pants can be part of a larger story. Mommy knows they are working on special projects in art, something for parents' night. Mommy knows that her child loves Friday because that is the day they have hot dogs for lunch.

Without those cues, I found I couldn't read my children, couldn't tell how they were doing, and it broke my heart. Suddenly, it was as if there was so much static in our relationship that the old lines of communication didn't work anymore.

The first week on my own, the week I had them with me in the apartment, we were too numb to do much more than watch videos and hug on the sofa. The boys were too confused to be able to talk about what was happening, and I was too relieved that they weren't crying every night to dig around and reopen the wound over and over.

But the second week, when they went to Ron's, was when the nightmare began for real. By every measure I was a good mother, yet here I was alone in a small apartment in a building filled with single people. I was so accustomed to the hubbub and focus of my children, I didn't have any idea who I was without them, and I didn't want to find out. At night I would lie on their beds among their stuffed animals and cry myself to sleep. Even now, that week is almost too wrenching to recall.

When it was finally Wednesday and my turn to have them for a night, I went to pick them up at the day care center. Jesse, startled to see me get out of the car, ran to the playground fence and said, in a cry of amazement, "You came back!"

All my explanations and reassurances had amounted to nothing. All he knew was what he felt, and it felt to him as if I had gone to the moon. Later, I mentioned the incident to a psychologist we were working with, and she shook her head. "No, he didn't think you went to the moon. He thought you had died."

Now I knew how people got holes in their hearts.

That first night back together I let them fall asleep curled up beside me in bed. I felt I would die if I had to let them go again, but the next day I took them to their schools, tried reassuring them over and over that they would see me again in a few days, then drove away. That night I lay in bed looking at the empty spot where they had slept the night before and I couldn't believe what I had done. I had started a process, pushed for a separation that had led to this. The hole in my heart was wide open, and a lifetime of grief seemed to be blowing through it.

Years later I was reading an article about birth mothers who give up children for adoption, and I shuddered with recognition when one mother talked about living forever with the unassuageable grief of losing one's child. It wasn't as if my children had died or disappeared, but more that I had abandoned them in some fundamental way that I hadn't meant and didn't want and now couldn't reverse. Something bad that I had started and now couldn't stop. When I'd had the children I knew that someday I would have to give them up, but that was part of the misty future, something that would happen in the natural course of their development. Maybe not when I was ready, but when they would be ready. Yet here I was, walking away from them when they were just three and five, an act that seemed so unnatural, so contrary to my instincts as a mother that I couldn't adjust.

I wasn't even sure if I should adjust. I questioned our joint custody arrangement—and my role in how it came to be—relentlessly in my head. David, overwhelmed by both a new school and a new living arrangement, was chewing holes in the sleeves of his sweatshirts. Jesse was suddenly kicking other children at day care and drawing stick figures with blood spurting from every inch of their bodies. I didn't know much of what was happening in Ron's house, but I could tell he was struggling to adjust to single-parenting, and not always with finesse. The kids didn't always look particularly well-groomed and they didn't smell like my children when they came from a week with him. I fretted about how often the sheets were being changed, whether Ron was giving them enough milk. Even worse, I knew that sometimes he lost his temper, and I worried myself sick many nights over the simple fact that I couldn't protect them anymore.

One day David left his favorite stuffed bear at school,

out on the playground, and I didn't know it was missing until he was back at my house a few days later. Even though it was dark, I drove over to the school with them and we searched through the woods around the field with flashlights, hoping against hope that Dennis the bear would miraculously appear, kicked up against a tree trunk or pile of leaves. But no luck. "Maybe Dennis was carried off by a squirrel that needed something soft for his nest," I told David, looking down at his sad little face. "Maybe there are squirrel babies nesting inside Dennis right now." It was the best I could do. As we drove slowly home I cursed myself for not having been there the moment David realized Dennis was gone. In the past I had retrieved blankets from restaurants, favorite toys accidentally lost in snowbanks, searched under radiators for wayward bits and pieces. Now, I couldn't even do that anymore.

This wasn't the divorce I had imagined. This was nothing like the way it was supposed to be. Divorce was supposed to mean me and the boys living quietly in the house, without interference. It was supposed to mean that I had control over choices about schools, doctors, discipline. It was supposed to mean that I got to set the terms of my children's lives, from the mood of their day to the color of their walls.

Instead, I was out on my ear, living in a cramped apartment, away from my neighbors, my familiar territory, my cats, and my home. I was still battling with my difficult spouse over everything from bed-wetting to lunch fixings. We were both unnerved by not knowing what the other parent was doing, and pried into our children's lives for clues, searching through backpacks, checking lunch boxes, asking subtle questions of day care workers and teachers. I learned to listen for small bits from the children, like the night David told me that Ron fed them lots of vegetables because he didn't think I ever made them eat them at my house. Whenever neighbors called to see what I was doing, I badgered them with questions: Does Ron still take the boys for a walk after dinner? Do you ever hear yelling coming from the house? Have you seen any women come by? And then I would gasp at the person I had become. I couldn't believe I had gotten to such a place. It felt like something out of the *Twilight Zone* to be so disconnected from the daily ebb and flow of my children's lives, to think that maybe my neighbors knew more about them than I did.

I had expected to feel better the minute I was on my own, and in many ways I did feel better—my private life was calmer, my space was my own—but that often just made me feel guiltier than ever. Because to improve my own life I had sacrificed the boys.

It was bad enough to have failed at marriage, but now I faced a much more troubling demon: I had failed as a mother. I had always feared that, deep down, I wasn't strong. Now my lack of strength, my paltry attempt to fight for more time with my kids, had resulted in a humiliating defeat. I hadn't been able to stand up to Ron in the marriage, and now I couldn't even do so in divorce. I had learned nothing. Despite my years at the *Washington Post*, despite the lessons of Al-Anon and numerous sessions with my therapist, I wasn't really the strong, centered woman I pretended to be. When push came to shove, it turned out that I was weak, fundamentally weak.

One night an image came to me in a dream, and I couldn't get it out of my mind: I was in a lifeboat sailing safely away from a burning ship while my children remained on deck in their father's arms.

I left them behind in a place where I could not breathe, and I wondered if they sometimes choked for air.

15

WITCHES' BREW

That hellish September finally ended, and when I flipped the calendar to October, I noticed that my thirty-eighth birthday was just a few weeks away.

"Mommy's birthday is coming up," I told the boys over breakfast one morning. "Maybe I can give you some money and Daddy could help you buy me a present."

David gave me a troubled look. "Maybe *you* can help us buy you a present," he said.

"Okay. Fine with me." Life was like this now, an on-going experiment. We had no idea how to do even the simplest things anymore.

"Are you going to have a party?" Jesse asked. "You could have a Halloween party."

"Oh, I don't think so. Grown-ups don't have parties every year, like kids do," I said. "Maybe we can have a party with your stuffed animals. They can sit at the table with us and wear silly hats."

"I think you should have a real party," David said. "A party with your friends. A witches' party."

"A witches' party?"

"Well, it's Halloween this month. All your friends are girls. So that's why a witches' party."

Indeed. A witches' party. My divorce had certainly brought my women friends out in force, helping with the move, bringing over meals the first few weeks, stopping by for coffee and huddled conversations over the kitchen table. Maybe a witches' party wasn't such a bad idea—celebrate the circle of women who had stood by me through the worst of it and try to turn the page on this bitter season. I sat and thought about it a minute.

"Yeah," said Jess. "All your mommy friends could come and wear *scary* hats!"

So a witches' party it was. I wrote up an invitation and told everyone to bring their favorite party food and a bottle of champagne. Annie, too far away in California to come, sent Halloween decorations, including fake spiderwebs and a witch's wig. The boys cut out pumpkins and bats from construction paper and stuck them on the walls, then helped me string the webs around the room. They wanted to stay, but it was a grown-up party, I said. Ron had offered to take them for the evening, and as I packed them off with kisses and bags of candy corn, I noticed a storm gathering in the west. Before I knew it, the wind was whipping the trees and then there was lightning and thunder cracking overhead. My friends came running in, rain-splattered and laughing, juggling dishes and bottles. "What a night for a witches' party," Sandy crowed. "Where's the cauldron?"

Boil, boil, toil and trouble.

We put the champagne bottles in the tub and covered them with ice, then handed out dry clothes for those who needed them and hung wet ones over the doors. Within minutes it felt like a slumber party, with everyone cozied up in my little living room, hugging their knees and tucking stockinged feet beneath them to make more space for the others. The conversation buzzed and before long we were deep in a passionate debate about the politics of divorce and the ways in which women were being cheated by the newfangled divorce laws. Despite the ubiquitous feel of divorce, few of my friends had been through it. But everyone knew a story—everyone had a sister or a friend or a coworker who had been through the divorce wars—and the stories flickered like kindling in the charged air. I spoke up occasionally, but mostly I sat perched on a corner of the sofa and listened, moved by the support I felt in the room but also troubled by the unspoken rules of the discussion. Women, invariably, were the victims in these stories. Divorce was a bad thing for women. Divorce law was evil—tipped in favor of men, who were getting away with all the money and, with the advent of gender-neutral custody laws, the children as well. In most of these stories, the main characters lost their individual qualities and fell into roles, and without exception the women wore halos and the men figured as villains and power-mongers.

It was a wonderful night, but it also brought back to me how contentious and frightening the issues of divorce and custody turned out to be for the women in the community around me. Divorce, because it threatens the fabric of society, is rarely treated as a private matter. My divorce was a social issue, an opportunity to make a stand, to fight for women's rights. While most of my close women friends understood what had happened, many female acquaintances were shocked to discover that I had given up partial custody to Ron. As a woman, I was weak and capitulating if I didn't fight for my kids and make the son of a bitch pay. It was assumed that I had been wronged, and that someone—my ex—should make reparations. It was a strangely contradictory feminist message: You deserve half of everything your husband has because the law is gender neutral, but don't forget, you're the mother. Don't give up the kids—you are entitled to them.

I was struck by how often the language of divorce seemed to come straight out of war manuals: fight, attack, offensive, scorched-earth, reparations. In this climate cooperation looked like weakness. Cooperation meant defeat.

It was a powerful but corrosive witches' brew, this mixture of New Age custody law, feminist politics, and old-fashioned expectations. Few people really understood how divorce law had changed in the previous decade or what gender neutrality meant. I was often puzzled when friends would warn me to watch out for problems that the law had dealt with years earlier, as if there were no protections at all. It felt as if everyone carried around with them their own private trove of divorce horror stories, bits and pieces they had heard through their lives and held close to their hearts. And few people could see that, despite all the politically correct rhetoric, what mattered to me was how my children were doing and how I could make this divorce easier for them. I didn't care about social statements, although I got plenty of messages that I should. I cared about what our life was going to be like. And I couldn't see any point to a scorched-earth policy.

When someone gets divorced, other people "read" what happens, and worry that it could happen to them. And their reactions then get iced over with their own fears.

I didn't care that Ron had forced me out of the house—I hadn't wanted the place, was happy to be in a small apartment that was easy to care for and didn't require a lawnmower. Yet one friend who came to visit started to cry sympathetic tears when she saw where we were living.

"Oh, Wendy," she said. "I had no idea it was this bad."

I looked around in dismay. The place was a bit messy, but it had everything we needed. "What's so bad?" I said.

"It's just such a, well, a step down from where you were, with your own house, and a nice yard." She began to falter, could see she had offended me.

"But this is a luxury apartment," I said defensively. "There's a pool in the basement. Every night we go swimming."

"I'm sure it's very nice," she said, backing away from her statement. "I think it's great you have a place this close to the boys' school."

I think there also was a deeper current, and one that I could understand. Most of my friends were other mothers, other good mothers like me, people who put their children first, who had worked to engineer jobs that allowed them time at home and the energy to parent. They all had partners, fathers who parented with a mix of ability and commitment, but in most of these families the lion's share of the child care fell to the moms. Although they were too polite to say so, I doubted any of these mothers could imagine themselves in my position. Like me before my divorce, these were mothers who never seriously believed a day could come when they wouldn't be with their children. And yet there I sat, just like them but childless. Childless and yet still alive, still functioning, even sipping champagne and laughing like the rest of them. All of a sudden I was impossible to understand and scary to contemplate.

There is nothing as unnatural as an unnatural mother. By fighting for joint custody, Ron got to be a hero. By agreeing to joint custody, I became something just short of reptilian—a mother who would give up her children; and woman after woman urged me to fight, to push for sole custody, the cost be damned. It was as if, by capitulating, I had let down the feminist movement in general and them in particular. When I spoke to people about Ron's rights, about his need for his children and the need for our children to be with both parents, they shook their heads. It'll never work, they said. The children will be too split, they'll be caught between you. It's a terrible idea. They need to be in one house and they need to be with you. These friends would look at me, their eyes smoky with fear. Because if I gave in, someday they might have to as well.

In the pit of my stomach, I understood their fear. The days without my children were still painful, hard to enjoy because of the guilt layered beneath the quiet. The trade-offs with Ron were tense and we were liable to flare into arguments because we were both still too raw to speak to each other easily. Inevitably, however, we each had information we needed to share with the other, a reminder about a field trip form, or a question about a missing sweatshirt, and then the exchange would start. The divorce books warned against sharing custody with an angry spouse, and I could see what they meant.

Yet occasionally one of us would crack through the armor of defensiveness each of us wore when we were together, and we would ask how the other was doing; then out would spill the anguish of missing the boys. The only thing that made me feel human about agreeing to the trial of joint custody was the genuine sadness Ron conveyed about his days alone. No one understood that better than I did. Ron was still the only person on earth who felt the same way I did about David and Jesse, and despite our differences I could feel that bond still holding there beneath it all. An anchor. I didn't realize yet how precious that would turn out to be.

Because most days it felt as if I had lost everything. Now that I was footing the rent and paying half of Jesse's high-priced child care by myself, I had little money left for anything more than groceries or clothes. I hadn't worried about money for years and now I was borrowing from my parents and worrying about debts backing up on my credit card. I was driving a ten-year-old car with bald tires and bad brakes. All our nice things I had left behind at Ron's until we had time to sort them out—china, silver, paintings, electronics. I slept on an old mattress in a borrowed bed, begged a secondhand television from my parents, and picked up kitchenware at garage sales. I didn't have a computer, didn't have a video camera, didn't have a microwave. In the evenings I would lug my laundry down the hall to the washer and dryer, and hope I had enough quarters. It was like being in college again—except that I was trying to raise children and work a full-time job. And I was nearly forty. I was supposed to be doing better by now.

I had grown up in a family that believed in a process of self-improvement, and had always felt that, in spite of my problems, things had been on an upward trajectory. My jobs got better, my income increased, I accumulated wealth, and I worked to make myself a better person. Leaving Ron had been part of this process, an effort to correct deeply troubling aspects of my life. But now it felt as if the divorce, instead, had sent me tumbling down the slope. I was starting all over again. I was poor, alone, with few resources and less chutzpah. Just when things were supposed to feel better, I was facing how much I had lost.

And it wasn't just household goods or property. I was beginning to understand that I had stepped outside society the day I left my marriage. I wasn't like everyone else anymore—I was different, an unsettling example of where an unhappy marriage could end. People who didn't know me very well—neighbors, school friends, colleagues—didn't have a clue as to what to say, because they didn't know if the divorce was a catastrophe or a liberation.

Sometimes I didn't know either.

Most days I struggled through the daylight hours as best I could, teaching my classes, caring for the boys, handling the round of errands while they were at their dad's. But later, when I summoned the courage to turn off the television and go to bed, I would find myself tortured by worry, a parade of problems that marched around my room in the darkness. I thought of them as the Four Horses of the Divorce Apocalypse: Money Problems, Bad Communication with Ex-Spouse, The Fearful Future, and Missing the Boys. In the pitch black it all looked bad, and I was responsible. I had started it. I had broken every promise—my vows to Ron, the unspoken but steely pledge I had made to my parents to make them proud by being a good person and a supportive mother and spouse. And then there was the promise I had made my children just by bringing them into the world—that I would protect them and do everything I could to make them happy and give them a world that was whole and strong. I had failed them all. And now I was alone.

16

THE BALCONY SCENE

Then, one night, there was a moment I think of now as the balcony scene. A romance, of sorts. As all balcony scenes are.

It had been an unusually contentious day at work. I felt trapped in a project with a colleague who was growing increasingly abusive in his treatment of me and I was angry with myself for having let it happen. I was supposed to be stronger than that now. I came home numb, fed the boys, watched a bit of television with them, then bathed them and put them down early. I felt I needed them out of the way, but I didn't know why.

After they were settled, however, I had no idea what to do with myself. The thoughts in my head circled relentlessly: There isn't enough money, this place is both too small and too expensive, the boys are unhappy and that is my fault, I cannot solve the problems with Ron, I cannot prevent myself from getting into bad relationships at work, I do not have the strength to do this. And then the worst thought: It will never be better than this. It will always be like this: struggling with Ron, worried about money, pushed around by jerks. I paced around the apartment, fiddled with things on my desk, riffled through papers, but I couldn't find a way to calm down. Finally I took a shower and got into bed, but I couldn't sleep. I lay there for hours, agitated, more than awake, staring at the ceiling with a mixture of despair and panic.

Go look at the kids, I thought. Maybe that will help. I rarely checked on them after they were asleep, mostly because they never needed it, but I went in and straightened their covers. They were out cold, little boy bundles of twisted jammies and tousled hair I could move about without waking. I looked at them but, oddly, didn't feel the usual surge of parental joy. I didn't lean over and kiss them because I didn't feel anything in particular. I walked out and shut their door. They didn't need me.

And then I went out into the living room and sat on the sofa and, for some reason, began to think about the balcony. I had never before thought about the balcony in that apartment other than as a hazard to the boys, and kept it secured with a padlock and a bar. I didn't want anyone wandering out there in their sleep or when I was in the shower. Tonight, however, the balcony seemed to have a different quality. It didn't feel like a hazard but, instead, like an opportunity, like a step. A step up and out, up and away to someplace. I stared at the balcony for a long time, and then I got up and unlocked the chain and moved the bar. I opened the door.

It was cold, early December, and I was barefoot and wearing only an old flannel nightgown. I stepped out onto the balcony, noting the cold cement beneath my feet but not particularly bothered by it. There was a pine tree a few feet away that presented a bit of a problem. I would probably hit it as I went down. I peered over the edge. There was soft sod at the base of the pine tree. Jesus, maybe I wouldn't even die. Maybe I would get seriously injured but still have to deal with all this stuff. Shit. I began to wonder about more failsafe methods. Knives? No, don't want the kids to find that. Pills? I doubted I had anything strong enough. The good thing about the balcony was that the kids wouldn't find me. The gardener would, or an early-morning jogger, a grown-up.

Then an odd voice inside me said, The hell with the kids. Don't think of the kids.

And that was all it took. All of a sudden I felt the cold under my feet, saw myself out on this balcony in the wind, my nightgown ghostly in the dark, thinking about—good Lord, what? I backed away from the rail and crept around the door, sliding it shut behind me. I padlocked the chain, put the bar back, then went into my bedroom and locked the door, as if locking it from the inside might make it harder for me to get out. I lay in bed a long time that night shivering, knowing now for sure that things were unbearable, that I had to make things better somehow, some way. I had already done the hardest things, so why did a balcony beckon like that now? I finally got up and wrote down the five worst problems—relations with Ron, money, the kids' unhappiness, the project at work, my dissatisfaction with my lawyer. I folded the paper into a ball and held it in my hand and finally said a prayer, offering the problems up to the universe because I just couldn't hold them anymore. Then I willed myself to sleep.

The next morning Jesse padded to my door and shook it, trying to get in, surprised to find it locked. I rolled out of bed, unlocked the door, then scooped him up and snuggled him in under my covers.

"Why couldn't I get in?"

"The door was locked. I must have locked it by accident."

"Maybe you were scared," he said, looking at me closely.

Out of the mouths of babes. "Maybe," I said. I didn't think he needed to know that Mommy was scared, though it was true.

"Did you have a dream about monsters?" he asked. Then his brow furrowed. "Sometimes I dream about monsters."

"I didn't have a dream about monsters, but sometimes I worry about things," I admitted. We lay quietly for a minute, contemplating our individual demons. His body pushed closer against mine.

"But you know what?" I said.

He turned his face toward me, hearing the upturn in my voice. "All I have to do is think of you and I feel brave. You make me brave because you are brave. And then the monsters go away. They only like people they can scare. If they can't scare you, they go away and try to find someone else."

The next evening I called my cousin Jean. I needed to tell someone, go public with this in some way. I sensed that Jeannie had been down this road herself, would understand it.

We talked a bit about this and that, her book, her cat. I finally steered the conversation around to myself, then eased in to the topic. We were talking about how I was managing and then, pushing myself even though this felt more difficult than I had imagined, I said: "I've had moments of thinking it might be easier if I just died. Easier for everybody."

She sucked in a breath. "Have you had any of these moments recently?" she asked. Then, razor sharp, "Do I need to come for a visit?"

"Oh, God, I don't know. It was just so strange. Last night I went out and stood on my balcony for a long time in the cold, but then I sort of woke up and came back in. I wasn't afraid at the time, but later it scared the daylights out of me."

She was quiet for a long moment. "That's probably a good sign," she finally said. "You know what? I don't think you have it in you. I don't think you're going to jump off the balcony."

For some reason, that offended me, as if my problems weren't dark enough to be worthy of serious depression or thoughts of suicide. "What do you mean?"

"You love your children too much. And you don't really think about death that much."

"You don't know that," I mumbled.

"Sure I do," she said. "You probably think about it occasionally, like most people, but you don't dream about it or obsess about it like true suicides do. You're not in love with the idea of dying."

I went silent because I knew she was right. I was too weak to ever commit suicide, I thought to myself. I was too weak to be able to fix anything in my life. Too cowardly.

"Besides," she said, more gently this time, "you're too good a mother."

I coughed. "I don't know about that."

"Oh, please. Would you stop this and just think about those boys for a minute? Would you ever agree to give Ron full custody?"

"No," I said quickly. "Of course not."

"See? You'll never leave them. Not you. They need you

too much, and you know that. Now will you please stop this and move on?"

"Oh, Jeannie," I said, starting to cry. "I don't know how to move on. It's all too hard, everything is a mess. I can't do it, I can't begin to untangle it all. I don't know where to start."

"Just start with the first thing. Just pick up one thing and fix that. This is a recovery process. You take little steps when you can't take big steps. The most important thing is to get up every morning and keep moving forward, even if you are just inching along."

"What if you can't even inch? What if you are sitting still?"

"That's okay too. Sometimes sitting still is as much as you can do."

"Okay."

"And get yourself some support," she said.

"Oh, I have lots of friends. I have you."

"No, I mean support from people with the same kinds of problems. People who are in the place you are, because no one else really understands it. Go find some group. There must be some in Washington."

"Okay."

"I love you. I'm coming east this spring. I'll be there in April, okay?"

"Good." But it wasn't good. April seemed years away, a stretch of time I couldn't imagine getting through. She could hear the disappointment in my voice.

"Look, you are going to survive this, because you are strong and you love your kids and because you must. If it gets really bad, I'll come sooner, I promise. All you have to do is call."

"Okay. I love you too. 'Bye," I whispered. When I set

down the phone I could feel that lonely whistling wind against my neck. I went and sat quietly in the boys' room, next to where they lay sleeping in their jumbled beds. Slowly I began to see something that I hadn't seen before, and that was the possibility that this divorce would warp me into somebody so different I wouldn't know myself. If I let it. I could see that there were a thousand directions open to me. I could become depressed, or I could become hard and bitter, or I could become even more obsessed with worries than I was already. I could become a bore to others, I could become a cross to my children, I could become weak and cringing. I could give up and step off a balcony. If I chose.

Or I could pull myself together and take care of my children. Because, where would they be without me? Motherless; now that was a hole for the heart. And there were a thousand ways I could leave them, even if I never jumped.

Their quiet breathing filled the little room, and I saw then that they were my anchors, the deep weight that would hold me fast against the winds whipping around me. They would keep me on course. They would keep me here. I could worry, and I could be scared, but I wasn't going to let myself feel that despair again because I wasn't about to abandon them.

I had just never anticipated that I'd find the worst monsters crouching there in my own heart.

17

GATHERING MY POWER

I'm sitting in a circle of strangers, in a stranger's living room, a plate with a few Christmas cookies and a slice of cheese balanced on my knee. Most of the people in the circle are older, in their fifties, but there are a handful of people my age. Most of them are women. Most of them look really sad but well groomed, as if this meeting was more about finding a date than sharing divorce stories.

There are two men in the room and both are bald.

I'm doing what Jeannie suggested—getting support. I'm at a meeting of a group called New Beginnings, a network of divorced men and women who meet to talk and socialize and generally help each other through the process.

Everyone introduces themselves by giving their name and a tidbit of their divorce story. Martha says she has been divorced for three years and is still finding the holidays difficult. Julie says she has been separated for eighteen months and is still fighting with her ex-husband over money. Stan says he's been divorced for seven years and thinks he may be ready for a serious commitment again. He smiles broadly at the group. He doesn't look nearly as unhappy as the women.

When it is my turn I say that I've been separated about three months and I feel like I'm doing okay. I smile bravely. Suddenly, everybody laughs. I look around, puzzled.

"That's really common in the first few months," the hostess says gently. "Lots of people think they are doing well in the beginning."

"It takes about a year to realize how bad off you really are," says another woman. "But that's when you get down to the serious work."

I don't say another word the rest of the evening. The talk circles around and finally everyone is focusing on a woman named Emily and her story. It turns out she has been trying to get her husband to respond to a settlement she first proposed four years ago. "He keeps saying he'll get the financial records together, but he just doesn't do it," she says, shaking her long, frizzy hair away from her face. "I'm just beginning to wonder if he is really serious."

Beginning to wonder? Before I can stop myself I stand up. I feel like I'm suffocating. The meeting isn't over yet but I make a show of checking my watch, mutter my regrets and thank-yous, and grab my coat. Losers, I think, as I hurry to my car. Anybody who would let a divorce drag on for four years has got to have screws loose. Some support group. Bald men and insufferable women. I'm not going to let that happen to me. Not me.

Right.

One of the painful truths of divorce is how pathetic we look as we march through the predictable steps. Divorce is depressing and boring, and the people in it seem to have little clue as to how hopeless and miserable they look from the outside. They talk incessantly about their problems, often sounding like they never move forward. They muck around in psychological ruins as if they can't let go, can't leave the past behind. They bore their friends and worry their families.

And the worst thing is we know we are doing it but don't seem able to stop.

A few days later I'm having supper with my friends Jon and Maggie, both lawyers, and talking—as usual—about my divorce. I'm trying to explain how I ended up agreeing to a trial of joint custody, and as the tale unfolds they begin to give each other meaningful glances, as if there's a subtext to this discussion I haven't figured out yet.

"What?" I finally say, when it gets really obvious. "What is it?"

"Your lawyer sounds, well, a little inept," says Maggie. "Do you like him?"

"I don't know. Not really. He doesn't seem to understand Ron very well."

"He also doesn't seem to understand custody law very well," Jon says. "Does he do lots of custody cases in the District?"

"I don't know. He seems to practice more in Virginia, though he has a D.C. office. Why? Would that matter?"

They glance at each other again. "Yes," says Maggie. "It can matter a lot."

So Jon explains it to me, how it matters if the judges know him and if he knows the judges. How my lawyer needs to understand someone like Ron, perhaps needs to be someone younger, someone who understands working professionals like us. How custody law is really tricky and how much the prejudices of individual judges can influence a decision. When I leave they give me a list of people to call, other divorce lawyers who practice in the District.

"Just call and talk to a few of them. Comparison-shop a bit. You have every right," says Jon. I hadn't thought of hiring a lawyer that way, but it's beginning to make sense.

"Then call the other guy and fire the son of a bitch," Maggie says. "You need someone to fight for you, if that's what you want. Nothing else is ever going to be as important as this."

There isn't a fiber in me that wants to fight, but my doubts about our joint custody arrangement gnaw at me night and day. I have agreed to extend the three months for another three months, mostly because my lawyer doesn't seem to have any other solution, and I feel deeply guilty about this decision.

The next week I go over to Ron's on a Sunday evening to pick up the boys and I find Ron pacing nervously on the sidewalk, the kids already packed up and seat-belted into the Volvo, ready to go. But something's amiss. Ron comes right up to me, his face working. "I'm sorry," he says, breathing hard. He starts to cry. "I just slapped Jesse."

"What?"

"I slapped Jesse on the face. He did something bad, but there's no excuse. I'm sorry. I'm so sorry."

I go to the car and open the door. Jesse looks up at me, ashen. There's a red mark on his cheek. He is very quiet. David is crying in the backseat.

I turn on Ron. "What happened?"

"He pushed a stone down the air vent of the car, even though I told him not to. It made me mad and I guess I lost it. I'm really sorry. I can't believe I did that."

Ron and I agreed early on as parents that we wouldn't spank our children, or use physical threats as discipline. There are times I've been tempted to swat a child who's seriously out of line, times I've even been told by grandparents and friends that spanking is appropriate. But I knew my children, and I knew their father, and I knew it wouldn't work for us. Now Ron has slapped Jesse, and it feels like a violation of some code Ron and I share. All of a sudden I realize we have a code, even if we haven't spoken of it before.

"We don't hit our children, Ron," I say, my voice rising. The fact that it's a blow to the face makes it seem more serious to me because I know it is more humiliating for the child. "We have an agreement about that."

"I know. It won't happen again. I promise." Ron leans inside the car, tells Jess he is sorry, but Jesse turns away.

I pull Ron out of the car door. "Don't make him forgive you right now," I say, my teeth clenched. I always hated that part, Ron's need to be forgiven when I was still mad as hell. "Wait until he is ready."

I close the car door, take the keys from Ron, and I can feel my power rising with my anger. "I'm going to have to speak to my lawyer about this. If you can't take care of them without hitting them, then I am going to have to reconsider my agreement about joint custody." I get in and drive away, leaving Ron standing silently on the sidewalk, his head down. He looks like he is crying.

The next day the red mark is gone from Jesse's face but I call several of the lawyers suggested by Jon and Maggie, then make an appointment to talk with the one I like best, a woman about my age, no-nonsense and tough on the phone, someone who works exclusively in the District and with the best divorce firm in the city. I'm not sure what I need to do, but if I need to fight Ron for custody I want some power in my corner.

I go down to her office and lay out the details of my case—how I ended up with a trial of joint custody, my concerns, my fears. Then I tell her about the slapping incident. She takes notes and listens intently, then chews on her pen for a moment. I tell her I'm concerned I may need to file for physical custody of the boys.

She stares out the window, thinking, then says: "If you

are going to fight for custody, I have to warn you that you need to be prepared to lose."

"Lose?" It has never really occurred to me that I could lose a court fight. I'm the mother, after all, and I don't slap my children. What could anyone say against me?

"Have you ever spanked them?" she asks, looking straight into my eyes.

"Well, yes, occasionally, when they were little and ran out in front of a bus or something. But I don't do it anymore." I don't like the way this is going. I shift in my seat uncomfortably.

"Look," she says. "You're the one who left the family home, you work full-time outside the house, and he makes more money than you. He hasn't abused the children or you. If forced to choose, many judges would say the kids would be better off with him."

"Slapping them is not abuse?"

"No. Slapping and spanking can be appropriate forms of discipline, at least in the eyes of the court. To show a pattern of abuse you need lots more evidence. Did you ever seek a restraining order against him? Did you ever go to the emergency room or doctor with injuries from him?"

"No, nothing like that. Ron would never have hit me." I can feel my power draining away. "But sometimes he yells."

"Everybody yells," she says dryly. "Here's what we would be dealing with: There are two judges hearing these cases in the District right now. One is an elderly black man who is more likely to lean in favor of the mother but is also not likely to see slapping as a problem, even if you could make that case. The other is Jewish, middle-aged. He's more likely to agree with you about the slapping incident, but he's also committed to gender neutrality. The fact that you're the mom isn't going to cut any ice with him. It's a crap shoot either way."

I sit silently, trying to fight down my rising panic. Better off without me? How could that be true? How could anyone see it that way?

"Do you have any idea what it takes to fight for custody?"

I shake my head. I can't speak for fear I'll cry.

"It takes thousands of dollars, often more than a hundred thousand. And to do it we would have to really go after your husband." She softens for a moment. "I'm not sure you want to do that. And even if we did that, we might not find anything particularly egregious. You could end up the visiting parent. I've seen it happen."

So it comes down to this, a horrifying cosmic gamble. I try to think of David and Jesse only visiting me on alternate weekends, not seeing them after school or helping with homework. Not packing their little lunches. Not playing ball with them in the backyard or taking walks with them in the evening. Not being there at night to read them stories and chase away the monsters. I look up at her. "I can't risk that," I croak. "I have to be in their lives."

"If I were you," she says, more gently now, "I would agree to joint custody and then do everything I could to help Ron be the best parent he can be. He wants to care for his kids. Is that such a bad thing?"

Over the next hour she charts a course. First she suggests we write his lawyer a letter detailing our concerns over the slapping incident and insisting that Ron agree to hire a counselor who could work with us on co-parenting skills and anger management. Then she says we should sign up for the free mediation service that is available to divorcing parents through the District courts and start working on a permanent agreement. Finally she looks at me with sympathy. "I know this is hard, but you will get through it. Your kids have two loving parents, and that's their greatest asset."

I staggered out onto the street, dazed by the sunlight and the harsh truths of this process. Justice, it turns out, is not what the courts are for—at least, not when it comes to divorce. Somewhere in my heart I imagined that someday a judge would stand up and say, Yes, she's right—she's the better parent, she's the patient one, the long-suffering one. She's the deserving one. She's the winner.

But now I saw that that would never happen, and perhaps that I wasn't more deserving than Ron, at least not in the eyes of society. I saw for the first time what was probably more true: that Ron and I were both flawed, both trying, both deserving, and both strong parents. The thought of becoming a visiting parent scared me to death— and I knew Ron had been facing that fear for months. No wonder he was fighting me.

It's a strange transition from everywoman to just your own unheroic self. The thought of spending the next fifteen years negotiating with Ron on everything from summer camp to doctors' bills made me feel worse off than ever. I was going to have to live with joint custody, and I was going to be a part-time mom. I knew agreeing to joint custody would worry my parents and trouble my friends, but I saw, through the haze of my sorrow, that my choices were limited. Once again, it was my sister Annie who lit the way. "Divorce is just like childbirth," she said. "You can't get through it unless you do it your own way. You and the boys and their dad are the only people who are going to have to live with the consequences of this. It doesn't matter what anyone else thinks. Do it the way you need to."

Now that I understood the legal landscape better, I could

see that my first lawyer, quick to console me but cowardly in the face of real difficulty, had not served me well. Some of his advice, in fact, had left me in a weakened legal position, particularly on the custody front, and some of his financial advice had been patently wrong. I shouldn't have moved out of the house, shouldn't have assumed I would get a particular level of child support. In fact, I shouldn't have assumed anything. It was more important, I could see now, that my lawyer protect my interests, even if that meant telling me things I didn't want to hear. It was a hard lesson, but I needed a lawyer who would act as a lawyer rather than a counselor, a pragmatist rather than a friend. I needed the truth.

I met my parents in Annapolis for lunch and asked if I could borrow the $5,000 retainer fee necessary so I could hire the new lawyer. I told them I wasn't going to fight for sole custody, but I was going to push to make sure Ron and I had a safety-net system in place so we could do a better job as co-parents. They didn't like it but they saw what I was facing and promised to do what they could to support both Ron and me as parents. They wrote me a check, then gave me hug. I hated that they were still bailing me out financially, but I swallowed my pride and tucked the check in my wallet. Just keep moving forward, I muttered to myself. Tiny steps if you can't take big ones.

It was difficult to give up the old dream of escape, difficult to give in and compromise, difficult to give my husband what he wanted when I got little more than my freedom—but it was the only way to broker a truce.

I called Ron that night and said I would agree to joint custody on a permanent basis if we hired a counselor to help us work out our differences. He agreed, then cried with relief.

18

FINDING MY FEET

Sleet. Just my luck. The boys and I have headed out to pick up a Christmas tree but frozen rain is bouncing off the hood of the car, so when we get to the hardware store I jump out and tell them to stay put. The cheapest trees are $5.99, which is all I can afford. I grab the nearest one bundled in plastic netting and start dragging it to the car.

"Don't you want to unwrap it, lady?" says the sales boy, eyeing me warily. "Don't you want to see if it's a good one?"

I stop for a moment and think about that. If I unwrap this tree, it's going to be harder to get it up the elevator and into the apartment. Besides, if I see what it really looks like I might break down and blow the rest of my money on a good one, like the ones they are selling for $10.99.

"No, I'm sure it's a fine little tree," I say, smiling at the boy with the scissors. "I'll just take it like this."

He accepts my money and shakes his head. "Well, if it's too ugly, you can bring it back."

The irony of this $5.99 Christmas tree is that finding the perfect tree was something of a Swallow family fetish. In my mother's house we marked celebrations with elaborate traditions, and the most famous one was that of the Christmas tree. Each year we went to considerable trouble to find the perfect tree, nosing endlessly through church parking lots or trekking out to tree farms. When we couldn't find the perfect tree, we sometimes wired together the perfect top from one tree and the perfect bottom from another. The year we moved into a contemporary house with a two-story-high living room we celebrated the first Christmas with a twenty-foot tree, decorating it from ladders. The neighbors were astonished, mostly by the effort it took to get it inside and set up. The next year, my father and I chopped down a tree we found in the far pasture of a tree farm near Gettysburg, only to discover that, while not as tall as the previous tree, it was so broad it nearly filled the living room. The ornaments disappeared into its dark green folds. It felt as if we had brought in a piece of the Black Forest.

But this first Christmas of my divorce, finding the perfect Christmas tree is the farthest thing from my mind. The holiday comes as a shock, comes before I am ready, before I have the strength to take on all that the season brings—dark afternoons, expectations encrusted with memories, the round of traditions that stretch before me like some sort of testing ground. Everything comes bundled with questions: Do I send cards to Ron's family? Do I go over to Ron's Christmas morning to watch the boys unwrap their presents or do I try to get invited home with someone else, like a lost cat? Do I admit to friends that I'm lonelier than I've ever felt, or do I swallow that down so they won't feel guilty if they can't include me in their plans? Money is tight, everyone else in the world is filled with purpose, and I stumble through activities, resenting tasks that every other Christmas I've done with pleasure.

When we get the tree home, it is indeed lopsided, with

large patches of awkward space between the branches. But the boys don't notice, so we decorate it with what we have, ornaments cut out of construction paper and glued with sparkles and feathers, and a single string of lights that blink in unison, as if the connection is bad. When the kids go off to their dad's for Christmas Eve, I sit alone before the tree unwrapping the basket of small present's my parents have sent me. They are sweet, simple gifts—candies, chocolates, pencils, small games—but I am struck by the overwhelming sense that my parents don't remember my tastes and preferences, don't seem to know me anymore. I'm the one who doesn't like licorice and balks at puzzles, yet there they are in my basket. I shake my head, angry with myself for feeling ungrateful. My parents know me well in countless other ways, and they would have been there with me if I had insisted. Still, the basket saddens me because I see for the first time that I don't belong to anyone anymore. By divorcing Ron, I have lost the only person in the world who knew those intimate and idiosyncratic things about me, my likes and dislikes, my favorite indulgences, my private concerns and pleasures. It isn't that I miss Ron, but I miss being at the center of a circle of family. I miss belonging to someone. I miss the boys more than I can even acknowledge. I sit staring at that pathetic tree, and the hugeness of what I have lost sweeps over me. And I have no idea how to get it back.

The first Christmas alone is always difficult. It comes up on you when you're still in that divorce fog, that disorienting place where emotions and worries swirl around in a ceaseless eddy. Holidays come laden with memories—some good, some bad—and they are difficult to escape. And then there are the children, and the effort to make the holiday as normal for them as possible. If we cannot make it normal, then maybe we can dazzle them, so we dash around trying to find the perfect presents and the best events to attend. And the children watch, befuddled, not knowing if they should admit to the mix of happiness and sadness that, inevitably, swirls about inside them as well.

That Christmas morning I went over to Ron's to watch the boys unwrap their presents. They still believed in Santa Claus, which can create all sorts of problems for divorced parents. We solved it that year by saying Santa would go to Daddy's. David was already troubled that Santa didn't visit the homes of our Jewish friends, so I didn't think he would buy the idea that Santa would visit both of his homes. Ron and I were still barely able to share the same space, but he offered me a cup of eggnog with brandy and we watched as Jesse ripped the wrapping from the train set that was his heart's desire and David labored to put together his Lego castle. It was so odd to be a visitor in that place—the living room of my marriage, with the Christmas tree decked out in the familiar ornaments, the children on the floor with their toys and the cats. I felt infinitely empty, but after I hugged the boys and said good-bye I also realized that part of the emptiness was the vacuum left by the evaporation of the pain and frustration that had so filled my heart in the years with Ron. Holidays had often been a time of tension and depression for Ron, and there were many years I packed away the Christmas ornaments wondering if we would still be together when the time came to unwrap them again twelve months later. Now, that pain was gone, and in its place was this astounding emptiness. Sometimes it ached, and sometimes it felt as if the wind was blowing right through me, but other times it made me feel as light as a bubble, able to float over anything. As I left Ron's house that morning, I danced down the steps. The awkward obligation was over, the children were happy, at least for today; I could go back to my safe little apartment and do anything I wanted. The world was mine to remake.

In January, at my lawyer's urging, Ron and I got down to the business of hiring a counselor to work with us—not to get us back together, but to teach us how to co-parent. We sent each other notes for a few days, warily circling one another, then finally picked up the phone and started working our way through the minefield of distrust left behind by the custody battle. We bickered for a bit about what type of psychologist it should be, and I began to despair again. The real experts on children of divorce all seemed to be forensic psychologists, the type brought in to testify in custody cases, but both Ron and I instinctively shrank back when we heard those words. It was as if we were being pulled into something we didn't want, but it was hard to say exactly what we feared. Ron, in particular, seemed skittish, nervous about where this could lead, and he vetoed one suggestion after another. Finally I saw what was holding us up.

"Maybe what we should do is agree that we won't call this person to ever testify against the other parent," I said. "Would that make you feel more comfortable?"

Ron was quiet for a minute, then said, "Yes," slowly, thinking it over. "Yes. Would you be willing to put that in writing?"

"I think so. Let's talk to our lawyers. Maybe we should look for a counselor more experienced with family systems than divorce. Maybe we are asking the wrong questions."

"Okay," he said. "Let's both come up with a few more names. I'll get back to you."

Some of my friends thought I was crazy to make this

deal with Ron, but my lawyer supported it. I knew it was risky, because it could cut off my access to valuable information if I ever felt I needed to fight for full custody, but it was also the first toehold up and out of the pit. I wasn't going to be able to co-parent with Ron if our relationship was riddled with distrust, that much was clear. And I needed to find a way to co-parent with him. As much as I didn't want to, my children needed me to work with their father closely over the next twenty years. I put my head down, said a quick prayer, and signed the document.

I'm too modern a woman to believe in a simple God, but I've learned an interesting lesson through this divorce: Since we cannot know the future, we might as well take advantage of the comfort that comes when we begin to trust the world again. I thought of it then as believing that there was some intrinsic safety in the world, as if the universe had an invisible net that would support me if I fell. It was about being able to put down the immense responsibility I carried all the time, the feeling that if I was not ever-vigilant, ever-awake, my children would die or disappear—that I was the only thing that stood between them and the abyss.

Once they went to live with their dad, I couldn't sustain that vigilance anymore. I had to start trusting that their father would watch them as I did, comfort them as I did, be there for them. He might need help with it, but I needed to allow him to be their father. My sister Anne, who had struggled so much with her ex-spouse, finally said one night after a tearful exchange: "Wendy, you cannot save your children from their other parent. You can do what you can to help him parent well, but you can't, ultimately, rescue them."

I also began believing that I would reap what I sowed. All through my marriage I had expected the worst from Ron, and I had often gotten just that. Now I decided to consciously expect the best from him, and to make those expectations clear. If he was late to pick up the kids, I assumed there was a problem rather than an attempt to ruin my evening, and, invariably, that was the case. If we missed our cues or had a misunderstanding, I would say it was my fault rather than blame him. I ignored small problems, and calmly addressed the bigger ones. To my surprise, I started to get the same treatment back from Ron. We started acting with a civility that sometimes astounded us, but seemed to make sense, as if it was a floor we could depend on to be there in our relationship. I started seeing him as an equal partner, and instead of hoarding information, I started sharing everything I heard from the boys' teachers and doctors. I started offering help when Ron seemed sick or overwhelmed, and those offers started flowing back to me, as well. Gradually, the tension between us began to ease.

Working with a recommendation from Ron's psychiatrist, we sat down one afternoon with the wonderful psychologist we would come to know as Dr. Mary. We asked her to be an advocate for the boys and to tell us when we were forgetting that they came first.

She nodded, then said: "For all you have been through, and the conflicts you still have with each other, I'm impressed that when it's a question of the kids' welfare, you drop it all and start working together. That's great. That's where we need to start, and you already have that foundation."

She outlined a road map: First, she wanted to talk with the boys and then confer with their teachers, so we could see how they were doing. Then she wanted to talk with us individually, to find out what was working and what wasn't, and then review the schedule of custody time. She warned us that she would have specific things for each of us to work on. We might have the right foundation, but clearly there was a lot we could do better.

While Dr. Mary started assessing the boys, Ron and I met one wet spring morning down at the big central courthouse in the District to sign up for mediation service so that we could start to unravel the tangle of pensions, debts, and assets, and come up with a settlement that would work for both of us. After our previous experience with a mediator, I was worried that mediation wouldn't work for us, that Ron would use the process to strip me of my fair share, as many of the divorce guides cautioned, or that I would feel pressured to give away too much just to move the process forward. But my lawyer assured me that it was nonbinding, and that she would review any settlement. We were assigned to a pair of mediators, a gentle-souled retired lawyer and a social worker. The lawyer was a soft-spoken man, keenly intelligent. The social worker, a woman about Ron's age, was savvy and experienced with mediation, tough but kindly. In the first session they set ground rules for discussions and suggested that our differing needs could be opportunities for compromise. With two mediators in the room, the power issues felt less threatening, and I left the courthouse that day feeling better than I had in months. Maybe we could do this. There was still a very long road before us—months of haggling over furniture and savings accounts and child support and vacation schedules, but it could be done. I could see that path, now, and once I could see it I could start to believe in it.

But when Dr. Mary called us in to review her assessment of the boys, I went with trepidation. What if she told me they had irreparable holes in their hearts? They seemed to be settling into the routine of going back and forth between my apartment and Ron's house, but I still worried that the divorce had caused serious emotional problems. It was clear they didn't understand what had hit them. David, who dimly remembered the fights between us, was unhappy but accepting. Jesse seemed to have no memory of life before the divorce, but for him it still felt like an earthquake—unexpected and devastating.

But Dr. Mary said she thought they were doing okay. Jesse's day care teachers said he had brought his kicking and biting under control, with their help, and David was no longer chewing through his sleeves. They were doing fine academically, if that could be measured in children so young. David, in kindergarten, was already reading, and Jesse was clearly quick with his letters and numbers. She wasn't worried about their schooling, and she said it was obvious they were deeply attached to both of their parents. But she was concerned about the schedule we had established—particularly the number of transitions it required of the boys—and said we would review that over the next few months. For now, she wanted us to start talking with them more about their feelings.

"Boys in our culture often have a hard time learning how to identify feelings," she told us. "I see boys ten, twelve years old who can't even begin to name what they are feeling—whether it is anger or sadness or frustration. David and Jesse can start learning that now. Get some of the divorce books for kids and start reading them in the evening, and see if you can get them to talk more." She then looked at us closely. "You have to let them know it is okay to talk about this. They will take their cues from you."

I realized, as I drove home, that she had already unearthed something about me. Since that awful night the boys had sat in the backseat of the car and I'd told them what was happening, I had subtly discouraged discussing our feelings. I had hidden all my own sadness and anger because I didn't want them to worry, and I hadn't been very willing to probe into theirs. But it was there, because I could see it in their artwork and their fantasy worlds. They both drew pictures of monsters and battles, and David seemed fascinated by pictures of elaborate traps. He drew all kinds of complicated contraptions, which he would imagine he could use to catch the bad guys. Jesse drew pictures of superheroes and, often, powerful dinosaurs that stomped around crushing people with their huge feet. It was a primal language of strength and destruction.

Yet when we sat down to read *Mommy and Daddy Live in Separate Houses* as Dr. Mary had suggested, the boys squirmed and complained. When I asked them how they felt about the divorce, they would stare at me, blank. Finally, when prodded, David would admit he was sad. Jesse would say only that he was "confused."

So one night, instead of talking about our feelings, I told them a story about a dinosaur family trying to cope with living in two caves. Although there were only two kids in our family, I put three in the dinosaur family: an older dinosaur like David, dreamy and earnest; a middle dinosaur like Jesse, clever but worried; and then a youngest who could give voice to the hysteria I knew both boys felt but couldn't claim as their own.

Night after night, the dinosaurs had adventures and faced problems, and in each tale the older ones helped the little one handle his fears. They thought up solutions, went to Mom or Dad for help, shared their toys and pillows. One night, after months of dinosaur-family stories, David sat bolt upright in bed in the middle of another tale. "Wait a minute," he shouted. "She's talking about us!" Jesse, by now heavily invested in the process, whipped around. "No she's not! They are animals, dinosaurs." And he wouldn't let me stop. He couldn't have me rip away the fantasy that allowed him to listen.

19

O B S E S S I O N

Until I got divorced I had always thought obsessions—intense, irrational attachments—were something that happened to crazy people. People who were grasping at straws, people who couldn't keep any rational distance in love, people with addictive personalities. People with screws loose. People other than me.

But it turned out I was wrong. Obsessive behavior was something anyone could learn, as long as the conditions were right. In fact, it turned out I had learned the habit in the climate of my bad marriage, with all that obsessive thinking about the other person, all that worry and concern fermenting in the brain. I came out of my relationship with Ron seriously infected, but I didn't see or understand how obsessions were warping my life until I fell in love.

It happened in March, during that slush time when everything is damp and chill and everyone gets the flu. I got a whopper of a cold one weekend after staying up late drinking scotch with an old college friend, then hiking around in wet boots the entire next day. By the time she left to go back to Pittsburgh, I was running a fever and my throat was closing up. I skipped the next few days of work, one of the few times I've canceled classes, and stayed home nursing myself. I felt at the time that I was finally running down, letting go of the tension from the divorce only to discover how infinitely tired I was by it all.

The second day I missed work an old friend called, someone I had known for years. He had heard I was sick and wondered if I needed anything. I said no, but thanks, and hung up. It didn't occur to me that his call was unusual, or motivated by anything other than friendly concern. I didn't get it at all.

A few days later he called from Chicago, where he was covering a story. By then I was better and I started wondering what this was about, but again, the purpose of the call seemed work-related and we didn't talk about much else. I was pretty sure he was married and, in some fundamental way, it never occurred to me that someone could be attracted to me. It had been so long since I had felt young and pretty, so long since I had cared about what I looked like. For months after I left Ron I doubt I even checked the mirror before leaving for work. My clothes were shabby, my haircut cheap. I felt that I'd come out of my divorce old, worn, out of shape, and dragging two children with me. No one was going to look twice at me.

It didn't seem to me that people my age fell in love, or had romantic adventures, although I could see it happening to others around me. Perhaps it was because my romantic reference points were from so long ago, my early twenties, and now I was thirty-nine, almost twice that age. Could it be anything like it was back then? Wouldn't dating be much more complicated now? Or would it be so simple as to be uninteresting, like having lunch with a business partner? I couldn't imagine it.

And then he called and asked if I wanted to go see an exhibit at one of the museums over my spring break. He didn't have anything particular in mind, just thought it might be a nice thing to do. I said sure, and we set a time. I thought about that a bit, but then dismissed it. Probably just being nice, taking pity on a lonely single divorcée.

The afternoon of our museum visit blew in warm and gusty, one of those singular March days that melts the slush and brings out the crocuses. We met at my apartment and rode the subway downtown, talking about his unhappy marriage and impending divorce. He said he and his wife had decided to split up but couldn't agree on who should move out. I remembered that stage, remembered the awkwardness of that impasse—the separate bedrooms, the tension in the kitchen, the efforts to avoid the other. I told him I was sorry for him, that it was too bad his marriage was failing. But he didn't seem overly distraught. "We've been unhappy for years," he said. "It hasn't been a marriage in a long time."

We got to the museum and walked around for a bit, then he took my hand and held it as we walked through a few more galleries. I was surprised but comforted by having someone hold my hand, and thought perhaps that he was looking for support, for a bit of warmth. But by then I also knew something was afoot. After a while we sat down on a bench in the middle of a gallery hung with beautiful paintings, with high school children on spring break swarming about us. "May I kiss you?" he asked. I didn't say yes or no, just closed my eyes. I was incredibly impressed that he had asked my permission.

By the time I got home, in the late afternoon, it was clear something was growing between us. I had several women friends coming for dinner that night and asked if he wanted to join us but he said no, he had promised to get home in time to feed his dog as his wife wasn't going to be home until later. He kissed me again, said he would call, and disappeared. It didn't occur to me to worry about his wife. Nothing outside his kisses seemed relevant.

That evening my friends marveled at me. "You look wonderful, you look ten years younger," they said. "Has something happened?" I peered at myself in the mirror when I escaped for a moment to the bathroom. It was true. I looked like a new woman. I barely recognized the person in the mirror—she was happy, flushed with life, eyes glittering with laughter. Jesus. Just a couple of kisses and look at me.

I finally confessed to my friends and they began teasing me, taunting me with dating advice and medical warnings. "It's different now," they said. "This isn't the sixties anymore and you aren't eighteen." They suggested I go buy new underwear, stock up on brandy. I served dinner but could barely eat anything myself. The night tingled with possibilities and I soaked it up, suddenly aware of the drought inside me. It had been years since I had shared a romantic moment with any man. Now, it looked like such a thing might be just around the corner.

As it turned out, the kisses in the museum led, in time, to a sweet if short affair. Finding someone who could gently lead me through the maze of fears and anxieties that sprouted whenever we got close to the bedroom proved to be an astounding blessing. Physical memories are oddly durable, and I found the only way to quiet them was to lay down other—better—memories, to bury them under happier times. With his help, I crossed that chasm I had feared for so long. Just being held, touched, even the smallest kiss, was like a warm blue bolt of electricity. I learned a thousand new things about myself through him—that I was desirable and that I could desire, that I was still young, and strong, and beautiful. Powerful lessons.

I began to arrange my life so I could stumble across him, which was no easy feat, as my life seemed circumscribed by the small triangle between the university, my apartment, and the children's school. I called friends who knew him better than I did, or who knew his wife, and surreptitiously questioned them. I began to look for his work in the newspaper, in magazines where I knew he published. I read his book.

But despite my increasing devotion, as the weeks passed I began to see that the affair was just that—an affair, not a romance. He seemed to enjoy my mind and my body, but didn't seem the least bit interested in my heart and soul, the places where I really lived. I didn't know how else to describe it, this powerful sense that he really didn't want any part of my larger life. He barely tolerated news about my children, seemed to ignore almost any topic except those we shared by profession. He seemed even less motivated to move out of his home, and it slowly dawned on me that he didn't really mean to leave his wife, or at least not yet. Because of her, we kept the affair secret. "Oh," said the few friends I told, vicariously enjoying the idea of a secret affair, "that must be so delicious, all that sneaking around." But that wasn't how it felt—it actually felt ridiculous and offensive. I was a grown-up, and I had not struggled out of my marriage to turn around and live a lie. We couldn't go out except to a few restaurants near my apartment. We never saw a movie together, and I wasn't allowed to call him. So I would wait, impatiently, hoping that he might get away for an afternoon or an evening. I watched myself do this and worried about it. But by then, I almost couldn't help it.

I found myself thinking about him all the time, even though we were seeing each other less and less. When I was with the boys, I was distracted, listening for the phone or checking how I looked in case he appeared at the door. When the boys were with Ron, I stayed home instead of going out with friends as I had done before, hoping against hope that he would call or surprise me. He couldn't remember my child care schedule, and often called at the last minute to see if I was free on evenings I routinely had the children, dangling the possibility of seeing him before me like a tease and irritated that I wouldn't even try to find baby-sitters.

I began to sense that this was turning crazy, but the harder it was to work out any semblance of normalcy between us the more it left me desperate to be with him and feel his affection. The need in me was so great, the empty space where love and respect should reside so cavernous, I could only stand in awe before it. I had had no idea, until someone paid me a little attention, just what I had been missing. I occasionally had lucid days, days when I could step back and see him for what he was—a confused, not terribly attractive man who had serious problems with intimacy. And yet I would see this and at the same time feel my heart leap if the phone rang. My hunger to be loved was something I couldn't control, and the more he hung back from me, the more I obsessed about him. My life narrowed. I exercised diligently when he wasn't around, worried about my wardrobe, got my nails done. I'd never had my nails done in my life.

And then my cousin Jean came to visit and it all began to fall apart.

. . .

I picked Jeannie up at Dulles on a bright May day, and she jumped in the car all trim and stylish in a gray pantsuit with pearls at her neck. It was impossible to look at her and guess that she was here for the Gay Pride march, and in fact she had had a wonderful conversation with some hapless chauvinist on the plane who was shocked to discover at the end that she was a lesbian and politically radical to boot. She loved doing that, upsetting people's apple carts. She laughed softly at the memory of the guy sputtering at her and trying to move to another seat. "As if I had cooties," she howled. "He really tried to move. Can you imagine?"

What I can imagine is that it must hurt to have another human try to move away from you just because you've revealed something intimate about yourself, but I don't say that. I almost never say those things to Jeannie because I'm not supposed to see that. I'm supposed to believe the bravado with which she shrugs off such slights. So I don't say anything.

"So tell me about this guy you are seeing," she says. "Do I get to meet him?"

"Maybe. It's a little hard to tell. His schedule is pretty crazy."

Her eyes narrow. "So what is he like? Is he treating you well?"

Treating me well. An interesting question. When we are together, yes, within the slim channel of our relationship. Yes. He holds doors, is polite, buys me little presents. "Oh, yes, he treats me well." I look back at the road. Jean has laser vision and I don't want her seeing through this.

But see through it she does, even though we spend most of her visit doing other things—marching in the Gay Pride parade together, going to movies, playing with my kids, speaking with my students at the university. What she sees is that I never seem to stop talking about him, yet he doesn't appear to be in my life. I invite him over for coffee Sunday morning to meet her, but he calls from a hardware store at the last minute and says he can't come after all, his wife is expecting him back. It would look too suspicious.

Jean looks at me as I try to explain this. I stumble, because there is really no explaining it.

"Sit down, sweetie," she says, firmly but not without affection. I sit down like an obedient child. She takes my hands. "This relationship has to stop. This isn't you. This isn't what you want."

I sit there pretending I'm listening, but I'm actually thinking like an addict. I smile and nod, but I'm really looking for the first opportunity to bolt.

"Okay. You're right," I say brightly. Maybe she'll stop now.

"No, you can't just say okay and I'm right. Listen to me. This is crazy. This seems good now but this is going to make you very unhappy. This is not healthy. He is not the man you need."

"Jean, I know you're saying this to help me, but you don't really know what I want in a guy. You don't even like guys. Why do you think you know what's right for me?"

She looked at me with great patience. "Wendy, I know this isn't right for you because I can see it in your face. You know it isn't right. I'm not sure what you want or what would be right, but I can tell that this isn't it."

She had me, and as we talked more I could see the entire romantic fiction I had wrapped around my lover beginning to break apart before my eyes. He wouldn't be the man who would make my life whole. He wouldn't be the gentle stepdad I sometimes imagined for my kids. He wouldn't ever be the one to build my hearth around. It wasn't going to happen. Yet the dream was hard to give up.

"Maybe I can see him while I try to meet other guys," I said. "No one knows we're going out anyway. This way I could have some companionship and still move on."

"Wendy, you know that's nuts. You need to have a vacuum there or you won't carry yourself like someone who is, well, open to love."

"Open to love?"

"Open. Friendly, curious about other people, open-hearted, adventurous. You have to be hungry or those things won't show. Now, tell me what you want in a man."

"What I want?"

"Yes. What you want. Let's make a list."

"I haven't made a list like that since high school."

"Need I say more?" She looked at me, pen poised, waiting. "Come on. You have to be able to envision it or fate won't bring him to you."

I thought that was a bit crazy, but I started listing qualities anyway, and somewhere down the middle of the list I started shouting things in a frenzy of details. "He has to be kind, and have a graduate degree, and be pretty athletic, and he has to like kids. No, he has to have kids. Okay, and he has to have good taste, and it has to be like mine, and he has to be responsible with money, and maybe he should be financially secure, and he has to like his parents, and he has to play a musical instrument—"

"Slow down!" Jeannie laughed. "I thought you didn't have any idea what you were looking for." She finished scribbling the list. "Anything else?"

"He has to have a dog."

"You really want me to write that down?"

"Yes," I said, pacing back and forth in front of the table. "I think a dog would say a lot about him."

"You could always get him a dog, if you want to live with a dog."

"No. He has to want one himself, and have a life where he could have one, and if he already had one, that would prove it." I stopped, breathless.

"Okay." She wrote down "dog." "Now how many of these qualities does your boyfriend have?"

I looked over at the list. "Maybe half." I didn't want to look at it too closely.

"Maybe," she said. "I think that's generous."

"Okay, I get your point. I'll break up with him. Soon. I promise."

As I dropped her at the airport the next morning, I swore again. "Really. I'm going to do it this week. I promise."

"You better, because I'm going to call, and I can always tell when you're fibbing."

That evening I sat for a long time looking at the list Jeannie had written, thinking about what I wanted and why it seemed so difficult to get. I thought about the idea of the vacuum, about appearing open in the world. It sounded easy, but that had always been difficult for me, because it had often proved dangerous in the past. But I wasn't four-teen anymore. I wasn't even twenty-five. Half my life was probably over. I didn't have lots of time to waste. I still looked fairly young, but that wasn't going to last forever. If I wanted to have a real relationship—one that might grow into something permanent—I needed to move on. I called my boyfriend at home, despite the ban. "I told you not to call me here," he hissed. "Why did you call?"

"I just wanted to tell you I can't see you anymore. It's over."

"Wait . . . ," he started to say, but I could tell his wife was there in the room with him. "Can we talk about this tomorrow?"

"Maybe," I said, as cold as a knife, because if I let myself thaw I would break down and start to cry. "I might not want to see you at all. 'Bye." And I hung up.

I went and drew a hot bath, then poured in a handful of bath salts. I undressed and sat down in the tub, sinking low so the water came up around my ears. A sadness seemed to settle on my chest, and I began to cry quietly. I knew it was best, but I was still hungry for love, hungry to belong to someone again, hungry to close the circle again and stand as a couple in the world. Eventually the tears ran out, but I didn't feel better. I felt as if I had given up my ticket to life itself.

There is a riptide in divorce, an undercurrent of longing to return to the world of the familiar and the safe by quickly becoming part of a couple again. It is an internal current, fed by the shock of loneliness that comes with the freedom, and it is an external pressure, a push from the larger world to tie up loose ends, fit back into the societal roles. It is difficult to love again without feeling drawn to the familiar steps—commitment, housekeeping, merging lives—because we know so little else. As the days passed that summer, and I put the affair behind me, I began to see that dating and love was hazardous territory for me. I felt unequipped for the world of men—burned by my marriage, hurt by the affair, distrustful of my own impulses and desires. I had little idea how to handle myself, or what my limits or goals should be. I could tell Jeannie what kind of man I would like, but I had no idea how to meet someone, or learn about him gradually, or how to manage the world of dates and singles bars. It was frightening just to carry myself as a single person, to feel men looking at me. So I shut the system down—I stopped thinking of love or men. I had lots to learn about myself before I could love again, and while I didn't want to do it, I saw that I needed to be alone to learn those things.

One night I was sitting with the circle of women from my Quaker meeting, sharing supper and our news, when I found myself saying that I was spending my time "obsessively trying not to obsess anymore." Because the obsession wasn't just about the man I had loved. It was a mental habit learned in the co-dependent blur of my marriage, a fixation with the other that I had first turned on Ron, then on my children, and finally on my lover. And when I recognized it for what it was, I saw that I was obsessing about nearly everything—money, my future, my work, my entire world. I wanted everything to be better now, but it wasn't better, and it couldn't be yet, no matter how hard I tried. And the effort was exhausting me.

Garrison Keillor has a saying that "in time, everything becomes appropriate," and I finally learned that I had to let go and allow time to do its gentle work. That I couldn't solve all the big problems right away. That my divorce was going to move forward slowly, that my future would unfold gradually, and that, in the end, all I could do was trust that I would be part of the world again. Until then, I could work to be happy when the day dawned and when I fell asleep at night, and for as many of the minutes in between as possible. As long as I didn't obsess about it.

20

IDENTITY CRISIS

My parents are visiting and my mother is eyeing the knee-high grass in the backyard of my new home, a rented house in suburban Maryland where the real estate is cheaper and the boys have room to run around. I have recently given up the expensive luxury apartment in Washington, but with mixed feelings. Yes, it was cramped and overpriced, but there was underground parking and someone else to take care of things like the landscaping. Now we have more space, a nice family next door, a yard big enough for baseball—and lots of grass, but it needs to be mowed.

"I hate to say this, honey, but houses are sometimes *condemned* for having grass that high," my mother says. "Do you plan to cut it, ever?"

Along with my concern for my children, the biggest barrier to getting divorced was the idea that I would have to do lots of things men were put on the planet to do, like haul the window air conditioners up from the basement every spring and struggle to get them into the windows without damaging a back or dropping the units. Or putting up the Christmas tree, a two-man task that, by its very nature, defies single-handed management. Or mowing the lawn.

I am not a big person, and I'm not particularly strong, and God did not see fit to give me a whole lot of mechanical horse sense. Living in a house—with a garage and a furnace and a dryer and a computer—requires a certain handiness that defies me. I spent a good year before my separation worrying incessantly about the air-conditioner problem, and then a friend suggested that maybe I could pay someone to carry them up and down for me, or rent a place with central air.

But the life-without-a-man problem persisted, and finally I had to learn to mow the lawn. My father helped me buy a secondhand electric mower and I laboriously pushed it up and down the lawn every Sunday, feeling ridiculous as I flipped the long cord out of the way. It just wasn't me.

But there were a lot of things that weren't me, and I was doing then nonetheless. In an effort to cut my rent and gain some space for the boys, I had moved to a more marginal neighborhood, one with working-class families of various national origins. There was more crime and little community feel. When a thirteen-year-old boy was murdered one afternoon at the local park—a place the boys and I visited frequently—a policeman stopped by asking questions about the neighborhood. When I told him I had recently moved in and knew only the family next door, he shook his head. "Nobody on this street knows anyone else," he said. "That's part of the problem." The house felt like what it was, a temporary residence. I was now a statistic—a woman who would probably move several times during the course of a few years, a woman who could barely afford housing in the Washington metropolitan area, a woman with no community to support her. Unhooked from the safety of marriage, I was floating away from all that was familiar.

There were countless new roles I now had to inhabit. When my family gathered for our five-year reunion, I was the one who slept on a couch in the hall when there weren't enough rooms for everyone. My married siblings got bedrooms and privacy. It wasn't that this didn't make sense, but along with my single status came a distinct loss of place, a demotion, a shifting of my role in the family. Now I was the maiden aunt, the one both more dependent on my parents and, at the same time, more responsible for them. It was easier for me to rearrange my life to go visit if one was sick, because I didn't have another adult to accommodate and I had days without my children. I no longer had a buffer between me and those old ties, someone to huddle with at night during a visit to the homestead, someone to help me reaffirm my adult identity. It became easier to slip back into being the child.

And everyone worried about me. Even though I soon gained tenure at the university, my parents worried about my financial future. They hired a locksmith to install special bolts on my doors, and counseled me not to drive around late at night, even though I'd spent years as a reporter interviewing strangers and often traveling around the city in the evenings. My siblings, lovingly, worried that I was lonely. Friends felt responsible for checking on me, and often asked me to join family gatherings or evenings out with other couples. I was moved by their concern, and deeply appreciated their efforts, but at the same time it also made me feel vaguely unsafe in the world. I had never been a charity case before—I had always been the one who took in the charity cases. Everyone hoped I would remarry.

But it was the role of childless mother that pinched the worst. Ron and I had switched to a custody schedule of splitting the weeks between us rather than alternating weeks, so the boys didn't have to go more than a few days without seeing their other parent. It worked well for us, but it meant there were some days—such as Sundays—when I never had the kids, and I sometimes found myself childless in places where I should have had them with me. Children at church who knew me as a mom were puzzled when I showed up without my boys, and their parents would stumble as they tried to explain. It was a measure of how far beyond the pale I had traveled that people hesitated to explain me to their children.

It turns out that intact couples seldom talk to their children about divorce. They would rather their kids didn't even know such a demon existed. I can understand their hesitancy—kids don't need to know the world is a scary place. But it makes divorce too much like death, too much of a taboo, too frightening to be discussed openly. And that taboo carries with it the implicit fear that—like death—it *could* happen. The taboo also boomerangs against children who go through a divorce, children who feel the adults around them whisper with concern, as if there is something too dark, too awful to be shared. As Jesse said to me once, living in two houses and having a mother who dated made him "weird." And he didn't want to be weird. He wanted to be like everyone else. He wanted parents he didn't need to think about.

In time there were other new roles, that of girlfriend, and that of potential stepmom. I learned, in time, how to shift quickly, dropping off my own children at their dad's only to go to my boyfriend's house to play a game of fish with his kids. Sometimes I mommied, sometimes I was the youthful single girl, sometimes I was the spinster sister helping my elderly parents, sometimes I was abandoned by everyone.

Nobody needs me. I'm lying in bed on a Sunday morning, watching the sun move across the wall, and I realize I don't know what to do with this new day because nobody needs me.

Most days this isn't a problem. When I have the kids with me, the day unfolds in its familiar pattern of need following need. First they need to be cuddled, then dressed, then fed. In between their needs I slip in a few of my own, get a kiss, toast a bagel. When I was married, during the worst years when the babies were young and the marriage had ceased to restore me, I often felt like a service station with cars lined up outside. Feed this one, bathe that one, talk with the other, fix dinner, fold the laundry. All I wanted on some days was a few minutes to lie in bed, with no one talking to me or needing to touch me. No one calling to me, or asking where something was. Every contact felt like a demand.

Now there are no demands, and the silence in the house echoes around me.

Most of us lose great chunks of ourselves in adulthood. There is no other way to grow up, especially if you care about the people around you. Yet in countless ways divorce sends us back to an earlier time in our life. It is as if fate rolls back the clock, so that we get a chance to go back to an old starting point and begin again. But it is not a clean slate, because we are who we have become. We are the older, experienced, weathered self set back in time, like in a science fiction movie where the hero who time-travels to an earlier era seems to be a genius just because he knows what will happen next. Maybe that is the problem—we know too much.

We know that we will never become famous sculptors, because just enjoying it isn't enough. We know that having children in our lives means that projects often go unfinished, and commitments get shortchanged. We know that piano lessons cost money and Sunday school teaching takes time. We know about obligations, and we are leery of them.

What we don't seem to know is which part of the life we are living is really our own, which are the pieces that we would choose again now that we have the chance. As I lie in bed on this bright morning, unable to get up because I do not need to get up, I wonder for the first time in two decades who I am—just me, Wendy. Not me as mother, or me as teacher, or me as daughter or friend or even as ex-wife. Just Wendy.

If I were to write a personal ad, I have no idea what I would say about myself. DWF, likes children and good food. No, that would never do—I sound like Betty Crocker. Do I like to travel? I don't really know, or rather, again, I know too much. I know it is expensive, and often excruciatingly lonely if you are by yourself. I know it is too much trouble with children, especially young children. I know that it is exhausting and exhilarating and dangerous and that it will probably not happen again in the foreseeable future because I have no money. So I don't know if I like to travel. Make me an offer.

I think of my sister Anne, who set up her easel in her little house by the sea when she first divorced, painting late into the night when her son was with his dad. Do I need a hobby? Perhaps, but I already have several talents I neglect shamelessly—my piano, my writing, my garden. I would feel too guilty to waste money on paints and canvases, too silly pretending that painting filled that void inside me.

Do I like to bike ride? Yes, but it's more fun with a friend, and all my friends are busy with their families on weekends. Do I like to hike? Yes. Maybe I should join the local Sierra Club.

This problem isn't just about activities. When I married I merged my personal style, my self, my life's culture with Ron and his culture in ways I only now fully understand, now that I've ripped those tangled vines apart again. Perhaps because his life was so rich in intellectual interests, so much more worldly and interesting than mine, I adopted many aspects of that world as my own. I also put aside many of my own interests and desires in the face of his, in selecting everything from bedding to pets. We owned cats because Ron did not like dogs, and I only remember now how I spent years as a child dreaming about the dog I would have someday when I grew up, poring over the American Kennel Club handbook searching for the perfect companion.

Now that I'm on my own, I strain to recover that original self, and what often answers back is just the echoing emptiness. Who I was the last time I was single—in my early twenties—hardly serves as a point of reference. I'm not that girl, and yet I'm not sure who she would have grown up to be in other circumstances. It is almost as if I have no definition, no outline, now that there is no one pressing in on me. By our nature as parents and employees and friends we move from job to job, changing shape to meet the demands of the moment. And then we wake up one day and find that, without demands, we don't know who we are.

This challenge is not just about what to do with my spare time either. It's about redrawing the outline, this time in bolder ink. It is about moving into middle age with a clear sense of who I am—not by default this time or someone else's vision of me—but my own vision, my own compass. It is also about taking responsibility for who I am, about no longer hiding behind someone else or blaming another for my life's problems. Spouses make great deflectors, great scapegoats. Now, I'm on my own. By standing alone in the world I stand more honestly, more nakedly than ever before. It's my story now. I'm no longer a footnote in someone else's book.

But finding who I will be is not easy. It doesn't seem to work to ask myself what I want. It's not that I don't know what I want, because I do know—it just seems absurdly unrealistic. I want to be loved by a man who will cherish and protect my heart. I want to feel financially secure again. I want my children to grow up healthy and happy. It is easy to say. It feels hopelessly impossible.

Instead, I ask myself what I miss. Somehow, that question brings me closer to figuring out what to do with my day and how to define myself. I miss cooking for someone who will appreciate a nice meal rather than for those little people who only want to know if we can have hot dogs instead. I miss music in my life, both listening to music and making music. I miss not having sunshine in my dining room while I read the morning paper. I miss digging in the garden in the late afternoon.

So I take these smaller absences and draw a line around them to see them better. I may not have a man to cook for, but I will invite friends over and cook for them. I pull out my old music books and stumble through a sonata, telling myself it is feeling the piano keys under my fingers that matters, not how it sounds. I buy myself a couple of potted plants, and start some tomato seeds in a cup. I do all this in baby steps.

It feels so unnatural to be alone in middle age. I knew I would be alone during my youth, and I fully expect to be alone through much of old age. But these years, the years while I am raising my children, these I never thought would find me alone. Maybe that is why thinking about what I miss helps me fill in the picture. If I think about the other things I miss, I don't think about missing the boys as much.

I have lunch one day with an old friend from the paper, also recently divorced, and I'm surprised to find him sporting an earring and a beautiful new leather jacket. He looks ten years younger. He's enrolled in drawing classes, and gotten a new guitar, he says. At night, he sings his children to sleep. When I murmur my admiration, he tells me he's made a list of things he wants to do before he dies, and he's working his way down it. "Nothing like a divorce to help you get your priorities in order," he says.

So I go home and draw up a list, then start to try out my wings again. I buy clothes in a newer look, sign up for a class in contra dance, go to a poetry reading with a poem of my own gripped nervously in my lap. I don't read it, but at least I consider reading it. I'm not sure this is me, the girl in the mirror with the shorter skirt, going to poetry readings, but I'm not sure it isn't me. It's a rare opportunity to remake myself. I trust I will find the pieces that will stick.

21

THE ENVY WARS

I'm sitting in a crowded restaurant in Bethesda with six old friends, three married couples, and I've silenced our small circle with my latest dispatch from the divorce front. Somebody asked how I was doing and I told them. The time without the boys is still hard, I say, but I'm learning to cope. Today, for instance, I lounged in bed over coffee and the newspaper, then met a friend at a bookstore for lunch, then took a long walk in the woods.

The men shift in their seats uneasily.

"That sounds, um, wonderful," says one of the women. Then in a quick rush of guilt, she leans across the table toward me and whispers, "How do you get them to take joint custody?"

There is an envy war in Washington between married and divorced people, and it rumbles around me. It is what makes me a loose cannon, the character in the play who walks onstage and upsets the status quo. I present the alternative, postcards from the other side. And the happier I appear, the more dangerous I am.

Many of my women friends, in particular, envy my space. Especially among the couples who juggle two careers with kids and households, the peace and quiet of having three days a week without my children—days to spend guiltless extra hours at work or meeting with friends in cafes and restaurants—seems like paradise.

And it's not just window dressing. In some ways, my life has never been easier. I do only three loads of laundry a week. The weekly grocery shopping rarely tops $75. Ron, eager to prove his worth, handles half the kids' dentist and doctor visits, organizes their sports schedules, and buys their equipment. What with cooking, cleaning, and homework, he does more for his kids than most fathers I know.

I had expected that I would be threatening to married couples, but I thought I would be threatening to wives because of my potential as a husband-stealer. In fact, the contrary has proven true: I'm threatening to husbands, who see me as some kind of modern-day pied piper leading women away from their families with tales of freedom and solitude. One close friend met me for coffee one night at a local diner, the only moment she could spare from her harried schedule, and then shook her head with resignation when I asked how she was doing. "I love my husband, but sometimes I think we should get divorced just so I could get some time to myself!" Wherever I go, to my book club, church, school, those women trying to manage jobs and families and working spouses follow the details of my life with unmasked envy. It makes me wonder how much the trend toward divorce might have something to do with the pace of the lives we all live, the staggering mound of responsibilities so many of us shoulder. Divorce, with its loss and ripping away, often brings a new simplicity. Life becomes simple, not as a choice, but because there is no other way to cope. And yet, from the outside, it can look incredibly inviting.

. . .

And then there is dating. This is how I know so many of my friends secretly envy me. It isn't that they don't love their spouses, it's that I get to live in the land of romantic possibility. Never mind that dating in middle age bears little resemblance to the high school version. Never mind that all the good men are already married, and never mind that it is frightening to admit I'm not getting any younger.

They hang with pleasure on the smallest details of the most boring dates. If I go out of town to a conference, they say, "Oh, you might meet someone," as if I would want to date someone who lives in Seattle. They want me to find the most perfect man. The only trouble is, nobody knows any.

To me, what they have—someone who loves them even if they are a bit round in the tummy and going gray—is the real prize. Marriage remains, in my eyes, the golden circle, the anointed space. To most people the couple who lives across the street from me would not seem special. They go to work, they come home and take out their trash, they plant pansies in the spring along the walk in their front yard. But they are an endless wonder to me because they do most of these things together, and happily. They even call each other "honey," and there are no suspicious undertones.

People who are married fascinate me. I watch them like a Peeping Tom, vicariously feeling the press of the hand against the other's shoulder, pretending on the subway that I'm reading while I listen to conversations meant only for two. I wish I could watch them more openly, as a scientist studies baboons on the Serengeti, because I have a scientist's curiosity about what makes their marriages work. I want to see inside to find out what makes them tick.

I wasn't like this when I was married, mostly because I couldn't see what marriage looked like from the outside. But now I know. Marriage looks like an astonishing achievement. Marriage, especially one that endures, seems little short of a miracle.

And it is amazing to me who has accomplished this miracle: all kinds of people. Average people, ugly people, fat people, stringy-haired people. In the grocery I can spot the women who are married—they have twice as many things in their baskets as those of us who are single. And I watch them. Sometimes I am baffled, because the woman I am watching seems no better than me. She is not prettier or nicer to her kids. Sometimes she is not nice at all, and yet she has achieved this miracle.

Truth be told, life would be easier for my family if we all lived in one house and were happy together, even if it meant more laundry. There would be someone to lean on, someone to listen to the routine bits and pieces of my life, someone else who cares just as much about my children. The ache to close the circle back up, find another to complete the portrait, is powerful indeed.

One summer I was visiting my sister Anne and her second husband, a man of many talents and kindnesses, and they began a minor squabble, only half-joking about their tendency to mutter endearments through gritted teeth when they are angry with each other. To their surprise and my own, I suddenly burst into tears, beside myself with envy that they had someone to mutter endearments to, whichever way. "You don't know how lucky you are," I hiccuped at them through my own gritted teeth. "You have everything; you are married."

It's ironic that as I build a happier life for myself in divorce I would still look upon marriage as the Elysian Fields. I know better in my brain, but my heart has a life of its own and it still seems to believe in fairy tales. Perhaps that is because being happily married is the part I have not been able to achieve. I have a successful career, a satisfying job with many personal and intellectual challenges. I have wonderful kids, and a host of loyal and loving friends. I get invited to plays, I seldom go to movies alone. But that is not the point. The point is that I am happy going to movies alone, and still I long to be happily married.

Mostly it is hard to live with no one there as a permanent support, and the boys sense my vulnerability, no matter how often I try to prove that a woman doesn't necessarily need a man. Once, when I was driving home from the grocery store one day with the boys, I was suddenly overwhelmed with a stomach virus. I pulled over in the heavy traffic and leaned out the car door. David panicked. "Mom," he yelled, "who's going to take care of you if you are sick? You should have thought of that before you got divorced!"

I did think of it. I just didn't think it would be like this.

I try to tell them that we have many friends and relatives here in Washington who will take care of me, because it's critical that they believe I am fully balanced. Because how will they ever be free to lean on me if they feel my precariousness?

Being children, they are sensitive creatures, and they feel that I never really relax. With friends and family I'm careful to lean lightly, and only momentarily. Over time it builds a tremendous amount of strength, and that sometimes feels like a curse. I fear I will become rigid in my independence. I fear I will become too happy ever to be willing again to make the compromises essential to partnership. I fear I am an alien species who will never have the right genes.

22

IN THE SHADOW

OF DIVORCE

I'm hunched in a tiny chair in my son's kindergarten class on back-to-school night, looking around the room and smiling at the other parents. The children have been finger-painting today, and I imagine my little boy in this bright and cheery place, squishing the paint between his fingers and watching the paper fill up with his hand prints. Then I notice that Jesse's desk is the only one without a painting laid out to dry.

"Did Jess paint this afternoon?" I ask, innocently enough.

The teacher looks at me and goes pale.

"But," she stammers, "he went home sick. Didn't you come get him?"

We stare at each other for a moment.

Then it comes to me. It was Ron's day to have the boys, so the nurse must have called him, or gotten him at work before she could find me. If Ron didn't tell me, then Jesse wasn't that sick. No big deal.

Then I glance around and every parent in the room is looking at me in horror. What kind of mom am I if I don't know my child went home sick?

Divorce robs us of much, and one of the worst things it takes away is the benefit of the doubt society gives to intact families. Whenever divorce is mentioned in the media, it invariably is in the context of something bad—the kid who guns down his classmates, or the man who commits suicide after he loses a custody battle. You never see a story of the math prodigy who happens to live in two homes, or hear of kids who do better because of a divorce. Over time, these stories accumulate in the public imagination, and in mine as well. If my kids do badly in school, or misbehave, it's the divorce that gets blamed, and not just by society—I blame the divorce too. Every time I read about some serial killer who grew up in a broken home, my heart goes cold. I forget that the serial killer's mom was a high school drop-out, or that his dad was unable to hold down a job, or that his mom's boyfriend dealt drugs out of the garage. What I remember is that his parents were divorced.

The boys and I live in the shadow of these stories, in the shadow of the statistics of divorce.

Before I got divorced, my children lived in a world where nearly everything predicted their success. They had intelligent, caring parents who could afford excellent schools and a stable life. Now, by the simple act of leaving their father, I have cast my children into a world in which they are vulnerable and at risk. According to the experts, kids of divorce are more likely to drop out of school, have sex early, and develop addictions to drugs or other substances. On top of these statistics is the conventional wisdom about children of divorce, which says that girls shut down and boys act out. That girls will fail to build healthy relationships, and that boys will do badly in school. Then there is the shadow message, that kids of divorce are more prone to depression, lifelong emotional problems, even suicide. It's a harrowing picture and from the first moment I read these numbers, I've kept a weather eye on my children. The day I walked out of their father's house, the vigil began.

All parents are well wrapped with worry when it comes to their children, and most parents cannot help but feel that their children's success is a reflection on their parenting. And so we push, and we cajole, and we plot and plan and prod to make sure our children do as well as is humanly possible. For those of us who are divorced, this equation is even more heavily weighted, bound up by a million worries and well-larded with guilt. If our children do badly, it really is our fault. If they start sniffing the glue in their model-building sets, or inviting their boyfriends up to their bedrooms in the unattended afternoon hours, or if they run away or jump off the roof, it's blood on our hands. Because if we hadn't gotten divorced, maybe none of this would have happened.

Maybe. But maybe not. Maybe, when the social sciences finally find an accurate way to measure these variable forces, it will turn out that it isn't divorce per se, but individual aspects of divorce that do the damage. Maybe for some children it was the loss of their daddy; maybe for others it will be the shifts in schools and homes rather than the divorce itself. Maybe the success of children of divorce will turn more on sheer economics than the fact of the divorce, or on how well their parents healed in the aftermath. Maybe, it will turn out that some children are predisposed to depression or addiction or suicide or mayhem, and divorce was just one of many factors that tipped a child the wrong way.

One of the refrains we hear when we divorce is that "kids are resilient," as if they can be expected to be more resilient than adults. I heard this so often during the years after I separated that I started grinding my teeth every time it surfaced. I was told all sorts of things designed to make me feel better but which obscured some hard truths. I was told not to worry too much about the boys, that "children adjust to what they have to adjust to." I was told that if I was happy, they would be happy. I was told to go on with my life so that they could go on with theirs.

There were surely days I needed to let go of my ceaseless worrying about the boys and move ahead, but I think it can become too easy during divorce to throw up one's hands and think, Oh well, the damage is done, I can't help it. And then we make decisions that force even more changes on our children, or leap into new relationships with little concern for them, or ignore the bad report cards because it just feels like too much to handle.

When Ron and I began working with Dr. Mary, she quickly let us know that we should try to do everything we could to reduce the number of changes happening in the kids' lives. She never said they were resilient; instead, she lectured us on the cumulative effects of stress, and said we needed to reduce their stress wherever possible, because they were already shouldering a sizable load. We talked about the custody schedule, trying to reduce the number of changes in a month and maximizing the hours Ron and I could be home with the boys after school. We decided that one of us, if possible, would stay in the house in the District where Ron was living, on the premise that keeping that as a permanent fixture in the boys' life would help stabilize them. If we needed to switch schools, she counseled us to think it out well in advance, and make a change that could be permanent if possible, one that would allow them to stay with their new friends through grade school and high school.

When it came to parenting styles, Mary challenged us both to try to move toward the middle, so there would be more consistency between the two houses. Because they were young, she told us we would get better results if discipline was similar and if as many rules as possible held for both households. Ron agreed to try to be more patient and follow Mary's guidance for effective discipline. I agreed to be tougher about a range of issues, from television to vegetables. "It's not fair to make Ron be the bad cop all the time," Mary would admonish me. "Let them see that you can be just as tough, and let them know it's okay to go to their dad for comfort."

What this meant was that Ron and I had to talk, frequently. We had to compare notes, share problems, admit to blunders. It wasn't something we were very good at, and the thought of bringing him into my parenting problems on a daily basis was demoralizing at first.

But then an astonishing thing happened: It began to work.

The truth is, single-parenting is exhausting and it doesn't stop until the children either go to sleep or back to their other parent. On any given evening, I was jumping from one room to the other, helping David with his homework, then pulling Jesse out of the bath before it got so cold he climbed out himself. But harder than the work was the feeling that I was alone with these children, that paralyzing sense that I was the only one worrying about them and mulling over their problems. As Ron and I worked with Mary, we began to see that instead of being enemies, we were each other's greatest asset. We were allies in the campaign to raise these children as best we could. There was no one else who cared about these boys like we did—we were all they had.

One day about a year after our separation, Jesse ran away from me in a bookstore, slipping out of the front door without anyone noticing and hiding behind some bushes by a bank down at the end of the block. It was the kind of thing four-year-olds do, but at the time it scared me to death. The store was on a very busy thoroughfare, and it was Saturday morning. Metrobuses were flying past, cars and pedestrians jockeying for position at every intersection. The bookstore was crowded from an event, and I didn't realize Jesse was gone until a few minutes had passed. By the time I found him, nearly fifteen minutes had gone by, long enough for me to sink to a level of serious panic. I didn't know if he had been nabbed or run over, but by the time I had him seated on a bench, I was doling out some serious punishments. We marched home and put all his stuffed animals in the closet for a week, then returned the video he had just rented for the evening—a tough blow, as it had been his turn to pick. I also told him he would have to sit on the floor next to my feet while waiting for me in stores until he could learn to stay close.

Then I realized I needed to check with Ron, because some of these punishments were going to spill over into his jurisdiction. I didn't really want to tell him what had happened, because Ron had often berated me for not keeping a closer eye on the children in public places, but when I described it Ron had a different reaction. "Jesus," he said. "Jess did the same thing to me last week. What do we do?"

Before the divorce, Ron would have said the problem was my fault, was a result of my lack of care. But now that he was single-parenting, he knew how these things could happen. I told him about the stuffed animals and the video, and the new rule about stores. "Whew, you're tough," he said. "But okay, whatever you say. I'll do it."

When I hung up I looked down at Jesse, by now contrite and missing his animals.

"What did Daddy say?"

"Daddy was upset you ran away too, just like Mommy, and he agreed with me about all the punishments."

An odd little look passed over Jesse's face—something like relief.

"So things are the same at Daddy's?"

"Yep. The same."

"Okay," he said. It seemed to make sense to him.

He never ran away from either of us again.

A few months later another surprising thing happened. I was angry with the kids about some typical children's failure—toys left on the stairs, homework ignored, dawdling in the bathroom when they were supposed to be getting dressed—and had been trying to negotiate a new rule when Ron called. He could hear the frustration in my voice and asked what was wrong.

"Oh, I'm just tired of having the same fights with them. And I'm mad at myself, because I'm getting too angry over this." I still had trouble admitting my failures to him, but at the moment I was too overcome to hide what was happening.

"Well, what I do when I'm angry with them is put myself in time out."

"What?"

"I put myself in time out," he said. "It really surprises them and gets me to calm down. Then I can go back out and talk rationally."

It turned out that, with Mary's help, Ron had devised a series of tricks for managing his frustration and anger. One day when I was miffed about some other offense and raised my voice, David suddenly shouted: "Mommy, if you are going to yell, you have to get on your knees."

"Excuse me?"

"If you need to yell, you have to get on your knees."

I was so dumbfounded it stopped me in my tracks. David explained that Daddy had told them to say that to him when he started yelling. "When Daddy is on his knees, he isn't as big, and so he isn't as scary," David said. "Also, he usually starts laughing. He looks silly when he tries to yell on his knees."

I was astounded. At one of the low points in the divorce, after the night Ron slapped Jesse, I told Ron that he needed to learn to manage his anger once and for all or he was going to lose the boys, just as he had lost me. Apparently, he had heard that.

He tried other tricks. He installed an intercom system in his house so he could call the boys down from upstairs without sounding like he was yelling. He read books on anger management, talked with his psychiatrist about different antidepressants. He was trying to get better, and he was doing it without my help. He was doing it for the boys.

Now that I was living in the Maryland suburbs, we decided to switch the boys from their Washington public school into the highly rated Montgomery County schools, where they could get better services and better teachers. I researched the test scores and budget initiatives at several elementary schools, visited a few, then sat down with Ron. My plan was to move to a new neighborhood, picked for its school, and rent there until I could afford to buy a house. I had to find a place that wasn't too far from Ron, with easy access between our two homes in rush hour, in an affordable neighborhood with a good school district. He approved my top choice, an older community with trees and small houses, and within a few weeks I found a place that had a manageable rent and a big backyard. The boys enrolled in the small, cozy neighborhood school for the following fall. I found out then that the school had a special group for kids of divorce called Banana Splits. They gathered, grade by grade, and talked with the counselor once a week about what it felt like to come from a family that was different—splitup, remarried, whatever. At the end of the year they had a Banana Split party. Yes, I thought to myself, this is what I've been looking for. A place where they can start to have a normal childhood, but one that accepts the realities of their life. A place where they won't feel so strange. A place where we can put down roots.

I know that—despite all we do—there will be subtle losses for my children. There are, inevitably, times when they feel neglected, because their on-duty parent is distracted by other problems and there's no one else to pick up the slack. There are things we don't do—activities, lessons, adventure travel—because we just can't manage it with only one adult. There are things I tolerate too much of—television, computer games—because I'm too busy to play checkers. And there will always be times when they ache for the parent who is missing, times when the one they need isn't there.

So I remain vigilant. I watch my children carefully, move in with solutions the minute a problem crops up. We keep Dr. Mary on the payroll and consult with the counselors at the boys' school. I'm careful not to worry in front of the boys about my adult concerns, and I refrain from blaming other problems—tight finances, limited options—on the divorce. Yes, things might be different if Ron and I had stayed together. But they don't need to know that.

23

M O N E Y

I'm chatting with a friend about music lessons for children, thinking it might be time for David to start learning to play the piano. David listens with interest when I practice, enjoys picking out tunes by ear. My friend's son has recently started taking lessons from someone he likes quite well, so I ask for the teacher's name and number.

Without missing a beat, my friend says: "Oh, you couldn't afford her."

Really.

He doesn't even give me the teacher's name. I push a bit, but he won't tell me, and I can't figure out if he is trying to protect me or if something else is at work. She's out of our league, much too dear for us, is the message. Hidden under this remark it feels as if there is another line: Maybe she's too good for us, as well.

When I was married this kind of thing never happened to me. In Washington in particular, most of the people I knew had similar levels of income. There were few very rich people around, and most of the people Ron and I counted as friends were working couples, wives and husbands bringing in the two incomes that are necessary if one is to survive in the Washington metropolitan area. No one could afford to live on one income.

And then I got divorced, and I tumbled over some invisible divide. The same income that used to support us in one household now had to support us in two, and because both Ron and I were caring for the boys, we both needed houses with bedrooms for them and yard space. Not surprisingly, we quickly discovered what it felt like to live on the edge.

In the past, neither of us had ever carried much debt, and both of us usually kept a cushion of funds in a money market account. During our marriage we had regularly contributed to our pension plans and IRAs, and had started putting money away for the kids' college educations.

But when we split up, that all changed. I scaled back my retirement contribution, gave up donating to charities, and neither of us had anything left over at the end of the month for the college fund. When we started dividing assets, Ron said he wanted to keep the Volvo we were leasing, but he soon found he couldn't afford the payments. He gave it up the second winter and he and the boys rode city buses for nearly a year, hauling groceries home from the corner store in the boy's red wagon.

The house we bought together and renovated the year David was born remained in both our names, although Ron lived there with the boys. The mortgage was a heavy load for him to carry alone, but the D.C. housing market was in a serious slump and Ron couldn't afford to buy me out. Not that it really mattered, though, because I was in no position to buy real estate myself. On my assistant professor's salary, I was just barely managing the rent and groceries. I didn't need to buy much for myself, but the boys needed clothes and toys. They were growing so fast and were so close in age that we could barely even hand things down from David to Jess. I got to know the secondhand stores and cruised them often, looking for the expensive items—winter coats, boots, games, even electronic equipment. My rent, high because of the excellent school district, ate up more than 50 percent of my take-home pay. According to federal housing officials, that made us the working poor.

This was new. I had been decidedly middle class since the day I was born, and in Mississippi I learned that the great advantage of being middle class was that you didn't have to think about money all the time. All the poor people I met, and most of the rich people I had known, were obsessed with money. Until I went to Mississippi I had never seen what a cash economy looked like. No one had checking accounts or credit cards—they cashed their paychecks, and then carefully doled out the bills as needs arose. If they still had money in their pockets, they could afford something. If they didn't, they didn't buy it. Nobody saved. People routinely came up short at the end of the month. I heard the jokes about fighting with the dog for the last can of beans, but I had no idea what that felt like. I had never been without the security of money in the bank, a credit card in my pocket, and a family within easy reach in case things got unusually tight.

I still had those things—although the nest egg in the bank was just barely enough to hold the account open—but my sense of financial security was gone. I could pretend for a while that I was doing fine, and then something would happen—a rental agent would insist my parents co-sign my lease—and I would feel that strange shame of needing to rely on them again. All around me friends solved their problems by throwing money at them, and it usually worked. If they couldn't be home with their middle school children in the afternoon because of work, they got a cell phone so the kids could call at any time. If their son was doing poorly in math, they hired a tutor. People were putting in second phone lines to accommodate their Internet use, buying sports utility vehicles so they would be safe while driving around the Beltway, adding computers and game systems and beepers to their lives. When life got too stressful, they packed everybody up and headed for Disneyworld.

We watched this and, sometimes, felt we were in a world apart.

"I'm the only kid I know who doesn't have a Nintendo," Jesse told me one afternoon. "It's like TV, Mom. You shouldn't have to grow up without one."

I was the only person I knew who drove a car without an air bag, or who kept track of the total cost of the things in the shopping cart so I wouldn't go over the weekly limit.

Not that we were impoverished—hardly. But the boys and I lived in the shadow of a genteel kind of poverty. Like the stories of Victorian spinsters who froze to death because they couldn't bear to burn the fine furniture, the boys and I lived hand-to-mouth for several years while trying to keep our standards intact.

I bought a computer to support my work and their schooling, then struggled to make the rent for the rest of the year. I watched the debt creep up on my credit card, worried because—no matter what I did—I couldn't quite live within my means. When I seemed overworked or tired, friends blithely suggested I get a massage, or hire a housecleaner, or at least get someone to mow the lawn. But each month I was a few hundred dollars over my budget. I knew I couldn't justify that kind of expense when I could clean the house perfectly well myself.

But we were far better off than many divorced people in the Washington area, and I wondered how other families did it. As I started meeting more single moms, I discovered that many of them lived with their parents, or in tiny apartments. Others felt pressured to remarry quickly, even if that wasn't the best thing for their kids. I met single mothers who worked second jobs—ringing up groceries at the local market until late in the evening or doing telemarketing from home when they should have been free to help their kids with homework—often to pay debts incurred during their divorces. I was much better off because I had a family I could lean on, and I earned enough to have choices. It felt like a gift from above.

Ironically, our struggles with money made it easier for Ron and me to talk with the mediators about settling the financial issues—who should get the house, how we should value and then separate the retirement money, how to split the debt and valuable items. In the beginning we were rigidly locked in disagreement by suspicion and distrust, but as we watched each other scraping by, our sympathetic understanding grew. Clearly, neither one of us had gotten away with the lion's share of anything. Over time the mediators gently helped us understand each other's fears. Although it would take several more years, we finally learned how to defuse arguments, seek the middle ground, and—most important—how to set aside the thornier problems until we could untangle them without losing our cool.

My younger sister, Penny, whom we both trusted, offered to divide the valuable household items, including the emotion-laden collection of wedding presents. She drew up a list that left each of us with a modest assortment of china and silver. Neither of us was going to be hosting dinners for twelve, but we could each host six if we weren't purists about the settings, and when we had enough money we could easily build our sets back up to eight. "No one feeds more than eight people these days, anyway," Penny said. I looked around my small kitchen; it didn't even have a dishwasher or a disposal. "I'm not entertaining a lot these days as it is," I said ruefully. "And when I do, we order pizza." But that was okay. The boys preferred it that way.

It is true that many women, most women, in fact, lose considerable economic ground when they divorce. Most will end up worse off financially than their ex-husbands, even if they get the kind of child support they are entitled to. And it is also true that joint custody takes the lion's share of child support away from women. Many people warned me about these possibilities when I separated from Ron, and encouraged me to go after him for all I could get. But over time I saw that our situation was different from the norm. The outcome, in our case, was much more even. We were both living similar lives. No one was taking fancy vacations or buying the boys expensive presents. The advice to "win" the financial battle just soured the working relationship Ron and I were gradually developing. I began to learn an important lesson about divorce: Question the advice and predictions you hear, and ignore those that don't apply to you. I wasn't a statistic, and the dire numbers didn't have to be a blueprint for my life. It was important to understand the dynamics and risks of divorce, but ultimately, I could do it the way I needed to.

One night my circle of Quaker women friends were talking about pointless fears, fears that once seemed large but that had evaporated over time. People mentioned different things, but finally one woman sat up and said the most pointless fear of her life had been worrying about money in the years shortly after she got divorced. "I still don't know how I did it, but I managed to keep my house and send my daughter to college. Today I have all I need to do the things I want to do. I used to worry we would end up in a homeless shelter, which was ridiculous. I wish I hadn't worried about it as much as I did, because the fears about money really corroded my life. But none of it ever came true."

I went up to her after the meeting and gave her a hug. "Thanks. That was the best advice I've gotten in years." Later that night I wrote down five ways to increase my income or cut our costs. We didn't have to be stretched like this forever. It was temporary, like much of the rest of my divorced life. Different from what I knew before, but not necessarily bad. At least my children were learning the value of a dollar and racking up some good stories to tell their grandchildren. "Why, when I was little we were so poor we had to haul groceries in our wagon! Through the snow!" I could already hear them.

24

WHAT I WANT

IN A MAN

Of all the divorce statistics I read, the one I hated the most stated that if a woman was going to remarry after being divorced, she would do so in the first four years. After that, the odds went way down.

Four years. I thought of the woman from the divorce group who had spent four years just trying to get her spouse to put together his financial documents so she could *get* divorced. Did that count? By now I was nearly three years out, but we weren't legally divorced yet. Did those years count, or was my clock still dormant, waiting for the moment the gavel came down on the judge's bench? Three years out and I had yet to find someone I wanted to date more than a few times, much less marry.

By now I had gone a long way toward rediscovering who I was, and felt more ready to try a serious relationship again. But one of the things I had rediscovered was that I was a girl with very high standards. I had managed to build a cozy life for myself and my boys, money problems were easing, I had friends to go places with and family to be there for holidays and vacations. I didn't want to risk that life for just anybody. I hadn't fought my way to this better place only to give it up for someone who wasn't perfect. So I would date people I met, then turn away at the end of the evening when they wanted a good-bye kiss. I had a hard time kissing people I didn't particularly like, and I usually came in after a date relieved to be alone again, in my own little house, free and unattached.

Maybe it was the people I was dating. I'm sure there are wonderful men in their forties out there, but most of them must be in hiding. Or in marriage. The men I met seemed to fall into one of three categories. First, there were the single men who had never married, or some who had married briefly but had never had children. Some of them were nice, but there was always some story that explained why they were so alone, usually some sad tale about the woman who got away—often after years of waiting for the guy to get off his duff and marry them. These men seemed truly mystified about what had gone wrong and spent their time with me going over the gory details. There was a lot of emotional wreckage in the past for these guys, and most of them preferred to sit picking through it rather than talking with me about their life now. Many said they had *wanted* kids, or they had *wanted* to be less consumed by their work, but it didn't ring true. Sitting over my plate of pasta, outside the circle of their attention, I was often struck by the smallness of their lives, and I couldn't quite figure out why they had asked me out. It was almost as if we were just going through the motions. There wasn't any *there* there.

With the second group there was plenty of *there* there, but usually more than I wanted to handle. These were the older men, the guys in their late fifties and early sixties. The advantage of these guys was that most had been through a real life, had done marriage and kids. And now they were finished and wanted some fun. That was supposed to be me. The younger trophy date who looked good next to them in the convertible.

Some of these guys were charming men, but they all seemed to be from a previous generation. Ron had been ten years older than me, but he had never looked or acted his age. These guys did, and it came through in everything from chauvinist remarks to their choice of restaurants and movies. As I fought off the hand on my knee under the linen tablecloth, I often felt as if I was trapped in some sort of James Bond fantasy. Fast women, high heels, martinis, and short skirts. They asked if I had ever thought about growing my hair long. They wanted me to go away for weekends in the country, waving away my concerns when I mentioned my children. "Get a sitter," they would say, grinning at me devilishly. "You need to live a little." They tossed money around to impress me, and usually only talked about their work in terms of their financial success. They didn't ask much about my teaching; somehow the idea that I was a professor let the air out of the fantasy.

With many of these men I felt as if I could have been just about anybody, as long as I was attractive and witty, because it was never about me. I often felt like a prop in a play—their play. I was perfect for them, they said, without ever asking if they were perfect for me. But I asked that of myself. Because I had too much to lose if they weren't.

And then there was the third group, the really bloody ones, the widowers and the ones left behind after horrible divorces. These were often the most promising men—men who loved being fathers, who had been devoted husbands—but their circumstances were just too harrowing. I went out once with a man whose beloved wife had died suddenly of a brain aneurysm, and there was nothing to do but talk about all he had lost. Even he knew it was a lousy date, but he couldn't handle anything more. I liked him but I wasn't willing to go through the long journey it would take before he was really free.

Then there was the one left behind with two daughters when his wife ran off with a lesbian lover. Again, the evening was consumed by a discussion of the wreckage. It would have been pointless to have tried anything more. I was beginning to feel more social worker than romantic prospect.

I went home one evening after another awkward date and looked at the list Jeannie had drawn up for me. Boy. I rarely got even a few of the attributes, much less the dog or the musical instrument. What I usually got were intelligent but self-centered guys, tortured guys. Guys with too much baggage.

Maybe my standards were the problem.

"There are plenty of men out there," said my friend Christy as she pushed her salad around on her plate. We were sitting in a sidewalk cafe on Connecticut Avenue, eyeing the lunch crowd. "The problem is that your vision is too narrow."

She knows what she is talking about. Although she has an M.B.A. and a highly successful career, her second husband has only a high school degree and sells furniture for a living. But it doesn't matter, because he is a prince of a man, and she is now happily ensconced in a wonderful marriage with two small children. "You're friendly, which is good. Now you just have to be more open-minded. Don't go for those dried-up, aging intellectuals. They're hopeless. They think too much. Look around you and be open to chance encounters. That's going to be your best bet."

So I go out into the world and I try to be more open-minded, but I quickly find that it puts a lot of pressure on my everyday life. It's one thing to put on mascara and a nice outfit for a date, but it's another thing to feel I have to do that every time I run to the grocery store.

One friend met her second husband waiting in line at the Department of Motor Vehicles. Another friend met her husband while trying to buy carpeting. The only problem with this approach is that not only do I have to look nice when I go to get my license renewed, I have to act nice. I'm usually friendly, but I'm in such a bad mood when I'm at the DMV, I'm not likely to be entertaining company.

It is the threat, promise, and pressure of the chance encounter.

And I'm convinced it is the only way I'm going to meet anyone worth dating. People in midlife, especially those who are married, just don't think about setting up their single friends. They know too much about them. They are subconsciously convinced that it won't work out, even before anyone gets a chance to try.

"So, ah, is your divorced, attractive, nice, successful friend—whom you love, so he can't be all bad—seeing anyone?" I ask. "Oh, God, no, you don't want to go out with him," they say. "He's a workaholic. You don't want that."

These friends seem to want more for me than I do. I just want to go to the movies with someone, but they want me to find perfect happiness. "No, he's kind of paunchy around the middle, you don't want that." "Him? You mean my office mate? No, well, I don't think you want to go out with him. I saw him smoke a cigar once."

When we were all younger, we met people through work, but now we are older, many of us in positions of responsibility and, well, it just isn't wise. We know how hard it is to work with anyone for ten years, but one you were in love with once? Ouch. Not worth the disruption, and too threatening to our stability.

And now that I'm a college professor, I feel like my work environment is the dating equivalent of Siberia. The students are too young—and off-limits for obvious reasons—and all my colleagues are, well, aging intellectuals. And most are married, or oblivious.

My friend Susan suggests I run a personal ad, but I'm not that desperate yet. Besides, I've noticed that most guys in the personals are looking for someone between the ages of twenty-four and thirty-nine. This is particularly disheartening for those of us who are bumping the upper limit, as if it's time to retire from dating. So I've stopped reading the personals, and have shelved thoughts of placing an ad. Instead, I ask Susan to go with me to a dance being held by one of the single parents' groups in Montgomery County. She looks at me, mildly appalled by this suggestion. "Come on," I coax. "We only have to stay for a half hour—promise. If it's really bad, I'll buy dinner later. We need to get out."

Susan is my single mom partner. She has a little boy of her own, and all the same problems I have—tight finances, juggling custody schedules with her son's father, navigating the world by herself. Like me, she's found lots of contentment in her single life, enjoying her son and riding through the hard times with grit and an abidingly high heart. I think she's terrific, and anyone who married her would be a lucky guy. She thinks the same about me.

So we doll ourselves up and drive out to the dance. It's a long way out, out in Gaithersburg, a stretch of town houses and planned communities that I think of as Singles

Land. "If we meet anyone out here, they are going to be geographically incorrect," Susan mutters as we wind through the area searching for the recreation center that is hosting the dance.

"Open-minded, now. That's what we are trying to be. We can't be snobs."

"That's it!" laughs Susan. "That's our problem. We're geographic snobs! Okay. Tonight I'm not even going to mention Georgetown." Susan lives in a cozy row house in one of the trendiest neighborhoods in Washington. I live just outside the Beltway, which is a step down, but not nearly as bad as out here in the farmlands halfway to Pennsylvania.

When we finally find the place, we park and go inside, paying our five dollars at the door and getting a stamp on our hands.

"Oh, God, I'm back in middle school," Susan says, her eyes widening. And she's right. It's a dance in a gym, only this time no one took the trouble to decorate. There's punch on a table in the corner, and lots of strange-looking guys standing around. There are fewer women and most of them are older than we are. We step inside and stand awkwardly near the entrance. "Jesus," Susan says. "You're going to have to buy me a really nice dinner."

Before we know it we both get asked to dance, so we go ahead, Susan flinging me one last look. I head out onto the wooden basketball floor with a guy who's a bit thick around the middle but with a nice enough face. He seems young, though, younger than I am. I'm wondering why he's here. After a few moments I'm wondering why he asked me to dance. He is looking only at the floor and has said almost nothing in response to the few questions I've asked: Where do you work? What do you do? Do you have children? He mutters his answers, looks away as if he can't talk and dance at the same time or as if he's already decided I'm not his type. I give up trying to be polite and just shuffle around, trying not to look self-conscious. At the end he asks for my phone number.

"My number?" I say, dumbfounded. "You're planning to call me? You don't know anything about me!"

At that he has to look at me, but his glance slides away after a split second. "Well, maybe we could go out. I can't talk in here."

"I don't think so," I say, and walk away.

Susan is standing by the punch table, behind a loud-speaker, as if she is trying to hide.

"You're not going to meet anyone standing behind this loudspeaker."

"That's the point."

We look at each other. Suddenly, it's over. We head for the door, laughing.

Once we are in the car again, Susan really lets loose. "We are not that desperate," she howls. "Tell me we aren't that desperate." We drive back into the city and go to our favorite restaurant and drink margaritas into the evening. We laugh and talk about the men we've known, and then about the fun we've had with our children and with our work. We understand each other and have such a wonderful evening we barely look up at the people passing by. At one point, a couple of guys in the next booth turn and ask us a few questions, but it doesn't occur to us until we're driving home later that maybe they were trying to start a conversation. We never try the singles scene again.

A few weeks later I go out to San Francisco for a conference and stay with my old high school friend Jamie, the one who talked me out of divorcing Ron years earlier, when

David was a baby. Jamie is single again as well, out of a long-term relationship and wondering about his romantic future. He drives me down to a beach just below the foot of the Golden Gate Bridge and we sit in the afternoon sun watching the ocean and talking about love. We've been best friends since eighth grade, but never a couple, never in love with each other. I tell him about my worst dates, the dance, then about my list. I ask if he thinks it's crazy to have such a list, if he thinks it's my standards that are making it so hard to find someone I like.

"I've dated so many people I've gotten it down to a system by now," he says. "There are five questions that seem to matter, and I can tell by how they answer them if I want to go out with them again. First, do they like their parents? Second, do they like their job? Third, have they had their heart broken? Fourth, do they have friends? And last, do they believe they will have to work at a relationship? If they can say yes to all of those, then I'm going to be more interested."

I think about the guys I've been dating. Most dislike their parents, and many dislike their jobs, even though they talk about them nonstop. Most of them have had their hearts broken, but few have gotten over the tragedy, and most of them seem more interested in those old wounds than in ever healing. Because they are tiresome to be with, most seem to have just a smattering of friends. As for working at relationships, that seems to be the big hang-up. Many of the guys who have been burned seem astounded to find that romance is tough, is something that isn't going to work like magic.

"Do you think having a dog matters?" I ask Jamie.

"Oh, Wen," he says, taking my hand in his. "You really are lost, aren't you?"

When I get home I take out Jeannie's list and look at it

again. With all those specific requirements, it seems to reverberate with the chafing of my marriage. He must be this, and be that, and get this right, and be right, and then, maybe only then, could it ever work out. God save me from such a man, and from being a woman who needs such a man. I tear the list up and stuff it in the trash.

It seems much simpler now. My list today has only four general demands.

First, he must be kind. That is still the base, the support for everything else.

Second, I want a man who loves children and knows how to parent. A man who can speak to kids when they're cranky. A man who sometimes gives in at the grocery store and buys Cocoa Puffs. A man who is happiest with a passel of kids in the van. A man who kisses his son as well as his daughter.

Third, I want a man who can go with me, happily, into old age. I want a man with plenty of sexual energy at forty so that there will be some there at sixty. I want a man who shares some of my interests or can teach me his so we'll have things to do together in our retirement. I want a man who takes care of his body—not so he will be handsome and svelte today, but so I can have some reassurance that he will not die and leave me alone.

Fourth, and this is critical: I want a man who lives an examined life, a man who can weather the inevitable changes life will bring. I want someone who will talk with me when things get rough, who will try to find the connections back, who can consider his strengths and weaknesses with honesty, and be fair to himself and me. I want someone whose instinct is to reach for me at the end of the fight. Someone who will meet me halfway in the middle of the bed. I want someone I can forgive without feeling that I have given myself away.

These feel like the clear needs, but there are other things below the consciousness of everyday life that surprise me when they surface. As I left San Francisco I told Jamie he was the sweetest man I had ever met. With wry wisdom he said, "Other than your daddy." And before I knew it I heard myself say, "True, but I need to find another one like you guys, so that when my father dies I won't fall off the planet."

Divorce is a time of great loss, but it is a loss we inflict on ourselves. We give up the family house so that we can get away. We forgo the stability of two incomes so we can gain our independence. We get many new possibilities with these losses.

But middle and older age bring other losses, losses not always compensated with new opportunities. The loss of parents and other friends as my generation moves closer toward death. The loss of little children as they grow into adults, changing wonderfully but irrevocably into someone else and passing through a time when they will not need or want us very much. I know instinctively that I will need support through these losses. I forgive siblings old wrongs; I work on long-term friendships so I can keep them wrapped around me; and I search for the man who will be there with me.

Knowing this somehow gives me a newfound sense of freedom and confidence in this search. Maybe his taste in furniture doesn't matter, as long as he will let me buy a few new things at Ikea. It's not so much about dogs or cats or children as much as about wanting a man who is happiest in a full house. He doesn't need to play a musical instrument if he will let me drag him to the symphony. I can probably learn to scuba-dive or learn to watch basketball. I can compromise on many things.

But he must be kind.

25

———

DATING AS

A FAMILY UNIT

Then, when I least expected it, I met someone kind.

The introduction was through a friend of a friend. "He's a great guy, and available," said my friend. "I saw him at the office picnic, and he was there with his sister, so obviously he is a nice person. They seemed to have a really good relationship, and he's got these two adorable kids."

"Great. What's his number?"

"His number? Don't you think we should do a real introduction, like, have you both over to dinner or something?"

"If you want, but that could take weeks to schedule. Just give me his number."

"You're going to call him, just like that?"

"You said he was interested in meeting me, right? So give me his number. We're grown-ups. I can handle this."

My married friends still don't get that dating when you are my age is different from when you are eighteen. Some of the traditional niceties get lost in the dust, others are best ignored. If put to the screws, I would have to admit I'm getting a wee bit nervous about the passage of time.

One thing I've learned from dating is that I can tell—within a few minutes—whether I want to spend any significant time with someone. A quick phone conversation should suffice.

I go home and call the guy that night after dinner. He sounds nice, but says he is juggling his kids—can he call me later? Sure, I say, thinking to myself that this will be the first test. "I'll call you tonight around ten," he says. "Promise."

I'm not sure if this is stalling or a ploy to gain time to gather intelligence, but there is a lot of kid noise in the background. Sure enough, he calls at ten, right on the dot. The first thing he says is, "I was really looking forward to calling you back. It made the whole evening feel exciting." I feel a little tingle of delight when he says that.

We talk for an hour, and then another hour the next night. We have a lot in common—young kids, joint custody, workable relationships with ex-spouses, jobs we enjoy. By the end of the week we've made plans for dinner Saturday night. When he picks me up, I'm surprised to find him more conservatively dressed than I had imagined, but he has a twinkle in his eye and a lightning-quick mind. He's funny and courteous. He's Southern, and it shows. A gentleman.

Over dinner he opens up and reveals that he's already done much of the soul-searching that comes with a failed marriage and divorce. He seems to understand what happened and how he would do it differently the next time. He admits to his faults, understands how they contributed to the problems. But best of all, he seems to be over it. Over the pain of divorce, over the shame. After dinner we walk around Bethesda, then play a little pool, where we discover that we both have a competitive streak. He takes me home and gives me a polite kiss. Nothing aggressive, nothing heavy-handed. The most promising evening in years.

Within a month we are spending as much free time together as possible, though that is limited by our custody schedules and our jobs. It's my first real relationship since my marriage, and while it is exhilarating, within a few months I feel the first twinges of worry. This is the first time I've had to venture back into that old jungle called commitment, thick with vines and quicksand, and this time the mission is complicated. I step carefully, but with determination.

At the time it seemed odd that I met him when I did, when I had finally learned to mow my own lawn and talk about auto insurance, when I felt as if life was a bright, open space built on the confidence that I could stand on my own two feet. But maybe that is what was attractive about me.

What attracted me most to him was that he was the first man I'd met who wasn't ambivalent. Perhaps he was ambivalent about me, but he wasn't ambivalent about what he ultimately wanted, which was to remarry and settle back into the life where there are four hands to help with children and someone to press against in the dark of the night.

I wanted that too. Even though I was past needing it with the desperation I had felt in the first year after my separation, I still wanted it. I knew when I got divorced that I didn't want to give it all up. But divorce is like clear-cutting: To get rid of the bad you must burn it all, and the only things left are the seeds of memory. There are many wonderful things about marriage, and most divorcing people miss them terribly. There is the balance another provides, the opposite weight to steady yourself against. There is another person to run to the cleaners, someone to help pay the bills, someone else to listen to the low-level static of living with kids. There is also the strength of older bonds, the history and shared experiences. Even when laced with pain, those bonds hug tightly. It explains, partly, why it is so difficult to divorce and why some divorced couples actually remarry each other, even though that rarely works out. And it explains why, after the struggle of getting out, we sometimes forget and feel nostalgic, even for the nightmare times. At least then there was someone to talk to, even if through gritted teeth.

So, gingerly, this new man and I started to get to know each other. After the string of bad dates I'd been through, his emotional openness was startling, and he continued to be a series of surprises. He called when he said he would. He remembered the details of our conversations, and told me things I had wanted to hear all my life. He was not afraid of building something with me, so we tentatively ventured into each other's lives—met each other's children and introduced them to each other, went to church together, double-dated with other friends.

Yet we were both as cautious as wild animals. We weren't ambivalent about the goal, but sometimes it felt as if we had no idea how to get through the maze of good intentions, habits, and old fears. We were suspicious of happiness because we knew it could blur our vision. We were terrified of becoming dependent again only to find out the other was not who we thought they were. With trepidation we revealed our flaws, slowly, one at a time. We spent months on our best behavior and wondered if what we were experiencing could hold up under the weight of everyday life. We were scared of what it would be like if we fought, so we did not fight. We wanted to be happy, and we were happy together; but we were both poised for flight.

Eventually, we learned to relax and wait for the answers to reveal themselves. There were many things about divorce I could only learn on my own, but there were other things, the pieces that were often the hardest to understand, that I could only learn by braving the entanglements of love again. In time, we even started fighting.

Despite my desire for partnership, I often balked at the compromises necessary, particularly when it involved our kids. Dating as a family is nothing like dating as a single person. Making dinner plans for six different people can be an emotional minefield—do you agree to go for Thai food when you know your youngest won't eat a bite? Do you suffer through the pouty glares from your kid, or do you whisper a promise of McDonald's later just to rescue the evening, even though you know that's not the best parenting? If you can't force him to eat, what does that say about you? And what if you admit your children have never even seen Thai food? Every dynamic reveals something, whether you like it or not. All the problems you used to keep confined to the privacy of your home quickly surface. And the whole time you are anxious, because if you can't control your children—if they are rude or hostile—maybe this new sweetheart will think better of it and head for the door.

At the heart of love is loyalty, and it is hard to partner with someone when you already are partnered in impenetrable ways with your children. As a single parent—an adult without anyone else to be loyal to—my attachment to my children had grown even stronger, perhaps too strong. I was more than a mommy lion when it came to them—I was a mommy Godzilla. I found it hard to push them to accept changes and disruptions when I wasn't sure yet if I was going to follow it up with a lifelong commitment to this new man. I didn't want to ask them to love him until I was sure I loved him, and I was careful not to become too enmeshed with his children. It didn't seem fair to drag them all through the experimental stages when we weren't sure of the outcome.

But life isn't as neat as a science project, and inevitably our lives overlapped. We settled into a routine that was built on conditions that ultimately proved unstable—I spent time with him and his kids, but he didn't spend that much time with me and mine. When my children went to Ron's on Saturday evening, I would head over to my boyfriend's house and spend the rest of the weekend with them, fitting into their life as best I could, like a visiting relative. In many ways, this suited him fine. We did the things they enjoyed, and I was there for companionship and to help with the kids. People saw us together and often assumed we were a family, which he liked, but which left me irritable. I didn't like it when people assumed I was the mother of his kids, both because I wasn't and because I didn't have the right to parent them—or love them or manage them—in the way I would my own children. I wasn't an aloof mother, but I looked like one when I was with them. And the assumption that my boyfriend and his kids were my family made me feel as if David and Jesse had vanished.

Learning to care about someone else's children was a bittersweet mixture of tension and joy. My boyfriend's children were loving, interesting kids. I was drawn to them, enjoyed playing and talking with them, but I was also leery of getting too close, of building bonds I might not sustain over time. I winced when my children discovered that I had done fun things with my boyfriend's kids, or when I had to leave mine behind to travel with them. And when his kids were difficult, as children inevitably are, I would feel a surge of guilty relief that the problem really wasn't mine to worry about.

I also chafed in the role of visiting girlfriend. I made dinners and cleaned up the kitchen, but was careful not to take on other chores. My boyfriend was often overwhelmed both by his demanding job and caring for his children and his house, but I was wary of falling into my old co-dependency habits, so I stayed in the background, helping but not directing. It was his house, his life, his children. I had my own. And I was far less willing to let him and his kids into my terrain on a regular basis because I feared the chaos that often ensued when we were all together. I had created a neat little life for myself and the boys. It turned out that that was far more precious to me than I had ever imagined.

What I began to see was that families each have their own culture, and those differences alone can make or break a relationship. This is not to say that one family culture is better than another, just that people find it hard to adjust to something unfamiliar. I have women friends I love dearly, but I look at the culture of their households and know I could never live with it. I know one family who thrives in an atmosphere of almost constant motion. Everyone talks quickly, the phone rings incessantly, cars come and go as children dash to sports and theater events. It's vibrant, exciting, and exhausting—at least for me. I know other families who live happily with mounds of clutter; families who restrict television and computer use to a few precious minutes a day. I know families who insist homework be done immediately after school, while others have the TV on all day, as if for company. Some families are noisy, some mousy. Some never sit down together for a meal, others serve dinner at tables often crowded with extra children and friends. It's all in what feels comfortable for that particular family.

One day my boyfriend and I were biking around a new development near his home and I was intrigued by models that appeared to be upscale duplexes.

"That's what we need," I yelled. "A duplex! We could have a common kitchen and master bedroom, but then each family would have a separate wing, with living room and children's rooms. That would be perfect."

He stopped pedaling and put his foot down on the pavement. "You're serious, aren't you?"

I hadn't been at first, but when he said that, I had to own up. When questioned, I would admit I couldn't imagine blending households and trying to negotiate the millions of small compromises that would entail, I told him. We disciplined differently, had different interests, ran our households on different principles. And I worried that both of us were too old to change our stripes.

The society around us, however, thought the whole arrangement was too perfect to abandon. When we went out somewhere with all four children, people would coo, "Oh, a Brady bunch! How cute!"

But it didn't seem cute to me, it often seemed tense and noisy, with someone always getting left out or ignored. When I watched *The Brady Bunch* reruns, I was struck by the Hollywood version. The Brady family dynamic worked because they had a full-time housekeeper who doubled as the resident psychologist and because Mom didn't have many responsibilities. (Mom Brady spends most of her time reading magazines.) I resented society's glib expectation that it would be a breeze to create a new family out of the broken pieces of two different designs, as if Hollywood had the secret formula for success.

The statistics on blended families, in fact, are the most depressing in the pantheon of frightening divorce data. Nearly 60 percent of second marriages fail, and for those with children, the number is closer to 75 percent. You don't have to be a math major to see what that means.

Over the years I met more and more divorced parents, and I got so I could spot the ones who seemed headed for trouble. One night Jesse and I stopped by an apartment complex to pick up one of his friends for a sleepover, and we were both surprised to find the child—an eight-year-old boy—climbing around on the kitchen counters and throwing boxes and cans of food on the floor in a full-scale tantrum. His harried mother, slim and soft-spoken, pleaded with him to stop but to no avail.

"He's looking for a box of macaroni and cheese, but I don't have any," she said apologetically as she stooped to pick up cans of soup rolling around the floor.

"I want macaroni and cheese for dinner!" the boy yelled. "Where is it?"

"But I thought you were going to have dinner with us," I said, puzzled.

"I am, but I want you to make me macaroni and cheese," he said.

Jesse and I looked at each other. Even he knew this was out-of-line behavior, and he was curious as to what I would do.

"But I'm not making that for dinner tonight, even if you can find some," I told the boy in a firm tone. "We're having pizza. I already made it, and I only cook one dinner a night."

The child stopped and looked at me to see if I was serious. Apparently, he wasn't used to being spoken to that way. His mom moved in. "Let's get you off the counter."

"But I want macaroni and cheese!" he screamed.

"Well, then, maybe tonight isn't a good night for a sleepover," I said, turning toward the door.

He jumped down. "Is it pepperoni pizza?"

"You'll have to wait and see. I think I can guarantee that you'll like it."

Jesse grabbed his hand. "Come on. Get your stuff."

As they went into the other room, the boy's mother sighed and pushed her hair back out of her eyes. "He's so out of control, but I don't know what to do with him."

"It's hard when you're single," I murmured.

"Exactly, which is why I'm getting married again."

"Really? Congratulations." I wished I could sound more enthusiastic.

"Well, it's all for him," she said, waving toward her son in the hall. "This time it's all about the children. My fiancé has three kids and they are very well behaved. I think they will be a good influence on Kevin. I can't handle him by myself."

As I packed the boys into the car, I felt myself grow sad. The thought of Kevin's mom remarrying to solve her son's behavior problems chilled me to the bone. I had married for the wrong reasons the first time around, and I couldn't imagine doing that again. Yet all around me I saw others tumble to the seductive power of remarriage, to the promise that partnering again would bring that elusive happiness and all the solutions they needed to make life right.

One friend remarried hoping it would help her win a custody case against her ex-husband. The marriage didn't last, and the ploy didn't work. She lost both the second husband and a significant chunk of her time with her kids.

All around me I saw single parents scrambling to right their lives, and for many the only path seemed to be remarriage.

It didn't help that many of those around me yearned to see me settled again, as if the boys and I were inherently unbalanced in our life by being just three. When two dozen long-stemmed roses appeared on my desk one Valentine's Day, an enormous pile of foliage that attracted some attention from my colleagues, my friend Wendell howled, "Just marry the poor guy and put him out of his misery!"

"He's really sweet, and he loves you," the others said. "You're not getting any younger, you know."

"Besides, he has a good income and a great future," my mother said.

"He's smart, he's kind," said my friend Christy. "Jesus, Wendy, what more do you want?"

What more did I want?

Something, but I couldn't put my finger on it.

I was beginning to feel like the heroine in a Jane Austen novel—refusing men everyone else thought I should be grateful for, just because of some ephemeral feeling that it wasn't quite right for me. And with the threat of being permanently single looming over my head. I seemed destined for regret.

I e-mailed Jamie in California, looking for guidance.

"I knew you would fall for the first guy who was nice to you," he e-mailed back. "But nice isn't everything. If it doesn't feel right, it isn't right."

And then Jean came for another visit, and she didn't like him.

It had been several years since Jeannie had been east, but I had gone west the previous fall to stand with her as she married her partner, Betsy, a strong and gentle companion, someone I hoped would have the deep patience and wisdom it would take to live with Jean. The wedding itself was a startling coming together of friends and family, including her own parents and others who struggled for a long time to accept Jeannie's confrontational brand of homosexuality. For Jean, who had wept with gratitude just a few years earlier when I had shown up at her public reading, being surrounded by no fewer than thirty blood relatives at her wedding was deeply moving. After the service she packed her life into a truck and headed north to Seattle, where Betsy worked. They bought a small house with a view of Mt. Rainier and in the backyard renovated a garage into a beautiful studio for Jean, complete with a small kitchen and a bathroom. In this quiet space—studded with jolts of blue and green pillows, bowls, pictures, fabrics—she surrounded herself with books, photos, file cabinets, and the hardware of her trade: telephone, fax, and computer. It was enough to make any writer envious. Outside the window of the studio, Betsy planted Jean's favorite flowers so she could see them from her desk. Jean was working on her fourth book, a collection of profiles of gay and lesbian families. I knew the interviewing and writing had been emotionally draining, but it was wonderful material. Along with the family book, she was working on her second novel and new poems that broke into fresh, shimmering territory.

She called to ask if she and her photographer for the family book could come and stay for a week while they interviewed people in the Washington area. She sounded upbeat on the phone, but when they arrived it was obvious the trip had taken a toll on their relationship. Jeff turned out to be a sweet, patient guy, but Jean was being unusually bossy and dictatorial. She seemed unwilling to allow him to contribute to the vision of the book, refusing to accept him as a fellow artist and trying to keep him in the role of assistant. I didn't envy him the job, and kept my head down when they argued late at night. It was like having a bad marriage come to stay.

One night my boyfriend joined us in Baltimore to attend a reading Jean was giving from her latest published book, one on the challenges of long-term recovery from alcohol. She was now thirteen years sober, but the book was dark and filled with images of death. Several of Jeannie's close friends had recently died of AIDS, which seemed to be the source of the shadows. My boyfriend commented later that it was an unusually depressing reading, but he also thought Jean's talent shone through. As was typical of him, he was trying to find nice things to say, trying to find ways to connect with this person who was so important in my life.

But Jeannie didn't make it easy for him. She kept her mouth shut when he was around, but he could feel her hostility, and the minute he left she would start in on me.

"He's Southern," she said.

"So?"

"Well, I know what Southern men are like, and he's not your type."

I suspected that he wasn't my type, but I didn't like the way she was stereotyping him.

"I don't think you're being fair," I said, immediately defensive because I was so deeply involved with someone Jeannie instinctively disliked. "You just don't like guys—I don't think you would like any guy I dated."

"Don't throw those homophobic clichés at me," she said, angry now but keeping her voice down. "I'm just trying to keep you from making a big mistake again. Or do you want me to butt out and let you ruin your life?"

I hung my head. On some level I knew she was right, but I hated being preached to, "No, I need to hear what you think, but you've barely met him and you're jumping to all these conclusions."

"I may be jumping to conclusions, but I still think I'm right. He's not your type. He doesn't have a dog, does he?"

"Oh, for Christ's sake, this isn't about a damn dog."

"Are you so sure?" she asked, eyeing me with that penetrating look. "I think you should go check the list."

"I threw that list away months ago. There are only a few things that are really critical, and he has most of them."

"So explain to me, then, why you won't let him into your life."

As usual, she could nail me.

She left unhappy with me, pulled into herself and overly polite about the good-byes. It wasn't as bad as the time she roared away on her motorcycle after fighting with me over Ron, but it left the same bad taste in my mouth. Unsure of myself, I stayed in the relationship, wondering if I was just afraid of commitment or if I should listen to my doubts. Listen to your gut, people said. But my gut was confused.

26

THE MONSTER

IN THE CLOSET

It must have been around dusk when Jeannie took the pills, more than three hundred of them, then wrapped herself in a sleeping bag and sat down to wait for death.

At the moment she decided to die, I was cozily tucked in the dim security of an Amtrak train three thousand miles away on the opposite coast, next to my boyfriend, returning to Washington after a weekend in New York. In a word, unavailable. It is hard for me to believe that the intense, loving, competitive relationship Jean and I shared for forty years could shut down without a word between us, but that is what happened. She didn't try to contact me, or others who could have helped. In the kitchen of her home in Seattle, she raised a steak knife over her head and threatened her partner, telling her to keep away. When a friend called to check on her, Jean lied and promised she wouldn't hurt herself. Then she locked herself in her studio. She left only three things on her desk: her will, a file fat with notes for her memorial service, and a quote from Primo Levi, the Holocaust survivor who eventually took his own life because he couldn't bear the memories anymore.

The quote was in Italian and nobody could read it, which

was probably the point. We found out later Levi had said something like "no exit" or "no other choice," but at the time we were mystified. Holding her secrets close, even at the end.

My mother called me at work. I had just finished teaching a class and was chatting with a student. It was the Tuesday after Martin Luther King Jr.'s birthday, the first day of the spring semester, and there were lots of people milling around outside my office. It seemed odd that my mother was calling midday.

"Honey," she said, her voice hoarse, "I didn't want to bother you at work, but I have something important to tell you."

"What, Mom?" Instinctively, I went still. I knew something was wrong.

"I don't know how to tell you this, but Jeannie has, well, Jeannie died yesterday."

"What?"

"Are you sitting down? Honey, she killed herself. She took an overdose of pills."

I was standing when I took the call, but when my mother's words formed and took meaning in my brain, I sank to my knees and bent double, squeezing the phone against my ear. "When? When did this happen?"

"Ah, I think yesterday afternoon, late afternoon. She went into a coma and died last night in the hospital. Aunt Cathy said her heart just gave out from trying to clear the toxins from her blood."

"Oh, Mom." I couldn't think. My student was trying to help me up. I pulled myself into my desk chair. "Oh, Mom. I never thought. I just never thought she would do this."

"I know, honey. I'm so sorry to have to tell you this at work. I'm so sorry."

"I was on the train, Mom. Maybe she tried to call. I wasn't home. She couldn't have gotten hold of me."

"Sweetie, this isn't your fault. Jean has never been happy, you know that. Maybe this was inevitable. But I'm so sorry, honey."

Penny comes over that evening to help me cope. She feeds the boys, then gets them into bed. I'm on the phone with Betsy, Jean's parents, Annie, my folks. I sit with my back against the refrigerator and cry. My children have never seen me like this, and new words circle in the air. When I go up to kiss them good night, they ask me what suicide means, and before I can think clearly about the consequences, I tell them.

"It's when you kill yourself."

"Is that how Aunt Jeannie died?"

I look in their faces and suddenly I cannot lie. I wish I could, but I can't.

"Yes, she did." They sit with this for a moment.

"How?" says Jesse.

"Why?" says David.

"She took a poison, honey. And I don't know why, really. She must have been very, very sad."

The room is quiet, and we can hear Penny doing the dishes downstairs.

"Daddy is sad sometimes," David says, looking away from me.

"You're sad now," says Jesse. "Are you going to kill yourself?"

Oh, God. "Honey, no. Just because people are sad doesn't mean they are going to kill themselves. There are different kinds of sadness, I guess. I'm sure Aunt Jeannie had a sadness that was very different."

My head is in a fog from the tension of the day, and I know I'm not doing a very good job of explaining this. "When someone commits suicide, it is more like they are sick—sick in the head," I say. "It's not really sadness. It's different from sadness. It's a sickness."

But as I turn out the light I can't help but see their serious little faces, propped on their pillows. Worrying. Already worrying.

My flight to Seattle for Jean's memorial service the weekend after her death gets rerouted through Dallas because of bad weather. I spend most of the day staring out at rainy runways and scratching angry notes to Jean on the back pages of my pocket calendar. *If you were sick, why didn't you trust me enough to ask for help? You always said we had an honest relationship, but in the middle of it was this big, fat lie— that you were well. That you were fine. That you would be there for me. Why did you throw this hand grenade into my life? And goddamn you for leaving me to get through this alone. Goddamn you. You had no right to end our relationship without asking me, to strip it of all the good stuff and leave behind only the toxins. You had no right.*

When I get to Seattle that night, I am swept into the circle of women who are Jean's family. Betsy is astonishing in her grief: quiet, sad, angry, and open. The last time I saw her was the day of their wedding, little more than a year earlier. That morning, before the ceremony, the three of us had hiked up the ridge behind Jean's house to share a few moments of quiet together. As the sun rose, we held hands and made each other promises of love and support. I felt at the time that I was handing Betsy something precious but also unbearably heavy, passing on the responsibility for Jean I had carried for so long. But they had been so happy. There was every reason to think it was a good thing.

The next morning, before the memorial service, Betsy and I go out to look through Jean's studio together. "I tried to do this earlier in the week, but I couldn't. I needed you here for this," she says to me as we step past the flower gardens, fallow now in the January chill. When we get to the door, we take each other's hand for a minute, steeling ourselves. Finally Betsy takes a deep breath and unlocks the door. Inside it is sunny but cold, and the place somehow reeks of depression. I look around and realize with a start that this is the crime scene, left as it was found. Jean's sleeping bag lies crumpled on the sofa. In the small kitchenette there are two jumbo-size aspirin bottles lying on the counter, along with the caps, the ripped-apart safety seals, the bag, and the drugstore receipt. The bottles are empty. We look at them, and then at each other, our eyes filling.

"What do we do with these?" Betsy says, her voice cracking.

"We throw them away," I whisper. I stuff it all in the bag, then deep in my jacket pocket. I'll dump it in a trash can somewhere far away, where Betsy won't stumble across it again.

I push down the tightness in my chest, and look around, trying to connect what's here with what I remember of Jean. And then I see them—hundreds of small mementos scattered all around that sacred space of her, small stones, fossils, colored pieces of glass, small statuettes of angels, feathers, candles, and dozens of photographs of family and friends.

"There is a story to each one," Betsy says as she sees me finger a tiny crystal egg. "Pick some out, because we want to put them in the church for the service." There are a few I recognize, a fossilized shell I found in Michigan and sent to her, a watercolor sketch of the family cabin on Cape Cod that Annie did for her. I don't remember her having all these mementos, and wonder what the sickness was that needed them. Each feels like a small anchor. Maybe there was so much bad stuff in her mind that she needed this tangible evidence to remember she was loved and had been happy.

At the church I busy myself arranging the shells and angels and stones. I feel better with them there—maybe there is some magic to them after all. Before long people begin to show up, including my cousins and aunts and uncles, those who were able to drop their busy lives and fly to Seattle. Jean's parents look unbearably old, and her dad grips me in a tight hug. For a long time, during the years Jean wouldn't talk to them, I was their bridge to her. They would call and I'd tell them what I knew, how she was doing, if she was okay. I knew they loved her, if imperfectly, and ever since then we've shared a special affection. My own family is absent, my parents in the middle of moving an elderly uncle into a nursing home and my sisters trapped in the hectic schedules of jobs and kids. I feel immensely lonely without them, but I hold on to my cousins, especially Jean's younger brother, a longtime friend.

During the service many people stand up to talk about their memories of Jean. Some people are angry with her, others more loving, forgiving. Many are perplexed, and everyone says something different. Few of her friends seem surprised—as if her depression was common knowledge—but, like me, they are shocked that she took such a devastating step. It's hard for us to believe she would leave Betsy and her book, which was not quite finished, or the many other good things in her life she had worked so hard to assemble.

Later, after the service, I drift among the people gathered, listening for more stories, trying to find clues in the conflicting impressions Jean left behind. Her ballroom-dancing teacher says she had stopped coming to lessons, and he knew something was wrong. An aunt comes up and says Jean had always had a cloud over her head and that looking through family photographs would prove she rarely smiled as a child. Three of our cousins, sisters, argue over Jean's anger, her tendency to "fire people" from her life, as one of them puts it. Julie admits she almost didn't come to the memorial service because Jean was so nasty the last time they spoke. But Laurie turns, surprised. "Jeannie nasty? She was never mean to me." They look at each other, both startled by the other's experience.

Finally one of Jean's oldest friends comes up and tells me she blames Jean's death on those in the drug and alcohol recovery community who shun antidepressant medications, considering them just another set of chemicals to use as a crutch. "If Jean had taken antidepressants, this wouldn't have happened," the woman tells me. "But she was terrified of drugs."

My last night in Seattle I sleep fitfully. Snatches from the memorial service swim through my head, and I am haunted by questions that don't have answers. Jean probably spent most of her life sick with depression, and yet she and I never talked about it, and now I can't think why. I watched her erratic, sometimes crazy behavior, but never called her on it. I listened when her anxieties and paranoia took over but rarely told her to stop. How could her depression have grown so powerful without some acknowledgment between us? Even as a child I knew I was her voice of reason, and now I wondered why I hadn't used that voice to speak up. If I had, would she still be alive?

When I say good-bye to her parents at the airport the next morning, I look into their grief-stricken faces and see all the same questions in their eyes.

I read for several months, and this is what I learn: People who are depressed tell a lot of lies. They lie to deflect inquiry, to keep up the facade that they are well. They lie to protect their feelings and the feelings of others. They lie because depression often becomes a strange, comforting, repetitive loop of despair that thrives in isolation. It takes on a life of its own and fights for its privacy. Jean's folder of notes for her memorial service included pages she had written in her twenties. There were detailed instructions for the service—who should sing, what should be said, even a menu for the reception afterward. She knew what she was talking about the night she said I didn't dream of death the way true suicides do. But now I know what it looks like, and it scares me to the bone.

Jesse and I are sitting at the kitchen table, snacking on apple slices after school. I ask the usual question, "Did you do anything interesting today?" and before I know it he tells me that in his Banana Splits session Maria said that she had a new stepdaddy and that she wants to kill him.

"Really?" I say, trying not to choke on my mouthful of apple. "What did the counselor say?"

Suddenly Jesse looks contrite. "Oh, I can't tell you. We aren't supposed to talk about what people say in Banana Splits. It's secret."

At our next meeting I relay this message to Dr. Mary.

She nods her head, and looks thoughtful for a long moment. We've been talking about the boys and the impact on them of the divorce. Now, layered on top, is my growing fear of depression, the role other people's depression has played in my life, and my abiding concern for Ron and the mood of his house when the children are there. She doesn't need to tell me what I already know: that my children are at risk of depression themselves, possibly even struggling with it now, at this tender age.

When one of them threatens to run away, as all children inevitably do, the alarm bells go off in my head. When they are sad I sit with them, trying to will the sadness away. I hover, I worry. I call them at their father's house every night, ostensibly to say hello but really so that I can take their emotional temperature.

"How are you tonight, sweetie?"

"Fine."

"Really? Are you doing anything fun?"

"No. We're playing with blocks."

"Oh. Well, how's Daddy?"

"Fine."

"Is anything wrong?"

"No, Mom. 'Bye."

Most nights, it goes like this, and I can't tell what's under the surface. They seem okay, but I don't trust okay anymore. I tell Mary my fears, my concerns. I have a long list of bogeymen, all looming large in the wake of Jean's death, and as I tick them off she listens patiently. When I'm done she looks at me with her eyebrows raised.

"Do you hear yourself?" she asks.

My obsessive worrying is still echoing around the room, and then it hits me.

"You think I'm going crazy," I say.

"No, not crazy, but I'm worried that you are becoming part of the problem."

I don't like being part of the problem so I make myself think about that. "It's like I'm raising them as tortured souls in training."

"Yes," she says. "They may be at some risk for future depression, but right now they are trying to be normal children. You need to let them be that, as much as possible. I don't mean ignore obvious problems, but remember that your boys are their own selves. They aren't their daddy, and they aren't your cousin, even if they are related to them. They are David and Jesse. You need to face your fears and control them. If the boys sense how worried you are, they will think there is something they really should be afraid of. They will take their cues from you."

In the months following Jeannie's death, I struggle to regain my footing in the world. I overextend myself at work, sink into a shallow depression of my own, lean too heavily on my boyfriend. In short, I cope badly, fretting endlessly about the boys, even as I try to stop.

One day I pick up the boys and David seems troubled, agitated and worried. When we get home I ask him what is wrong, and he says that Daddy is sad, and there doesn't seem to be anything he can do to help.

"I tell him I love him, but it doesn't make any difference," he says. "It's like he doesn't care."

David is only nine—what can he understand of adult depression? "Daddy does care, honey," I tell him, pulling him close. "Sometimes Daddy gets depressed. It's something that happens inside his body, and it makes him feel sad. It has nothing to do with you or Jess. It just happens. I'm sure that it makes Daddy feel better to hear that you love him, but you have to understand that it isn't your fault or anything you are responsible for."

"But how can we make him better?"

I look at my son's worried face and it feels that Ron and I will be forever linked, forever operating in each other's lives. But maybe that isn't such a terrible thing.

"The best thing you can do is tell me when Daddy is sad, just like you are doing now. I'll talk with Daddy. I can help him get help."

Maybe Mary is right—that the big lesson in the sky is that I finally have to learn to face this monster. Instead of running from it, as I ran from Ron's depression, or ignoring it, as I did with Jean's, maybe I need to stand up before it with a chair and a whip. Tame it, force it to yield. I become, over time, something of a militant about depression. I read more about it, speak up when I suspect friends or students are feeling that cold wind on their backs, confront Ron when I hear that life in his house is growing dark and dreary. Offer help, push him to seek help, talk with the boys about their father's moods. Fortunately, he is open to my meddling, seems, in fact, to appreciate that I will act as his reality check. And when the boys seem low, or troubled or sad, we sit down and talk seriously about their feelings— and then we get up, make ourselves milk shakes, and try to feel better. Mary says I need to teach my children to see the gray in life, to teach them that everything is a weave of good and bad, that each day will be a mix rather than a fantasy of either perfection or misery. It's a delicate act, this balance between listening to my children's sorrows and keeping these sorrows manageable. As Mary has suggested, I need to be careful not to breathe life into the fears, not to anticipate problems we don't have, not to post my own demons around the house. But at the same time I need to be vigilant. I need to listen, acknowledge, be willing to hear the frightening thoughts. It's similar to how I've learned to behave through my divorce: concerned but calm, realistic but hopeful. I must trust life again, trust that my children will grow up whole, but keep a weather eye on it.

It is a year later, the anniversary of Jean's death, and I scramble through my day coping with the small crises of the week. David's arm is in a cast, the result of a sledding accident, and he needs to go to the doctor for another X-ray. Jesse forgets his lunch box. People are usually sad on these anniversaries, so I watch myself for signs of grief. I'm quiet, but it is less that I am saddened than that I am haunted by the events of a year ago. I am glad it is not that time again, with the crying and the anger, the harried trip to Seattle for her memorial service, the confusing shifts of moving into her dark world for a few days, then the wrench back to my place here in Washington. The doctor looks at David's X-ray, then tells us the arm is healing nicely. David smiles. In breaking his arm he has discovered his mortality, so I am glad to see him reassured. "Children are very resilient," the doctor says. He expects me to smile but instead I narrow my eyes. "Some are," I say back. For David's benefit I smile and ruffle his hair. "I think this one is."

But I'm not sure. That evening I cut up pears for the boys and we play fish while having our before-bed snack. I watch them, looking for clues. They each have their own set of risk factors for depression, some characteristics woven tightly into their personalities, some experiences suffered at the hands of their parents and the world. I worry about their genetic history—my genetic history—and a future I cannot predict, cannot see.

I consider phoning Jean's parents, but choose instead to play with the boys until bedtime. Life has swept on, past the grief around Jean, past the vacuum she created by dying. I feel her fading, and then I think: She always wanted more attention than everyone else. It's somebody else's turn.

27

THE FINAL BREAK

By the time Ron and I had been separated for four years, I was beginning to wonder if I would ever be settled again. We had been in mediation for nearly three years, and while we had crafted a strong child care agreement, we were still snagged on the financial settlement, particularly the division of the property and the pensions. I was tired of moving, tired to the bone of living in ugly rental properties with rugs that smelled of other people's pets. One night I was talking with my parents about my deep wish to buy my own little house, and tears welled in my eyes.

"I'm so sick of white walls. I'm sick of sleeping in a basement. I'm sick of tending someone else's garden," I said, trying to explain what was beginning to feel like a minor obsession.

"But, honey," my mother said gently. "You may want to hold off for a few more years. Yes, it would be nice to get into your own place, but what if you remarry? You will probably want to move then. You don't want to be saddled with two properties."

I doubted I was remarrying anytime soon, and I didn't like the idea that I had to wait for a man to come into my life before I could settle in a community, get to know the neighbors, or join the local swimming pool.

"I don't think we should hold our breath for me to remarry," I said, looking away because I hated disappointing them. "And I don't know if it is smart to live like a vagabond in the hope that I'll meet the perfect guy tomorrow. I don't want to get married for the wrong reasons again. If I ever remarry I want it to be really simple—not for money, not for security, not for real estate."

My parents shifted uneasily in their seats. I think they sometimes didn't know quite what to think of me, whether to worry or throw up their hands.

"Besides," I said, growing more passionate by the minute, "do you have any idea what it is like to be my age and not have a permanent home? Not be able to paint the rooms the colors you like? Not be able to rip up the carpeting? Not be able to know if you will still be living there when it's time to harvest the tomatoes? I lost my hearth when I moved out of Ron's house, and this divorce is not going to be over for me until I get it back." I had to stop, then, because my voice was shaking.

"Well," said my dad, "if you could get your equity out of Ron's house, you could probably afford it."

"That's right," I said. "I've already talked to some banks. That's what it would take."

I went to Ron the next week and told him we had to find a way for me to get my money out of the house in D.C. He said he understood, and that he was already considering selling it so that he could move out closer to me and the boys' school in the Maryland suburbs. We decided to put it on the market, and I agreed to help him clean the place and pay half of the painting and repair costs to get it ready.

Over the next few weeks, I gradually got pulled into his orbit again, as we worked together to hire a real estate agent, dickered with handymen about the repairs, and started to clean out closets still loaded with jointly owned property. It was the last thing I wanted to do, and everyone around me thought I was crazy to help him clean and paint a house he had been living in for nearly four years. But I felt responsible for a share of the mess, and I needed us to get the best price possible in a sagging real estate market. For several weeks before the house went up for sale, we both painted like furies, inevitably sinking into arguments and yelling again as time ran out and the tension mounted. It felt like the worst years of our marriage. Yes, I could still leave at the end of the day, but not in the middle of a job. I would go home at night, peel off the paint-splattered clothes, and collapse into tears. Maybe I was handling this all wrong. Maybe everyone I knew was right, this was insane. As I had before, I wondered if I had really changed at all.

But the worst was soon over, and the last weekend we bought marigolds for the window box and weeded the yard. The house looked great. We waited anxiously for several weeks, as a trickle of people passed through to see it, but there were no serious buyers. The real estate agent met with us and suggested we lower the price. Even with that, he cautioned, the market was saturated with similar properties, and very few houses in the District were selling. Families with kids were bailing out for the suburbs, and few singles could afford our neighborhood. He said it might make sense to wait a few more years to see if the market recovered.

.　.　.

A few days later I went by Ron's to get the kids, and he asked me to sit down at the dining room table. He had a proposal for me.

"Look," he said, "the house isn't worth as much as we thought. Maybe we could figure out what we could realistically sell it for, then add what we would have to pay for all the transfer costs—real estate agent, taxes, whatever—and then I'll buy out your share at that amount. I think I could get a loan through my credit union that would cover it."

We sat down and came up with an estimate that felt generous to both of us, because we could avoid the nearly $30,000 in fees if he bought me out as part of the divorce settlement. We looked at the numbers on the piece of paper and realized this was a deal we could both be happy with. I would get my equity, Ron and the boys could stay in the house. With that decision, suddenly the dam that had been holding up our financial settlement burst. Over the next few hours, we quickly traded assets back and forth, experimenting with different combinations, all in the spirit we had learned from the mediators—trying to find solutions to both our problems. Instead of fighting over every piece, now the goal was to find a way to let each parent come out whole: able to own a house, to take vacations, to contribute equally to the boys' needs, both financially and emotionally. We knew by now that if we fought, most of it would go to lawyers or the IRS. If we could compromise, we could keep our assets to support the boys. By the end of the afternoon, the agreement was in place. We took it into the mediators and they were thrilled to see we had reached a resolution. They quickly whipped it into legal shape, then told us to take the entire agreement—the child care section and the financial settlement—to our lawyers for approval. Once we got their okay we could schedule a court date.

When I showed it to my lawyer, her only comment was, "This is the most intimate divorce agreement I've ever seen, but if it works for you, I guess it's okay."

"We've been living by these terms for over four years," I said. "Everyone seems to be doing fine with them."

"Okay," she said. "Let me look over it carefully, but I think it's a deal."

One day soon after I was trying to negotiate a crowded parking lot after a soccer game. Ron and David were in Ron's car, because we were all headed to a pizza party down the street, and Jesse was with me. As I pulled out, I nearly hit Ron, who was angling out of a space nearby.

I braked quickly, then laughed. "Wouldn't that be funny, if Mommy ran into Daddy's car?" I said, not thinking much about such a question.

But Jesse glanced around, his face cloudy with concern. "No, it wouldn't be funny. You and Daddy would get in a fight."

"Oh, I don't think we would get in a fight. Mommy and Daddy don't fight like that anymore," I said.

"You don't?"

"No, Daddy and I don't need to fight anymore, sweetie."

He thought about that for a moment.

"Then when are you going to get back together?" Four years after our split, Jesse was still hoping.

Ron and I have a relationship today that most people, including our children, find puzzling. On the surface we get along, which makes some wonder why we can't get back together.

But that isn't the whole story. Our relationship now is like a good business partnership. We have a common objective—to raise our children in a climate of wholeness and strength and support. Our relationship is built on trust, but this time the trust is more measured, more pragmatic, undoubtedly more fragile. To keep it healthy we tend it carefully, with politeness, tolerance, consideration. We slip occasionally—sigh in exasperation over the phone, or say something tinged with bitterness—but we can feel when we get off track and usually try, within a few days, to get back on. We can't afford to have the fabric of our relationship fray. We see everything through the prism of how it will affect the boys, and that enables us to be humane to each other, even when we don't want to be. It is odd to build trust with an ex-partner again, odd to allow the goodwill and friendly exchanges that build such trust. We are constantly bumping against the borders of intimacy, sharing something of our inner selves, then retreating again behind our walls because it feels too much like it used to feel, too close. It's an ebb and flow, but over time we've managed to establish the limits of the territory.

Through the years I've met many divorced parents, and most of them have told me they couldn't do this, that Ron and I must be unusually saintlike, or that we can only do this because our relationship must never have been that bad to begin with.

This always makes me uncomfortable, because separating us out that way isolates us, puts us in the realm of the impossible. Besides, we are decidedly unsaintlike, both of us. We are no different from most divorcing couples. We could have made it nasty, we could have hardened our positions, we could have struggled for years in that intimate anger that marks so many divorces. When people say they couldn't do this, I answer that more families could if they knew it was possible, if forgiveness and healing could become part of our cultural vocabulary about divorce, rather than our fixation on brokenness and blame. Society is not particularly comfortable with the idea of a good divorce, a healthy divorce. On some level divorce needs to remain a demon or too many of us would flee. I understand that, but at the same time, that societal attitude, and the legal structures that support it, make it easier for divorced people to demonize each other. And when there are children involved, that only damages them. Our adversarial approach to divorce breaks families apart more than may be necessary. When Ron and I started this process, it felt as if there were few models for a better way, and few people believed we could do it—or, if we could, why we didn't just remarry.

To be honest, there were some important things we had working for us. The breakup of my marriage was the most painful thing I've ever experienced, and yet it could have been worse. Both Ron and I had an instinctive understanding that it would be better not to complicate it with relationships with other people before we agreed to split, or to break some of the essential ties of trust that still existed between us. I had many fears about what would happen, but in the end neither of us did anything particularly unusual. Neither one of us stole the children away to New Zealand or had an affair. Limiting the damage meant that it was easier, eventually, to forgive and let go.

Our child care agreement is studded with stipulations partly because we were able to anticipate certain details about our futures. We knew it was unlikely either parent would move out of the Washington area while the kids were still in school. We knew we would keep our jobs—

Ron with the government, me as a tenured professor at my university. We knew what we could probably afford in the future, and we knew that each of our incomes would probably stay within ballpark range of the other's. These stable elements helped us craft an agreement that serves as the base for everything else.

But I learned some surprising things about myself through this process: that I can compromise and still retain my dignity; that I can voice my concerns without criticizing; that to be trusted I have to be trustworthy; that I can protect myself better by horse-trading than by grandstanding. Ironically, I also learned that my pacifist nature—the thing that made me a girl who wouldn't fight back—is perhaps one of my greatest strengths, not a shameful weakness. I no longer distrust my inclination toward compromise and conciliation; I follow it, honor it. It is a valuable tool, perhaps the most important one I have to resolve the problems that rise before me.

But mostly I've learned how sweet life can be when you forgive and move on.

After several years of indecision, I broke up with my boyfriend, ultimately convinced that I needed to trust my heart. He was a wonderful man with many fine qualities, yet he wasn't the man for me. Our strongest common interest was our children, but I suddenly saw that the children wouldn't be with us much longer. David was closing in on middle school, and Jesse wasn't far behind. If I remarried, I needed to pick someone I would be happy with through my retirement, and that meant sharing the deeper interests, the strong bonds that would carry us through our old age. I still wanted what my parents had—someone who would want to watch *Masterpiece Theater* with me, who would enjoy the opera with me, who would put down his own project to help me in the garden if that was what I was doing on a Sunday afternoon.

I know that if I ever fall in love again I have some serious work to do on myself. That I will have to confront the looming question of loyalties, that I will have to love someone as much as I love my children, even if that seems unnatural. That I will have to give up the delicious sense of control I have over my own house and daily life. Yes, it would be nice to have someone to help with the trash and run to the bank. It would be nice to never mow that damn lawn again, never have to shovel the walk. But in exchange, I will have to give up my hegemony over our lives. I will have to consult with another, compromise, consider, possibly even live with ugly furniture. Sometimes, when I'm savoring one of those wonderful moments of solitude, I worry that I've been single too long to be able to make the transition back to a partnership. I have no idea what it would be like to live again in a house that is always full, always echoing with another's step.

Yet I still believe in marriage—good marriage—as the sacred circle, the secret garden of the heart. I know, though, that if I marry again it will not be the same as it was the first time. It will never be as it was supposed to be. I've lost the chance to raise my children while loving their father; I've lost the chance to grow toward someone for so long that our separate selves become inexplicably entwined; I've lost the chance to achieve what my parents achieved— fifty years together, through thick and thin. I've lost the chance to believe again that anything is possible. I'm more realist than romantic now. I may have to learn, all over again, how to lose my heart.

. . .

Knowing what I've lost makes me vigilant about other people's marriages, nervous when I hear friends casually drop hints that they are beginning to think they might be better off without their spouses. Sometimes I talk with someone and I can see that divorce fantasy flickering in their eyes. "It wouldn't be so bad," they say, "because I'm sure my husband would agree that the kids should stay with me. And I would get the house, I think."

"You don't have any idea," I tell them. "You can't count on anything."

A friend from college calls and tells me about a long-time office mate who one day suddenly kissed her in the elevator.

"It was so exciting," she gushes. "I haven't felt this way in years!"

I think of her kids, children I know. I can't bear to think of this happening to them. "Please think of your children," I tell her. "When you start thinking about the kiss in the elevator, think instead of them. Don't ever stop thinking about them."

I can often see the difference, now, between the couples who are just struggling with life and those who really shouldn't be living together. The bad marriages leap out at me, the ones that echo with that too-familiar tension. The couple who snipes at each other continuously through their son's birthday party, criticizing each other over the smallest of errors. The pair who works their life as a complex tag team, never really living together in the same space at the same time. The people whose conversation is filled with blame and distrust. The people who suck up all the air in the room as they try to make you see, beyond a shadow of a doubt, that the problems are all because of the spouse and the things he or she does. The people who make me sad because I know that, one day, they may set out on this most harrowing of journeys. And yet I listen, respectful of their misery, remembering my own. Knowing that everyone needs to talk themselves through it, at whatever pace they can muster. Sometimes these conversations bear fruit, and I find, months later, that the person has indeed separated from his or her spouse. Other times the desire to divorce dies on the vine, and when we get together there is an unwritten rule that we shouldn't speak of it. That's fine with me. The fewer divorces, the better.

One day David comes home from school and says that his friend Stephen doesn't get to live with his dad; in fact, he only sees him in the summer. This is the first time he understands that some kids of divorced families don't get to live with both parents, and he is horrified. I count it as a bookend to my conflict over joint custody and finally let myself off the hook. I've found that my children carry their own story about this divorce, and that it continues to evolve. That they will revisit it again and again as they grow and mature. They are too old now for dinosaur-family stories, but they like to hear me make up stories about their futures—about the full and interesting lives they will lead when they grow up. In these tales I marry them off to women with goofy names, send them to the Antarctic to study penguins, make them into baseball heroes or poets or nerdy scientists. Sometimes I make up stories about the children they will have, and they listen, rapt, absorbing my hope for them.

It has taken me years, but over time I've managed to make peace with the statistics about children of divorce. Despite the dire predictions, the boys appear to be doing fine. They are sweet and friendly. They are doing better in school than I ever expected. They are usually respectful, and always loving, and seem busy with their buddies and their sports. I've learned that the numbers don't have to be a manifest destiny, that, in fact, I can make them not be true if I work at it hard enough. I've met many other divorced people and what I've found is that I have many advantages that put me and my children on the outer fringe of the data. I have a good job and a viable income, which means I have choices. I am lucky to have Ron on the other side, someone who shares my values about many critical issues, from education to religion. The boys know what it looks like to have a father fold laundry, just as they've seen me struggle with the lawn mower. I'm lucky to co-parent with someone who tries, again and again, to get it right, to do it better. We've been able to afford good counseling, and we've caught many problems before they've become unmanageable. I have a safety net of family and friends. My children know they live inside a thick web of loving bonds and that their father and mother are woven together, for better or for worse, as long as they live. Because I've finally let go of the divorce fantasy that Ron would someday vanish off the planet and leave us alone. The thought that my children might lose their father, in fact, would be the worst thing that could happen to us. Because then we really would be alone.

Ron and I got divorced on a clear February morning in 1997.

Nearly five years had passed since the evening I hid the kitchen knives in the basement and told him I couldn't stay in our marriage any longer.

Five years is a long time, too long for a divorce, most people would tell you. Perhaps, but by the time Ron and I stood before the family court judge in Washington, D.C., we had shed our lawyers and the anger that had so warped our marriage. Instead, we stood there with a co-parenting agreement thick with connections. The judge shook his head, muttered, "If you can work this well together, I don't know why you can't stay married," then slammed his gavel down. After it was over we stood awkwardly outside the courthouse for a moment, unable to believe that the long years of custody struggles and mediation were really finished. Then Ron looked at me, his eyes suddenly twinkling in that impish way of his. "Want to go have lunch? We could go over to the National Gallery." So we walked down the hill and sat under a fern in the palm court, and talked about the boys and summer plans. It was so civilized and hopeful, a fitting end for two people who had sworn in court to work together peaceably as co-parents for the rest of their lives. Ron asked for a hug as we said good-bye and I went home to collect the boys from school, then took them to a movie and, after ice cream sundaes, tucked them into bed. It wasn't until I was sure they were asleep that I tossed back several fingers of bourbon, got into the shower, and cried. Even five years later, I still wasn't over it. I would never be over it.

A few months later I decided I needed to test my wings, try something more difficult with the boys now that they were older. We decided to go camping together in Canada, visiting friends along the way, but doing much of it on our own. We would see Niagara Falls, Toronto, then head north along the shores of Lake Huron, up the beautiful Bruce Peninsula, and crossing to the north shore of the lake, only returning to the United States through Sault Sainte Marie. The boys wanted to see the locks where the big ships came through from Lake Superior. We were gone several weeks and logged more than two thousand miles on the car. We camped in places where the only shower was a dip in the lake, where the mosquitoes descended at dusk, where the bears prowled at night. We hiked across lovely pine tree–covered islands, cooked over a fire, played baseball with other families, fended off the concerns that a single mother was camping alone with her kids. It was a wonderful adventure, just the kind of trip I had always imagined taking with a husband. But it turned out I could do it on my own.

Last summer I bought a house filled with light and air, in the neighborhood where the boys were already enrolled in school. I immediately put down thick rugs in all the bedrooms. The night before the moving van was to come, the boys and I unrolled our sleeping bags in the still-empty house and began planning our life.

"Can we build a tree fort?"

"Yes, of course. Let's ask Grampy to help."

"Can we get a dog?"

"Maybe. How about a cat?"

"Can we have a party for our friends?"

"Yes, a housewarming. We'll tell everyone to bring presents."

"Can we join the pool?"

"Sure. Right away."

After a while they tired and snuggled down in their bags. "I like this house, Mom," Jesse said quietly. "Maybe it's been waiting for us."

"Yeah," David said. "It feels like our house."

It was then that I knew I had recovered, that the long journey was finally over. The next day I would go out to buy tomato sets and look for a kitten to raise. We were home. We were finally home.

EPILOGUE

Biologists who work with peregrine falcons have an interesting way of judging whether mated pairs have been successful parents. They don't get the merit badge until their offspring have offspring. If their children are too weak, or too badly schooled in nest-building or hunting to raise their own, then they have failed. It's not just having children, but raising children who can raise children that is the test.

Every day I wonder if my children will grow up whole enough to marry and raise my grandchildren. Sometimes I stop to consider what they have learned from watching this divorce, from living this split life.

They have learned that love can die, although I think they know it doesn't die between children and parents. They have learned that in life bad things can be hidden just around the next corner, although I think they also know that bad things can be survived and even overcome.

They did not grow up with parents who loved each other, but they did grow up with parents who respected each other and themselves, and who were not afraid to work for a happier place. They have seen us compromise, watched us push down our anger and bite our tongues. They have seen us behave as grown-ups. Whatever life brings them—sickness or health, better or worse—I have to believe this will prove to have been a valuable lesson.

What I discovered in the end about divorce was that we were both to blame—and we were both to be forgiven. Forgiven by each other, by the community around us, and, someday I hope, by our two boys. Forgiveness is an odd place to go. It isn't very popular these days, old-fashioned and sparsely settled. Many of my women friends find it highly suspect terrain, just bordering the badlands of powerlessness. But it has a mysteriously healing atmosphere, and I know firsthand it is a place where children thrive. The key to forgiveness, perhaps, is accepting the lesson it took me so long to learn: that life is complex. The question is no longer whether life is fair or kind or cruel or just. It is none of those things and all of those things. I am complex, my ex-husband is complex, and the picture we leave behind for our children is riddled with contradiction. Ron and I cooperate well as co-parents, yet sometimes we can barely sit in the same room together. We loved each other once, yet now the intimacy of being in the other's house often feels like an affront. We kiss the same children, rush back into partnership the minute one of them is threatened, strategize as a team to map their futures and their happiness. Yet when left alone together, we stare at the floor. Intimacy between people, as it is for all social creatures, is a delicate ballet of love and power—and former intimacy is a dance all its own. We will never get it quite right, but we will keep trying and trying. That effort, perhaps more than anything else, is the legacy we leave our boys.

Instead of lying awake at night fretting over a list of problems, I am now more likely to lie awake counting my blessings. I have a wonderful job, enough financial security to keep the demons at bay, good friends and a loving circle of family. A snow-white cat lies curled at my feet. With my parents still healthy and the boys deep into Little League, I see now that these are, in fact, the halcyon days, the days we will always remember.

When I think of the disruption and sadness my divorce has caused my children and the others I love, I try to balance that pain against the memory of the dreams, those frightening dreams from the darkest years of my marriage. The one that came back again and again was the one of slowly going blind, or sometimes losing the use of my legs or arms. Despite my obvious disability no one in this dream believed me. I was told to quit complaining and get on with things. And the panic would rise up inside me because I couldn't see or move and no one would listen.

I don't have that dream anymore. I haven't had it since the day I moved out. I have other nightmares, but in these dreams I am always whole and strong, and able to save my children.